PROGRESSIVE Skills in English

Level 1 Course Book

Terry Phillips and Anna Phillips
with Nicholas Regan

Garnet
EDUCATION

Published by
Garnet Publishing Ltd.
8 Southern Court
South Street
Reading RG1 4QS, UK

First edition 2011

ISBN: 978-1-85964-676-2

British Library Cataloguing-in-Publication Data
A catalogue record for this book is available from
the British Library.

Production
Project managers: Richard Peacock, Nicky Platt
Editorial team: Emily Clarke, Sarah Mellowes,
                    Richard Peacock, Nicky Platt, Rod Webb
Research: Lucy Phillips
Design: Ed Du Bois, Mike Hinks
Illustration: Doug Nash
Photography: Clipart, Corbis, Digital Vision, Getty
                    Images, Image Source, Photodisc,
                    Istockphoto, Shutterstock
Audio and DVD: EFS Television Production Ltd.

Every effort has been made to trace the copyright holders
and we apologize in advance for any unintentional
omissions. We will be happy to insert the appropriate
acknowledgements in any subsequent editions.

The authors and publisher would like to thank the following
for permission to reproduce from copyright material:

Google for results listing on page 28

Printed and bound
in Lebanon by International Press: interpress@int-press.com

Contents

Listening	Speaking	Reading	Writing	Knowledge area
1 Freshers' week	Systems of education	Living and working at university	A Personal Statement	Education
2 Concepts	Human behaviour	Personality and behaviour	Extroverts and introverts	Psychology and sociology
3 How to be a good employee	Summer jobs	Choosing a career	The interview process	Work and business
4 The scientific method	Diagrams and explanations	Temperature and time	A laboratory report	Science and nature
5 Geographical location	Location and physical features	Encyclopedia research	Advantages and disadvantages	The physical world

Skills

Listening	Speaking	Reading	Writing
1 • waiting for definitions	• organizing a talk • choosing the tense	• preparing to read: title / heading / introduction • recognizing advice and instructions	• spelling: /iː/ • organizing information into paragraphs: grouping information
2 • recognizing time signposts	• taking turns: starting a turn • taking turns: recognizing the end of a turn	• preparing to read: illustrations	• spelling: /ɑː/ • gathering and recording information • organizing information into paragraphs
3 • hearing important words: more loudly	• how to make a good impression • taking turns: extending a turn	• dealing with new words • preparing to read: section headings	• spelling: /g/, /dʒ/ • organizing information into a flow chart • chronological markers
4 • predicting the next word from context	• giving a scientific explanation • asking about pronunciation	• finding and using topic sentences • looking for examples	• spelling: /ɜː/ • choosing between present and past • referring to tables
5 • understanding location	• introducing a talk	• transferring information: to a table	• spelling: /ɔː/ • descriptions

Grammar

Listening	Speaking	Reading	Writing
1 • grammar of definitions: *an X is a Y* *X is -ing*	• present simple vs past simple	• imperatives for advice • time phrases – present and past	• writing about self: present simple vs present continuous
2 • recognizing past time	• modals: *can / can't*	• frequency adverbs	• writing about others • joining with *and*
3 • modals: *must / mustn't* • joining with *because*	• closed questions + short answers • closed questions with a choice	• basic SV (O/A/C) patterns	• present simple passive • joining with *because / so*
4 • recognizing articles • recognizing introductory phrases	• *this* vs *these* • joining with *and / but / because / so*	• comparatives • sentences with post-modification	• past simple passive • passives in longer sentences
5 • *there is / there are* • *it is / they are*	• prepositions of place • joining with *which*	• superlatives • sentences with preceding prepositional phrase	• modifying a noun • building the noun phrase

Phonology, Everyday English and Portfolio work

Listening	Speaking	Everyday English	Portfolio
1 • vowels – short vs long: /i/ vs /iː/ • consonants: /p/ vs /b/	• vowels – short vs long: /i/ vs /iː/	• asking about words and phrases	Activities and clubs
2 • vowels – short vs long: /æ/ vs /ɑː/	• vowels – short vs long: /æ/ vs /ɑː/ • consonants: /n/, /ŋ/, /ŋk/	• asking for information	What kind of person am I?
3 • consonants: /g/, /ʤ/, /j/	• consonants: /g/, /ʤ/, /j/	• asking about times and days	Jobs
4 • vowels – short vs long: /e/ vs /ɜː/ • consonants: /θ/ vs /ð/	• vowels – short vs long: /e/ vs /ɜː/	• offering and requesting help • accepting and rejecting help	Natural events
5 • vowels – short vs long: /ɒ/ vs /ɔː/ • consonants: /s/ vs /z/	• vowels – short vs long: /ɒ/ vs /ɔː/ • consonants: /s/ vs /z/	• getting around town	Comparing countries

Introduction

This is Level 1 of *Progressive Skills in English*. This course is in four levels, from Intermediate to Advanced. In addition, there is a remedial / false beginner course, *Starting Skills in English*, for students who are not ready to begin Level 1.

Progressive Skills in English is designed to help students who are at university or about to enter a university where some or all of their course is taught in English. The course helps students in all four skills:

Listening – to lectures
Speaking – in tutorials and seminars
Reading – for research
Writing – assignments

Progressive Skills in English is arranged in five themes. Each theme is divided into four sections, one for each skill. Each skill section has five core lessons as follows:

Lesson 1: *Vocabulary for the skill*
pre-teaches key vocabulary for the section

Lesson 2: *Real-time practice*
practises previously learnt skills and exposes students to new skills; in most cases, this lesson provides a model for the activity in Lesson 5

Lesson 3: *Learning skills*
presents and practises new skills

Lesson 4: *Grammar for the skill*
presents and practises key grammar points for the skill

Lesson 5: *Applying skills*
provides practice in the skills and grammar from the section; in most cases, students work on a parallel task to the one presented in Lesson 2

In addition, there are three extra elements in each theme:

Everyday English	presents and practises survival English for everyday life
Knowledge quiz	tests students on their learning of key vocabulary and knowledge
Portfolio	offers extended practice and integration of the skills in the theme

Theme 1

Education

- Freshers' week

- Systems of education

- Living and working at university

- A Personal Statement

Listening: Freshers' week

1.1 Vocabulary for listening — Academic life

A Activating knowledge

1. 🔊 1.1 Listen and discuss some statements about education.

> At school, English is more useful than Mathematics.

2. 🔊 1.2 Listen to some students. Do they agree or disagree with each statement?

> I think that's true.

> Actually, I don't agree. Maths is much more useful than English.

B Developing vocabulary

1. Complete each sentence with a word or phrase from the list on the right.

   a. The ___academic___ year in my country starts in October. All the university students go back then.

   b. When does the second _____ start? Is it in February?

   c. Which _____ are you in? Education? Mathematics? Modern Languages?

   d. Which _____ gives the Science in Education lectures?

   e. How many _____ are in the Faculty of Education? I mean, how many people work there?

   f. Where is the student _____ at this university? Where do the students live?

   g. This is a large _____. There are ten faculty buildings, the library, the Resource Centre and the Students' Union.

   h. A university student is called a _____ in the first year.

2. 🔊 1.3 Listen and check your answers.

C Building connections between words

🔊 1.4 [DVD] 1.A Listen to two words or phrases. What is the connection between each pair? Use the phrases below.

- *They are both ...*
- *They both + verb ...*
- *They are opposites.*
- *A(n) X is a(n) Y.*

academic (*adj*)
access (*n* and *v*)
accommodation (*n*)
article (*n*)
assignment (*n*)
bursar (*n*)
campus (*n*)
contribute (*v*)
crèche (*n*)
deadline (*n*)
dean (*n*)
degree (*n*)
faculty (*n*)
fee (*n*)
field trip
fresher (*n*)
graduate (*n* and *v*)
hall of residence
head (*n*) [of]
in charge [of]
lecture (*n*)
lecturer (*n*)
librarian (*n*)
look up (*v*)
participation (*n*)
professor (*n*)
projector (*n*)
research (*n*)
resource centre
responsible [for]
schedule (*n*)
semester (*n*)
sixth form
sixth form college
socialize (*v*)
staff (*n*)
Students' Union
subject (*n*)
tutorial (*n*)
undergraduate (*n*)
vice chancellor (*n*)

A   Activating background knowledge

Tick the jobs below that you find in a university.
What does each person do?

☐	bookseller	☐	cook
☐	car park attendant	☐	gardener
☐	caretaker	☐	lecturer
☐	cleaner	☐	librarian
☐	manager	☐	teacher
☐	nurse	☐	waiter
☐	receptionist	☐	hairdresser
☐	secretary	☐	guard

B   Understanding introductions

You are going to watch an introduction to the Faculty
of Education at Greenhill University.

1. What is Mr Beech saying? DVD 1.B Watch the first part of
   his talk, with the sound turned right down. Guess some
   of his words.

2. 1.5 DVD 1.B Listen to the talk now and check your ideas.

3. What does each person in the faculty do?
   Write notes next to the names on the list on the
   opposite page.

C   Understanding words in context

You are going to watch a short talk by Mrs Pinner.
She defines several words in her talk. 1.6 DVD 1.C Watch
the talk. Tick the correct definitions.

1. campus	☑	money for a course
2. resources	☐	Senior Common Room
3. fees	☐	the university buildings
4. Welfare Office	☐	accommodation for students on campus
5. JCR	☐	things to help with studying
6. SCR	☐	place to go if you have problems
7. hall of residence	☐	special place for students
8. Students' Union (SU)	☐	Junior Common Room

D   Transferring information

Study the campus map on the opposite page.

1. Which places are mentioned in
   Mrs Pinner's talk? Find and circle them
   on the map.

2. What can students do in each place?

> What does a dean do at
> a British university?

> He or she is responsible
> for a faculty.

E   Remembering real-world knowledge

1.7 Listen and answer the questions.

Greenhill University
Faculty of Education

Dean of Education   (Peter Beech)   *responsible for Fac. of Ed.*

Bursar   Mrs Pearce

Head of Year 1   Pat Pinner

Accommodation Manager   Bill Heel

Resource Centre Manager   Ben Hill

Head of ISS   Tim Mills

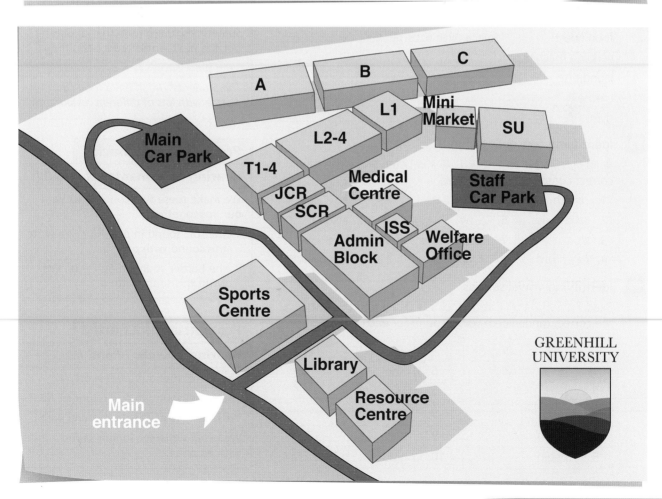

A   Reviewing key words

🔊 **1.8** Listen to the stressed syllables from some words in this theme.
Number the words below.

☐ schedule	☐1 education	☐ accommodation	☐ union
☐ bursar	☐ lecture	☐ responsible	☐ resources
☐ campus	☐ library	☐ semester	☐ faculty

B   Identifying a new skill

1. 🔊 **1.9** DVD **1.D** Watch another talk. Match the words
and definitions.

    a. assignment   ☐ academic magazines
    b. deadline   ☐ a small discussion
    c. research   ☐a a piece of work to do on your own
    d. journals   ☐ the time to give in an assignment
    e. tutorial   ☐ reading articles

2. Read the Skills Check.

3. How does Mrs Pinner introduce each definition?
🔊 **1.9** DVD **1.D** Watch again. Tick the phrases you hear
in the Skills Check.

C   Listening for definitions

🔊 **1.10** Listen to some speakers. They define each word below.
Write the definition in each case.

food court	_place with lots of diff. rest._
vending machines	
laundrette	
crèche	
gym	

D   Identifying consonant sounds

Read Pronunciation Check 1. 🔊 **1.11** Listen and write the
correct consonant in each word.

1. _b_ oth	5. jo___	9. ___eo___le
2. cam___us	6. ___ay	10. ___ersonal
3. clu___	7. res___onsible	11. ___lace
4. ex___lain	8. ___ursar	12. ___ro___lem

E   Identifying vowel sounds

Read Pronunciation Check 2. 🔊 **1.12** Listen and tick under
the correct (underlined) vowel sound for each word.

		/ɪ/	/iː/
1.	in	✓	
2.	fee		
3.	teach		
4.	mean		
5.	begin		

		/ɪ/	/iː/
6.	free		
7.	meet		
8.	ill		
9.	it		
10.	give		

Skills Check

Waiting for definitions

People often define words **after** they
use the word for the first time.

Example:

*I'm the **Head of Year 1** – that means
I'm **responsible for the schedule**.*

When you hear a new word, listen
carefully. You may hear a definition.
Listen for these phrases:

That means …
That is … / That's …
I mean …
In other words, …
… which is / are …

Sometimes, there is no special phrase,
but **the next words** are a definition.

Example:

*The Students' Union has a food court –
a place with lots of different restaurants.*

Pronunciation Check 1

Hearing consonants: /p/ and /b/

We make these two consonants with
our lips together:

1. the soft sound in *pen* – /p/. We write
this sound with *p*.

2. the harder sound in *Ben* – /b/. We
write this sound with *b*.

Pronunciation Check 2

Hearing vowels: /ɪ/ and /iː/

The vowel sound in *fill* is short: /ɪ/.

The vowel sound in *feel* is longer: /iː/.

We usually write the short sound with *i*.

We often write the longer sound
with *ea* or *ee*.

We can define a noun with a general word plus more information. ①

subject	verb	general word	more information
A food court	is	a place	with many different restaurants.
A dean	is	a person	in charge of a faculty.
A vending machine	is	a machine	with food and drinks.
An article	is	a text	in a newspaper, journal or on the Internet.
A schedule	is	a list	of days and times.

A Defining with subject-verb-complement
Study each photograph below.
1. How can you define each person, place or thing?
2. ⊙ 1.13 Listen to some definitions. Which word or phrase is the speaker defining in each case?

a cafeteria   a lecture hall   a lab   a degree   a graduate

a projector   a theatre   a sports centre   a field trip   a librarian

We can define an action with *means* / *is* and another verb in the gerund. ②

subject	verb	gerund	more information
Research	means	finding	information in books or on the Internet.
Access	means	getting	in.
Greeting	is	saying	hello.
Socializing	is	meeting	people in your free time.

B Defining with subject-verb-gerund
⊙ 1.14 Listen. How does the speaker define each action below?
1. revising
2. contributing
3. parting
4. graduating
5. advising
6. disagreeing

> What is revising?

> It's going over something again, something you studied before.

A Activating ideas

The pictures on the right are from a talk by Mr Mills of ISS. What can you see in each picture?

B Predicting content

🎵 1.15 DVD 1.E Watch and listen to the introduction to the talk. What is Mr Mills going to talk about?

C Practising a key skill

1. 🎵 1.16 DVD 1.F Watch and listen to the rest of the talk. What is the custom in Britain for each of the items in the pictures? Complete Table 1 below.

Table 1: *Some British customs*

custom	notes
greetings	Pleased to meet you. How do you do? Hi. / Hello.
handshakes	
eye contact	
social distance	
gender equality	
participation	

2. Which of the customs are the same in your culture? Which ones are different? How?

D Transferring information

Define each of the words and phrases in the first column of Table 1.

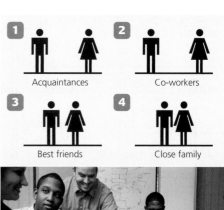

1 Acquaintances 2 Co-workers

3 Best friends 4 Close family

Speaking: Systems of education

1.6 Vocabulary for speaking   Education systems

A Activating ideas

Read these statements. Do you agree or disagree with each one?

1. All schooling should be mixed, not single-sex. There should be girls and boys in the same class.

> Schooling should be mixed.
>
> I disagree. I think girls learn better in single-sex schools.
>
> I agree. It's better.

2. Children should study all the subjects on the curriculum. They should not drop Geography, for example, at the age of 14.
3. All children should learn a foreign language.
4. There should not be physical punishment of children at any age.
5. Children with different abilities should be in different classes.

B Practising new vocabulary

1. 🔊 1.17 Listen. Complete each dialogue with a word from the list on the right. Make any necessary changes.

1 A: When do you _____ national examinations?

B: In Britain, we _____ them at 16 and at 18.

2 A: Is education _____ in your country?

B: Yes, up to the age of 16.

3 A: When did you start school?

B: When I was three. I went to _____ school.

4 A: Who was your best teacher?

B: Mr Jarvis. He _____ us as adults.

2. Practise the dialogues in pairs.
3. Write and say two more lines for each dialogue.

C Developing independent learning

Study the dictionary entries for two words from this theme. The pronunciation is between two forward slashes (//).

1. What do the red symbols represent?
2. Identify the words below.

/ɪ t/   /f iː t/   /f ɪ l/   /g ɪ v/

/iː t/   /r iː d/   /f iː l/   /m iː t/

---

sit (v) /s ɪ t/ 1. use a chair
2. take an examination,
e.g., *When do you ~ the IELTS exam?*

---

fee (n) /f iː/ 1. money you pay for a professional
service 2. money you pay for a course of study;
USAGE NOTE: OFTEN PLURAL,
e.g., *The ~s for this course are very high.*

---

ability (n) [= skill]
behaviour (n)
best (adj)
certificate (n)
college (n)
compulsory (adj)
cram (v)
curriculum (n)
degree (n)
dictionary (n)
dormitory (n)
drop (v) [a subject]
examination (n)
form (n)
graduate (n and v)
keep (v) [order]
kindergarten (n)
last (v)
mixed (adj)
nursery (adj) [school]
primary (adj) [school]
punishment (n)
pupil (n)
residential (adj)
reward (n)
secondary (adj) [school]
semester (n)
set (v) [an exam]
single-sex (adj)
sit (v) [an exam]
stay on (v)
take (v) [an exam]
tertiary (adj)
treat (v)
  [= behave towards]
tutorial (n)
worst (adj)

A Previewing vocabulary

1. 🔊 1.18 Listen to the words on the right. Tick the correct column to show the number of syllables.

2. Mark the stressed syllable on each two- and three-syllable word.

3. 🔊 1.19 Listen again and repeat the words.

		1	2	3
a.	ꞌafter		✓	
b.	children			
c.	level			
d.	nursery			
e.	primary			
f.	secondary			
g.	called			
h.	exam			
i.	school			
j.	sixth			

B Hearing a model

You are going to hear a short talk from a student to his study group at university.

1. 🔊 1.20 Listen to the first part of the talk. Complete Table 1.

2. 🔊 1.21 Listen to the second part of the talk. Tick in Table 1:
   - the **schools** he went to.
   - the **exams** he took.

3. How does the student organize his talk?

4. Which tense does he use in each part of the talk? Why?

Table 1: *Education in the UK*

type of school	age range	exams at the end
nursery		

C Practising a model

1. Study some of the sentences from the talk below. Underline the important words or phrases in each sentence.

a. Britain has four kinds of school. They are nursery, primary, secondary and sixth form.

b. Children don't take exams at nursery school.

c. At four or five, they move to primary school.

d. They stay there for six years and then they move to secondary school.

e. Secondary school lasts five years.

f. Children take exams called GCSEs at the age of 16.

g. You can leave school after GCSEs or A levels. However, about 50 per cent of British teenagers go on to university.

h. I didn't go to nursery school.

i. I was good at primary school and I liked the teachers.

j. I went to secondary school.

2. 🔊 1.22 Listen and check.

3. Practise saying the sentences.

D Producing a model

1. Make some notes on:
   - the education system in your country.
   - your own education.

2. Give a short talk.

A Activating ideas

What can you remember about these phrases?

- nursery school
- GCSE
- sixth form
- A levels
- primary
- take an exam / make an exam

B Studying models

Cover the conversations in Exercise C.

1. Look at the questions on the right. They are from conversations between students and tutors. What is the rest of the conversation in each case?
2. ◉ 1.23 Listen to the conversations. Number the sentences on the right 1 to 6 in the order you hear them.

☐ Do you *take* an exam or *make* an exam?

☐ Does *primary* mean *first*?

☐ Is sixth form for 17- and 18-year-olds?

☐ What does *GCSE* mean?

☐ What are A levels?

☐ What's a nursery school?

C Practising conversations

Uncover the conversations. Practise in pairs.

1 A: What's a nursery school?
    B: It's a school for young children.
    A: How old are they?
    B: They're between three and five.

2 A: What does *GCSE* mean?
    B: It's an abbreviation.
    A: I know. But what does it mean?
    B: It means *General Certificate of Secondary Education*.

3 A: Does *primary* mean 'first'?
    B: Yes, it does.
    A: So does *secondary* mean 'second'?
    B: That's right.

4 A: What are A levels?
    B: They're exams in Britain.
    A: When do you take them?
    B: You take them at 18.

5 A: Is sixth form for 17- and 18-year-olds?
    B: Yes, it is.
    A: Why is it called *sixth form*?
    B: Because it starts with the sixth year of secondary school.

6 A: Do you *take* an exam or *make* an exam?
    B: We use the verb *take* with exams.
    A: And what about assignments?
    B: You *do* assignments.

D Real-time speaking

Work in pairs. Ask and answer questions about some words and phrases. Use patterns from the conversations above.

Student A

1. Look at the information on page 173. Learn the meanings of some words connected with education.
2. Ask B about the other words.
3. Answer B's questions about your words.

Student B

1. Look at the information on page 177. Learn the meanings of some words connected with education.
2. Answer A's questions about your words.
3. Ask A about the other words.

A   Saying vowels

1. Say each pair of words on the right. Make sure your partner can hear the difference.

2. Look at the transcript of the talk in Lesson 1.7 (pages 183–184).

   a. <u>Underline</u> some words with the vowel sound /ɪ/.

   b. ⟨Circle⟩ some words with the vowel sound /iː/.

	A	B
1.	fill	feel
2.	still	steal
3.	will	wheel
4.	list	least
5.	ill	eel
6.	sit	seat
7.	this	these
8.	hill	he'll
9.	his	he's
10.	is he	easy

B   Identifying a new skill (1)

1. Read Skills Check 1. How is the talk in Lesson 1.7 organized?

2. What can you remember about the talk in Lesson 1.7?
   • General facts?
   • Personal experiences?

3. Look at the extracts below from a talk about drama. Mark each sentence *G* for general facts or *P* for personal experiences.

		Children learn a lot about themselves in Drama.
G	1	Drama is a very important subject.
P	1	I took Drama for GCSE.
		I got a good pass in the examination.
		I was the main person in one of the plays.
		I wasn't very good, but I had a lot of fun.
		Most secondary schools in Britain have Drama classes.
		Some children take examinations in Drama at GCSE or A level.
		We did a lot of drama games, and we put on a play every term.

4. Number the *G* sentences in a logical order.

5. Number the *P* sentences in a logical order.

C   Identifying a new skill (2)

1. Read Skills Check 2.

2. Look again at the extracts in Exercise B. Underline all the present simple verbs. Circle all the past simple verbs.

D   Rehearsing a new skill

Practise saying the sentences in Exercise B in order. Remember to stress the key words.

> *Drama* is a very important **subject**.

E   Using new skills in a real-world task

Make a few sentences about this topic:
Popular subjects at school in my country and my favourite subject.

Skills Check 1

Organizing a talk

You must organize information in a talk in a logical way.

In the talk in Lesson 1.7, the student wanted to describe:
• education in **general**;
• **his own** education.

The best organization in English is:
• **general** facts; then
• **personal** experiences.

Within each paragraph, the best organization is:
• **chronological** – earliest to latest, e.g., *nursery, then primary, then ...*

Skills Check 2

Choosing the tense

You must choose the correct tense for each part of a talk.

1. We talk about general facts which are true now with the present simple.

   *There **are** four kinds of school in Britain.*

   *Children **go** to primary school at four or five.*

   *Secondary school **lasts** five years.*

   *Children **don't take** exams at the end of primary school.*

2. We talk about events in the past with the past simple.

   *I **was** good at primary school.*

   *I **started** primary school at five.*

   *I **didn't take** the 11+ exam.*

In English, there are two kinds of verb, the verb *be* and other verbs. ③

1. The verb *be*: present simple

subject	verb	complement*	extra information
The 11+	is	an exam.	
A levels	are	exams.	
School	isn't	compulsory	after 16.
Classes	aren't	small	at secondary school.

*The correct name for any words after the verb *be* is the *complement*.

2. Other verbs: present simple

subject	verb	object	extra information
Many children	begin	school	at five.
Primary school	lasts	six years,	from five to 11.
Children	don't take	exams	at nursery school.
Primary	*doesn't mean*	*second.*	

A **Talking about general facts**

My country has three kinds of school.

Read the facts below about the education system in Britain.
Give a general fact about the education system in your country.

1. Britain has four kinds of school.
2. They are nursery, primary, secondary and sixth form.
3. Many British children start school at four or five.
4. Education is compulsory up to the age of 16.
5. Pupils can leave school at 16.
6. Many pupils go on to sixth form.
7. There are exams called A levels at 18.
8. Fifty per cent of pupils go on to university.

1. The verb *be*: past simple ④

subject	verb	complement	extra information
I	was(n't)	good	at primary school.
The exams	were(n't)	easy	at 16.
I	was(n't)	a prefect	in the sixth form.

2. Other verbs: past simple

subject	verb	object	extra information
I	started	school	at five.
I	took	ten GCSEs	at the end of secondary school.
I	didn't leave	school	at 16.

B **Talking about past facts**

I started school at four.

Read each fact about the education system in Britain.
Give true information about your own education in the past.

1. Many British children start school at four or five.
2. Many children like their first school.
3. Pupils take exams at 16.
4. Many pupils don't like doing exams.
5. Some pupils leave school at 16.
6. Many pupils stay at school up to the age of 18.

A **Reviewing sounds (1)**

1. Study the dialogues below.

   a. <u>Underline</u> the words with the vowel sound /ɪ/.

   b. (Circle) the words with the vowel sound /iː/.

   1 A: How do you feel?

   B: I'm really ill.

   2 A: Did you eat the eel?

   B: No, I didn't!

   3 A: Is he his brother?

   B: No, but she's his sister.

2. Practise the dialogues in pairs.

B **Reviewing sounds (2)**

Say each pair of words below. Make sure your partner can hear the difference.

	A	B
1.	bit	pit
2.	buy	pie
3.	bought	port
4.	open	Oban
5.	cab	cap

Table 1: *Good and bad teachers*

good	bad
keep order (= stop bad behaviour)	sarcastic (= make fun of)

C **Researching information**

1. Work in two groups.
   Group A: Read the text on page 177.
   Group B: Read the text on page 173.
   Underline the new words.

2. Ask the other members of your group about the new words.

3. Complete the correct part of Table 1.

4. Add any ideas of your own to your column.

D **Giving a short factual talk**

Stay in two groups, A and B.

1. Read Assignment 1. Which talk are you going to give?

2. Prepare your talk. Remember:
   - Choose the correct tense for each section.
   - Form the tense correctly.
   - Give definitions of new words.
   - Underline key words and phrases in your talk.

3. Practise giving your talk to your group.

4. Make new groups. There must be students from Group A and Group B in each group. Give your talk.

5. Ask about any new words.

Faculty of Education
Assignment 1

Reflect on your experiences of being a student. In the next tutorial you must give a short talk.
Either:
- give your idea of good teachers and talk about the best teacher you ever had.

Or:
- give your idea of bad teachers and talk about the worst teacher you ever had.

Reading: Living and working at university

1.11 Vocabulary for reading   English-English dictionaries

A   Developing vocabulary

Find nine words or phrases in the list on the right connected with computers. Match the words to the meanings. Use a dictionary to check your answers.

1. domain _____ a type of website, e.g., .ac = an academic website, probably a university

2. _____ a program which finds websites and webpages

3. _____ the way computers in different locations are linked together to share information

4. _____ one page on a website

5. _____ a set of webpages on the world wide web

6. _____ an entrance on the Internet to a set of resources

7. _____ a program which damages computer documents or programs

8. _____ a connection between two Internet documents

9. _____ a way of protecting your computer or documents on your computer

B   Building background knowledge

Complete the text below with words from the list on the right. Make any necessary changes. Use a dictionary to check your ideas.

> At university, lecturers often give assignments with deadlines, for example: 'You must write 2,000 words on a particular _____topic_____ by next Tuesday.' You must do research for an assignment in the library or on the Internet. This is called _____ research. You must find out about the research and ideas of other people. However, sometimes you must do _____ research. This is 'first' research. It means doing an _____ yourself and _____ the results. You must then analyze your _____.

C   Developing independent learning

1. Study the extract from a dictionary. What do the letters in brackets ( ) mean?

2. How many meanings of *record* does the extract show?

3. Use your dictionary to find the part(s) of speech and the meaning(s) of these words: *save, access, mark*.

> **record** (*n*) /ˈrekɔːd/
> **1.** a piece of information in writing; *Have you got a ~ of her name?* **2.** a plastic disk with information on, usually music; *CDs are more popular than ~s nowadays.*
>
> **record** (*v*) /rɪˈkɔːd/
> **1.** to put information in writing; *I ~ed the results in a table.* **2.** to put information into electronic form; *The group are ~ing a new album at the moment.*

---

accurate *(adj)*
analyze *(v)*
attachment *(n)*
  [= document]
cut *(v)* [= take out]
data *(n)*
domain *(n)*
efficiently *(adv)*
experiment *(n)*
extracurricular *(adj)*
heading *(n)*
(the) Internet *(n)*
link *(n)*
manage *(v)*
mark *(n and v)*
opinion *(n)*
out *(adj)*
  [= not in a library]
password *(n)*
paste *(v)*
permission *(n)*
plagiarism *(n)*
plagiarize *(v)*
portal *(n)*
primary *(adj)*
  [research]
program *(n)*
record *(n and v)*
relax *(v)*
remind *(v)*
respect *(v)*
search engine
secondary *(adj)*
  [research]
sensibly *(adj)*
source *(n)*
subheading *(n)*
topic *(n)*
virus *(n)*
webpage *(n)*
website *(n)*
wireless *(adj)*

A Activating ideas

You are going to read an article (opposite). Read the heading.

1. What is the article about? Make a list of possible ideas, e.g., *schedules*.

2. What sort of information do you expect to find in the article? Tick one or more.

☐ jokes   ☐ information
☐ news   ☐ advice
☐ explanations   ☐ rules

3. What tense(s) will be in the text? Why?

4. Read the subheading. Do you agree with the statement? Why (not)?

B Making and checking hypotheses

1. Read each section heading. Write **one** piece of advice for each section under **my advice** in the table below.

S	my advice	in the text
1.	*eat sensibly*	✓
2.		
3.		
4.		
5.		

2. Read each section of the text. Tick your advice or write something new in the right-hand column above.

C Understanding vocabulary in context

These words in the text may be new to you. Match each word to a dictionary definition.

1. sensibly   ☐ (*v*) organize or control; *They ~ their money very well.*

2. extracurricular ☐ (*n*) personal idea or view; *In my ~, the library is better than the Internet for most research.*

3. respect   ☐ (*n*) allowing someone to do something; *Have you got ~ to be here?*

4. efficiently   ☐ (*v*) make someone remember something; *The lecturer ~ me to give in the assignment tomorrow.*

5. opinion   ☐ (*v*) show someone you have a good opinion of them; *You should ~ people who are older than you.*

6. permission   ☐1 (*adv*) in a correct or practical way; *He does not always behave ~.*

7. remind   ☐ (*adv*) with no waste of time; *If you do this job ~, it will only take a short time.*

8. manage   ☐ (*adj*) after lectures; *There are many ~ activities at this university.*

D Developing critical thinking

Discuss these questions.

1. Which piece(s) of advice in the text do you agree with?

2. Which piece(s) of advice do you disagree with?

Life ... at university

University life is different from school life in many ways.

1 **University life sometimes means living away from home.**

Now you are responsible for your life. In the past, perhaps, your parents managed your life. Perhaps they made meals for you, took you to school and reminded you to do homework or revise for a test. Now, you must do everything for yourself. Buy a calendar. Mark all the important dates and times on it – lectures, deadlines for assignments, the dates of tests and examinations. Never miss deadlines, and always prepare for tests and examinations.

You are also responsible for managing your health. Eat sensibly and get enough sleep. Work hard, but relax too. Do extracurricular activities – join social clubs at the university or in the city.

2 **University life sometimes means sharing accommodation.**

You don't have to make friends with flatmates. But you must respect them. Don't use their possessions. Never go into their rooms without permission. At home, perhaps, you only had to clean your bedroom. But in your hall or flat, clean the kitchen and the bathroom after using it.

3 **University life usually means working harder at your studies.**

You probably found school work hard sometimes. But university work is usually much harder. Don't worry about this. Most university students feel the same. Always do your best. Spend at least two hours on private study for every hour of lectures.

4 **University life sometimes means learning new language skills.**

You learnt English at school. Your English is good. But you need new language skills at university. Learn how to listen to lectures. Learn how to participate in tutorials. Learn how to do reading research efficiently. Learn how to write essays.

5 **University life always means developing critical thinking.**

At school, you wrote essays with titles such as 'Describe the water cycle.' 'Compare and contrast the physical features of two small countries.' But at university, lecturers often give titles to make you think. For example: 'Schools are like prisons. Discuss.' Research the topic. Find out the facts and the ideas of other people. Give your opinion at the end if the lecturer asks for it.

2 Life ... at university

A Reviewing vocabulary

Make a phrase with each of the verbs below.

manage your life

manage eat respect do miss spend think listen participate write

B Identifying a new skill (1)

1. Read Skills Check 1. What should you look at before you start reading?

2. Study the titles and introductions below. Match each title and introduction to one paragraph on the right.

3. What other information do you expect to read in the same text?

Skills Check 1

Preparing to read

1. Read the **title** or **heading** of an article. Think: *What information is in this text?*

2. Read the **introduction** or **first paragraph**. Think: *Is my prediction correct?*

---

1 Staff at Greenhill University
We are delighted to welcome you to the university. We would like to introduce you to some of the staff so you know who to go to if you have any problems.

2 University Sports Club
Do you want to get fit, or just have some fun with friends? Come and join the university's own sports club in the Sports Centre near the main entrance.

3 Using the projector
It is easy to use the projector in each tutorial room if you follow these simple instructions.

4 IT Services and Support
We're here to make sure you stay connected everywhere on the campus.

5 IMPORTANT NOTICE
Portable Electrical Equipment
In accordance with the Electricity at Work regulations 1990, we must test all electrical equipment for safety.

☐ **Using your own PC/laptop**
All rooms in the halls of residence have Internet connections free of charge. Note: This is not wireless. You must buy a cable from the IT Support Office.

☐ **Inspection day**
Please leave all electrical equipment on your desk on the day of the inspection. Each item costs £1.10. The inspector will put a sticker on each safe item.

☐ **Mr Mills** is in charge of ISS, the International Student Support service. Go to Mr Mills if you want extra help with your English, for example.

☐ **Opening hours**
7.00 a.m.–10.00 p.m. Monday to Friday
9.00 a.m.–6.00 p.m. Saturday and Sunday

☐ • Switch on the device. (The Power On switch is on the underside.)
• Switch on your laptop.
• Go to PowerPoint on your laptop.

C Identifying a new skill (2)

1. Read Skills Check 2.

2. Underline all the pieces of advice and all the instructions in the texts above.

Skills Check 2

Recognizing advice and instructions

We use the **imperative** to give advice.

Buy a calendar.

Don't worry.

We also use the imperative to give instructions.

Switch on the device.

Imperatives have no subject. We make the negative with the auxiliary *Don't*. We can sometimes make ⑤ the sentence stronger with *always* and *never*.

	verb	other information
	Relax!	
	Be	happy.
	Buy	a calendar.
	Eat	sensibly.
	Revise	for tests.
Always	do	your best.

auxiliary	verb	other information
	worry!	
	be	worried.
Don't	use	their possessions.
	write	carelessly.
	go	into their rooms.
Never	use	their possessions.

A Predicting advice with imperatives

All the phrases below come from a leaflet about using the Internet safely.
Read each verb and think: *What will the advice be?*

1. Be careful ...
2. Don't click ...
3. Don't open ...
4. Install ...
5. Never give ...
6. Protect ...
7. Turn off ...
8. Don't believe ...

Time phrases tell you the time of a sentence. Time phrases can come at the beginning or the end of a sentence. ⑥

time phrases	subject	verb	other information
Now,	you	are	responsible for your life.
In the past,	your parents	managed	your life.

B Predicting time with time phrases

What time is the writer talking about in each of the phrases below? Tick **present** or **past**.

	present	past
At one time,		✓
At that time,		
At the moment,		
At the present time,		
Currently,		
In her childhood,		

	present	past
In the 20th century,		
Last week,		
Now,		
Nowadays,		
Then,		
Yesterday,		

Web Images Videos Maps News Shopping Mail more ▼

Google

plagiarism   Search

About 5,160,000 results (0.11 seconds)   Advanced search

Everything

News

Books

More

The web
Pages from the UK

Any time
Latest
Past 2 days

Standard view
Wonder wheel

More search tools

Free Check For **Plagiarism**   Sponsored links
www.Grammarly.com/**Plagiarism**_Checks   Check Your Papers For **Plagiarism** And Correct Grammar Errors Now!

Online **Plagiarism** Checker
WriteCheck.Turnitin.com   Originality checking for STUDENTS From the makers of Turnitin

Plagiarism.org
Welcome to **Plagiarism**.org, the online resource for people concerned with the growing
problem of internet **plagiarism**. This site is designed to provide the ...
www.**plagiarism**.org/ - Cached - Similar

Plagiarism - Wikipedia, the free encyclopedia
Plagiarism, as defined in the 1995 Random House Compact Unabridged Dictionary, is the
"use or close imitation of the language and thoughts of another author ...
Etymology - Sanctions - Defenses - Self-plagiarism
en.wikipedia.org/wiki/**Plagiarism** - Cached - Similar

Plagiarism I Define **Plagiarism** at Dictionary.com

Sponsored links

Plagiarism
Software checks for **Plagiarism**
Plagiarism and Anti - **Plagiarism**
TurnitinSafely.com/**Plagiarism**

Plagiarism Software
Use the automatic tool for
avoiding and eluding it.
Synonymizer.com.ar

Dissertation Proofreading
International Students:
Get up to 20% better grades!
www.CorrectandPass.com

See your ad here »

A Reviewing vocabulary

What can you ...

1. be responsible for?   3. revise for?   5. respect?   7. spend?   9. record?
2. manage?   4. miss?   6. worry about?   8. share?

B Predicting content

You are going to read the text on the opposite page.

1. Read the heading and the first paragraph. What is the text about?
2. What advice will the text contain? Make some predictions.
3. Read the section headings. Check your predictions to see if they were correct.

C Understanding advice

1. Read the text. Tick the advice from the text. Correct any pieces of advice which are wrong.

   a. Do a lot of research.   ✓
   b. Always do research in a library.   ✗   Go to the library if possible.
   c. Never use the Internet.   ☐
   d. Don't read sites with .co.uk or .com.   ☐
   e. Don't read private sites.   ☐
   f. Don't read sites with .org or .gov.   ☐
   g. Always start with Wikipedia.   ☐
   h. Report information in your own words.   ☐
   i. Cut and paste interesting parts of websites.   ☐

2. Why does the writer give each piece of advice?

   a. Because you will get good marks.
   b. Because a library is organized, the information is checked and the librarian can help you.

D Present or past?

Read the final section, **Avoid plagiarism**, again. Mark the sentence(s) of the paragraph which:

- give general facts (*GF*)   • talk about the present (*PRES*)
- talk about the past (*PAST*)   • give advice (*ADV*)

Research at university

You must do a lot of assignments at university. For most of the assignments, you must do research. Do a lot of research. Then you will get good marks. But you must do *good* research.

1. Go to the library

At one time, students did research in the university library. Nowadays, most students do research on the Internet. But the university library is still there. It is still an excellent place for students. Try the library first! Firstly, the information is organized. Secondly, it is checked. Thirdly, the librarian can help you. But perhaps the library is closed or the book you want is out. Then you must use the Internet.

2. Use *academic* sources

Type 'What is a good teacher?' into Google. You get nearly four million webpages! But a lot of those pages are commercial. Look for the domains .co.uk and .com. Don't read these sites. They want to sell you something. Other webpages are private sites. A tilde (~) says 'This is a private site'. Don't read these sites either. Nobody has checked the information on these sites. Look for academic sites (.ac and .edu). Look also for .org and .gov. These are not commercial sites.

3. Use more than one source

Do not get all your information from one source. Firstly, perhaps the source is not accurate. Secondly, perhaps the source does not have complete information. Finally, you risk plagiarism – see below. Choose at least three academic sources. Never use Wikipedia! It is not an academic site. Take notes from each source. Then use your own words to report the information. Always record your sources. At one time, it was easy to find the source again. Nowadays, it is often hard to find a website a second time. Copy the complete web address of the article. Write the date of your search. Keep it with your notes.

4. Avoid plagiarism

Plagiarism is copying someone's work. The word comes from Latin. It means to 'steal or kidnap'. At one time, students stole paragraphs from webpages. Lecturers accepted their work. But in 2001, a lecturer at an American university checked student assignments. He had a new computer program. He found 158 cases of plagiarism. Forty-eight students had to leave the university. Nowadays, all university lecturers use computer programs. They find plagiarism easily. Don't cut and paste from websites. Sometimes, the lecturer gives no marks for an assignment with plagiarism. Sometimes, the university asks the student to leave.

How much have you learnt about education in Theme 1 so far?
Test your knowledge and your partner's knowledge.

1 How many parts of a university campus can you name?

2 What do you know about these customs in the UK?

3 What do these pictures show?

4 How many types of school are there in the UK? What do you know about each type?

5 What is a good teacher?

6 What is a bad teacher?

Writing: A Personal Statement

1

Getting into a university

A Activating ideas

How do you get into a university in your country? Explain the process.

B Understanding new vocabulary

Complete the leaflet below. Use words from the vocabulary list on the right. Make any necessary changes.

How do I get into a UK university?

1. You can ...apply........ direct to the university of your choice.

2. You must complete an .... form, in paper or online.

3. The form asks for personal ...., such as name and address.

4. These details include information about your education and your ....

5. You must demonstrate that your language .... is high enough to take a tertiary course in English.

6. You must also .... a Personal Statement.

7. This statement tells the university your reasons for .... for a particular course.

8. You must also tell the university about any work ...., full-time or part-time.

9. Some admissions officers at university want to know about your .... and interests.

10. You must supply the name of a .... – a teacher in your own country, for example, who can write about your suitability as a university student.

C Developing independent learning

In English-English dictionaries, words with the same **root** appear near each other. See the example below.

1. Study the dictionary entries for some words from this theme. What is the root?

2. Use your dictionary to find words related to some of the words in the list on the right.
   - the noun from *delete*
   - the noun from *organize*
   - the verb from *qualification*
   - the noun for a person who *edits* a book
   - the plural of *hobby*

---

applicable (*adj*) fitting the situation, e.g., *Is this rule ~ to me?*

applicant (*n*) a person who applies for a job or a place on a course; *~s must write a Personal Statement.*

application (*n*) a document, usually a form, with information about an applicant, e.g., name, address, nationality; *Please complete the ~ form in block capitals.*

apply (*v*) 1. send information about yourself to get a job or a place on a course; 2. fit the situation; *This rule does not ~ to me because I am a student at the university.*

---

address (*n*)
applicable (*adj*)
applicant (*n*)
application (*n*)
apply (*v*)
appropriate (*adj*)
block capital
collect (*v*)
complete (*v*)
contents (*n*)
date of birth
delete (*v*)
detail (*n*)
edit (*v*)
employment (*n*)
experience (*n*)
form (*n*)
full (*adj*) [name]
hobby (*n*)
interest (*n*)
level (*n*)
lower case
membership (*n*)
organize (*v*)
paragraph (*n*)
participate (*v*)
print (*v*)
punctuation (*n*)
qualification (*n*)
referee (*n*)
require (*v*)
rewrite (*v*)
select (*v*)
space (*n*)
statement (*n*)
status (*n*)
subject (*n*)
surname (*n*)

A   Understanding a discourse structure (1)

1. Find and circle the instructions on the form below.
2. What mistakes has the person made in completing the form?

University Sports Club

	Application form	Do not write in this space
Title	Mr Mrs Miss Ms ~~Dr~~ (delete as applicable)	
Sex	M / F ✓ (circle as appropriate)	

Please PRINT one letter only in each space. Use BLACK ink only.

First name(s)	R	i	c	a	r	d	o		G	u	i	ll	e	r	m	o
Surname	M	o	r	e	no											
E-mail address	r	i	k	12	@	h	o	t	m	a	i	l	.	c	o	m

Membership required	Single [X] Family [ ] Swim and Gym Only [X] (Tick one)
Date of birth (DD/MM/YYYY)	20th October 85

B   Performing a real-world task

Complete the application form below with true information about **you**.

University Sports Club

	Application form	Do not write in this space
Title	Mr Mrs Miss Ms Dr (delete as applicable)	
Sex	M / F (circle as appropriate)	

Please PRINT one letter only in each space. Use BLACK ink only.

First name(s)																
Surname																
E-mail address																

Membership required	Single [ ] Family [ ] Swim and Gym Only [ ] (Tick one)
Date of birth (DD/MM/YYYY)	

C   Understanding a discourse structure (2)

Study the application form and the Personal Statement on the opposite page.

Complete the Personal Statement with information from the application form.

D   Producing key patterns

Study the openings of sentences from the Personal Statement. Complete each sentence with true information about you.

1. My name is ....
2. I was born ....
3. I attended ....
4. I am studying at ....
5. I am taking ....
6. Out of school, I ....

Greenhill University
Application form

By completing this form, you consent to the university passing your personal details to our agent in your region.

Please complete the form in BLOCK CAPITALS.

Title	Mr ~~Mr~~ ~~Mrs~~ Miss ~~Ms~~ ~~Dr~~ (delete as applicable)											Official use only
First name(s)	O	L	I	V	I	A		A	M	A	N	D	A
Surname	M	A	R	T	I	N	S						

Status	SINGLE
Place of birth	LONDON, UK
Date of birth (DD/MM/YYYY)	15/04/1992
Nationality	BRITISH
Course applied for	BA EDUCATION (SPECIAL INTEREST: PRIMARY TEACHING)

Schools	School	From (month/year)	To (month/year)
	PENNINGTON PRIMARY SCHOOL	SEP 98	JUL 04
	LYMINGTON SECONDARY SCHOOL	SEP 04	JUL 09
	BROCKENHURST SIXTH FORM COLLEGE	SEP 09	NOW

Qualification(s)	10 GCSES, INC. MATHS, BIOLOGY, FRENCH A LEVELS (EXAMS IN JUNE 2011 + EXPECTED GRADE) ENGLISH (B), PSYCHOLOGY (B), DRAMA (C) TRAINED IN FIRST AID LIFE-SAVING CERTIFICATE
Employment	PART-TIME FOR PUBLISHING COMPANY - RESEARCH FOR PRIMARY SCHOOL BOOKS
Hobbies and interests	FOOTBALL (CAPTAIN AT SEC. SCH.), GUIDES, LOCAL YOUTH THEATRE

Personal Statement

My name is Olivia Amanda Martins and I am __eighteen__ years old. I am British.

I was born _____. I am _____. I live in Lymington on the south coast of England.

I am applying for _____. I want _____ because I enjoy learning about this subject very much. I am particularly interested in _____.

I hope to become _____.

I attended Pennington Primary School from September 1998 to July 2004. I went to Lymington Secondary School _____. Then I enrolled at sixth form college.

I am studying at Brockenhurst Sixth Form College now. I _____ in September 2009. I _____ English, Psychology and Drama in the sixth form.

At the end of secondary school, I obtained _____ in a wide range of subjects, including Maths, Biology and French. Next year, I hope to get _____.

I am trained in first aid, and I also have _____.

At secondary school, I was _____. Out of school, I go to Guides. I also participate in _____.

At the moment, I _____ part-time for a local publishing company. I _____ research for a series of books for primary children.

In conclusion, I am a hard-working student. I get on well with people of all kinds. I believe that primary teaching is the career for me because I like working with young children.

A Developing vocabulary

All these words from the theme have the same vowel sound. What is the sound? What is the correct spelling?

1. Write one or two letters in each space.

   a. incr_ea_se   f. stud_____
   b. eight_____n   g. t_____ch
   c. facult_____   h. m_____n
   d. r_____d   i. l_____ve
   e. d_____tails   j. degr_____

2. Read Skills Check 1 and check your answers.

3. Write some more words with each pattern, e.g., *agree*.

B Identifying a new skill

1. Read Skills Check 2.

2. Study the list of paragraph topics below. Read the sentences from a Personal Statement below. Write the number of the correct paragraph next to each sentence.

   1. Personal details   5. Qualifications
   2. Course + reasons   6. Hobbies and interests
   3. Schools in the past   7. Work
   4. School now + subjects   8. Conclusion

   ☐ I also participate in a small music group.
   ☐ I am applying for the BA course in Engineering.
   ☐ 1 │ I am married.
   ☐ I am not studying at school now.
   ☐ I am particularly interested in machines.
   ☐ I am working full-time as a sales assistant at the moment.
   ☐ I enjoy playing the guitar and writing music.
   ☐ I believe that engineering is the career for me because I like working with machines.
   ☐ I finished school in July 2009.
   ☐ I live in Madrid.
   ☐ 5 │ I obtained the International Baccalaureate (IB) in 2009.
   ☐ I studied at the American School of Madrid.
   ☐ I want to become an engineer.
   ☐ I scored 38 points in the IB.
   ☐ My name is Pablo Juarez and I am Spanish.
   ☐ In conclusion, I always try hard in my studies.

Skills Check 1

Spelling the /iː/ sound

There are five main ways to spell this sound.

e	*me, we, he, details*
ee	*green, see, degree, eighteen*
ea	*read, teach, mean, leave, easy*
ie	*achieve, believe, thief*
y	*history, very, study, faculty*

Skills Check 2

Organizing information into paragraphs

In English, we put all the information about one subject into the same paragraph.

The first paragraph of Olivia's Personal Statement (Lesson 1.17) contains personal details – name, age, nationality, etc.

My name is Olivia Amanda Martins and I am eighteen years old. I am British. I was born in London on 15th April, 1992. I live in Lymington on the south coast of England.

When you are writing, choose a subject for each paragraph. Then decide the information to go into each paragraph.

C Producing key patterns

Study the openings of more sentences from the Personal Statement. Complete each sentence with true information about you.

1. I want to study _____.
2. I hope to get _____.
3. I am particularly interested in _____.
4. I hope to become _____.

We use the **present simple** to write about **general facts**.   ⑦

Table 1   Table 2

subject	verb *be*	complement
I	am (not)	Brazilian.
		17.
		married.
		from Santos.
		at secondary school.
		interested in medicine.

subject	other verbs	extra information
I (do not)	live	in São Paulo.
	participate	in many activities.
	get on with	people well.
	play	tennis.
	have	a certificate for life-saving.
	go	to a local youth theatre.

A   Writing about yourself (1)

1. Cover the **complement** column in Table 1. What sort of information can follow the verb *be*?
   nationality

2. Cover the **extra information** column in Table 2. What sort of information can follow each verb?
   live + in a town or city

3. Write one true sentence about yourself with each pattern.

We use the **present simple** to write about **likes**, **wants** and **hopes**.   ⑧

subject	verb	extra information	
I	like	working	with children.
	enjoy	education	very much.
	want	to study	education.
	hope	to become	a teacher.

B   Writing about yourself (2)

1. Cover the table above. Rewrite the sentences below correctly.
   a. I am like studying science. *I like studying science.*
   b. I love teach young children new things. ....
   c. I enjoy to learn mathematics. ....
   d. I want doing a course in medicine. ....
   e. I hope becoming a doctor. ....

2. Write one true sentence about yourself in each pattern.

We use the **present continuous** for actions **happening at this time** (but perhaps not at this moment).   ⑨

subject	verb	object
I	am studying	Biology and Mathematics.
	am working	part-time.
	am doing	research.

C   Writing about yourself (3)

Write three true sentences about yourself with the same pattern as in the table above.

A   Reviewing vocabulary

What noun or noun phrase can follow each verb?

1. apply to   *a university*
2. attend
3. complete
4. enrol at
5. have
6. lead
7. obtain
8. play
9. study
10. take

B   Key writing stages

Study The TOWER of writing. What are the five stages in the TOWER of writing?

C   Thinking

You are going to write a Personal Statement for a UK university. What information must you give? Brainstorm.

name, nationality, course

D   Organizing

Design a writing plan. Make notes about yourself for each section.

E   Writing

Write your Personal Statement. Remember to use:

- the present simple for general facts.
- the present simple for likes, wants and hopes.
- the present continuous for actions happening now.
- the past simple for events in the past.

F   Editing

Exchange statements with a partner. Read his/her statement.

1. Do you understand it? If you have any problems, put a *?* next to the sentence.
2. Are there any:
   - spelling mistakes? Write *S*.
   - grammar mistakes? Write *G*.
   - punctuation mistakes? Write *P*.

G   Rewriting

Read your Personal Statement again. Look at the *?*, *S*, *G* and *P* marks on your first draft. Write the Personal Statement again.

The TOWER of writing

 T   **hink**
- Who is it for?
- What is it about?
- Where can I find more information?

 O   **rganize**
- What is the writing plan?
- How many paragraphs do I need?
- What information should be in each paragraph?

 W   **rite**
- The first draft = *Writing for the writer*

 E   **dit**
- Does the first draft make sense?
- Have I made any mistakes in spelling, grammar or pronunciation?

 R   **ewrite**
Correct any mistakes.

A　Activating ideas

1. Look at the photographs above. What are the main activities of each club?
2. Which of these clubs would you like to join? Why? Which of these clubs would you hate? Why?

B　Gathering information (1)

1. Divide into two groups. Group 1: 🎧 1.24, Group 2: 🎧 1.25. Listen to the information about two clubs at Greenhill University – the IT Club and the Debating Society. Make notes to answer these questions.

   a. Who is the club for?

   b. Where do the meetings take place?

   c. When do they take place?

   d. When do they start?

   e. When do they finish?

   f. What do people do at the club?

2. Work in pairs, one student from Group 1 and the other from Group 2. Exchange information about your club. Make notes.

3. Can you join both clubs? Explain your answer.

C　Gathering information (2)

1. Work in groups of three. Read one of the texts about social clubs – the Drama Club, the Volleyball Club or the Geography Club on pages 38/39. Make notes.
2. Explain the information you read about to your partners. Your partners should make notes.

D　Giving a talk

Choose one of the clubs from your portfolio notes – the IT Club, the Debating Society, the Drama Club, the Volleyball Club or the Geography Club. Write a short talk. Give your talk in a small group.

E　Researching

Do some research into two or three local clubs. Design a table for collecting information about them. Make notes in the table.

Drama Club

Do you like acting?

The Drama Club meets at 3.45 every Tuesday in the Drama Studio. We finish around 6 p.m.

This club is run by the Year 3 students, but it is open to anyone.

We put on a play every semester. Our next production will be Ibsen's *A Doll's House*.

If you want to be part of this production, come along on Tuesday 14th September.

We do not audition for the roles. We just give people parts.

Everyone in the club is involved in the production in some way.

VOLLEYBALL CLUB

Do you like sport?

If the answer is yes ...

Can you play volleyball?

Don't worry if the answer is no, because the Volleyball Club is for good players and complete beginners.

We meet for one hour at 12.30 on Friday lunchtimes on the netball courts.

You must wear sports clothes and trainers.

Good players practise with the volleyball team. Beginners learn the game and have fun!

Geography Club

How many continents are there?
Where is Peru? Where are the West Indies?
What is the longest river in the world?

If you can answer these questions, come and join the Geography Club.*

Where in the world are we?

We meet for one hour in Room 24 (on the second floor).
Meetings start at 4.30 p.m. on Mondays.

Come along for:
• help with assignments • geography games • projects

We also go on many field trips to local areas of interest,
for example, nature reserves.

*Don't worry if you can't answer them! Come anyway!

Theme 2

Psychology and sociology

- Concepts

- Human behaviour

- Personality and behaviour

- Extroverts and introverts

2.1 Vocabulary for listening | What groups do you belong to?

1   2   3   4

A Activating ideas

Look at the pictures above. What groups do they show?

B Understanding vocabulary in context

1. Study the figure below. What does it show?

2. 🔊 2.1 Listen. Complete the text below with words from the list on the right. Make any necessary changes.

A person is an ...*individual*.... Psychology is about individuals. _____ ask

questions like: *What is the* _____*? How does it control* _____

behaviour? People have _____ with other people. _____ is about

human behaviour in groups. Sociologists ask questions like: *Why do people*

_____ *groups? Why do groups sometimes* _____ *badly?* In the

diagram, the circle for **my family** is _____ from the other three circles.

Why? Because my family is _____ from my friends, my neighbours and

my colleagues. Why are these three circles _____? Because some of

my friends live in my neighbourhood and some of my friends are also my

colleagues. _____

call the four inner circles the

_____ groups. The people

in your primary groups are very

important to you.

The human race
My colleagues
My family
My neighbours
My friends
My country

C Developing vocabulary

1. Discuss the difference in meaning between each pair of words below.

2. 🔊 2.2 Listen to a student explaining one word in each pair. Tick the word.

a. ☐ sociologist   ☐ sociology
b. ☐ psychologist   ☐ psychology
c. ☐ primary school   ☐ primary group
d. ☐ mind   ☐ brain
e. ☐ people   ☐ human race
f. ☐ individual   ☐ identity

D Developing critical thinking

Draw a figure to show the groups you belong to.

act (*v*)
aim (*n* and *v*)
alone (*adj*)
ancient (*adj*)
behave (*v*)
behaviour (*n*)
brain (*n*)
century (*n*)
cognitive (*adj*)
colleague (*n*)
control (*v*)
different (*adj*) [from]
form (*v*)
friendship (*n*)
group (*n*)
human (*n*)
human race
identity (*n*)
individual (*n*)
key (*adj*)
link (*v*)
medicine (*n*)
memory (*n*)
mind (*n*)
neighbour (*n*)
pattern (*n*)
personality (*n*)
philosopher (*n*)
primary (*adj*) [= main]
psychologist (*n*)
psychology (*n*)
relationship (*n*)
religion (*n*)
rights (*n*)
rule (*n*)
separate (*adj*)
social (*adj*)
sociologist (*n*)
sociology (*n*)
term (*n*) [= name]
the same as

_____

_____

_____

A Activating ideas

Discuss these questions.

1. When did humans start to live in groups?
2. Why do people live in groups?
3. When do groups of people behave well?
4. Why do groups of people behave badly?

B Predicting content

Look at the first slide from a lecture on the opposite page. Which phrases will you hear? Tick one or more.

1. ☐ a man called
2. ☐ at that time
3. ☐ he said
4. ☐ he wrote a famous book
5. ☐ human behaviour

6. ☐ in mathematics
7. ☐ in the 14th century
8. ☐ in the future
9. ☐ in the past
10. ☐ next year

C Showing comprehension

🎧 2.3 DVD 2.A Watch each part of the lecture. Tick the best way to complete the sentence about each part.

Part 1. The lecture is about …

a. ✔ sociology in the past and the present.
b. ☐ sociology in the past.
c. ☐ sociology in the present.

Part 2. Sociologists …

a. ☐ study human behaviour in groups.
b. ☐ try to understand human behaviour in groups.
c. ☐ study, try to understand and try to predict human behaviour in groups.

Part 3. People first became interested in human behaviour …

a. ☐ a long time ago.
b. ☐ in 1838.
c. ☐ in the 4th century BCE.

Part 4. This part of the talk is mainly about …

a. ☐ Plato and Ibn Khaldun.
b. ☐ two German sociologists.
c. ☐ Max Weber.

Part 5. Anthony Giddens believes that …

a. ☐ groups make people.
b. ☐ people make groups.
c. ☐ the relationship between people and groups is two-way.

D Remembering real-world knowledge

1. Complete the information on each slide opposite.
2. DVD 2.A Watch the lecture again and check your ideas.

E Developing critical thinking

Read the quotations on the slides opposite. Which ones do you agree with? Which ones do you disagree with? Explain your answers.

Social Studies (Module SSU24)

Lecture 2: Introduction to the science of sociology

- Aims
- History: Key names and quotes
- Sociology today

'To study, understand and _____ human behaviour in groups.'

Auguste Comte

'The Father of Sociology'
Key date: _____

'Human behaviour has _____ and _____.'

Plato

Key date: _____

'People live in groups for _____ and _____,'

'Groups must have _____ of behaviour.'

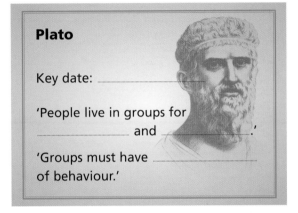

Ibn Khaldun

Key date: _____

'Groups are like _____. They are born, they grow and then they die. This happens to all groups.'

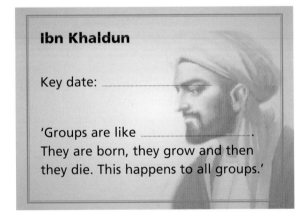

Karl Marx

Key date: _____

'People from different groups must _____ each other.'

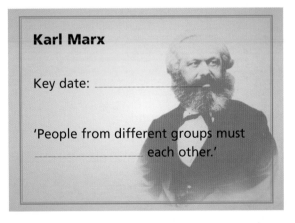

Max Weber

Key date: _____

'There are three important things for groups. They are _____, _____ and _____.'

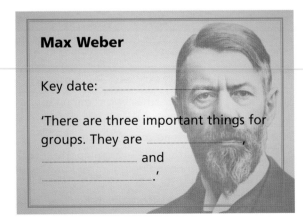

Anthony Giddens

Key date: _____

'People make society ... then _____ makes _____.'

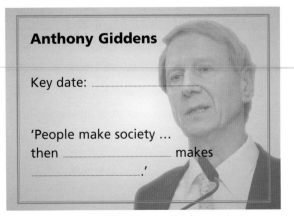

A Reviewing key words

1. Study the pairs of words on the right.
2. 🔊 2.4 Listen. Tick the word you hear in each case.

> a. *Nowadays we call the study of groups 'sociology'.*

B Identifying a new skill

Read the Skills Check. Look at the transcript for Lesson 2.2 on pages 185–186. Underline all the time expressions.

C Recognizing time signposts

🔊 2.5 Listen to sentences from other lectures. Is each sentence about the past or the present?

> 1. *In 1789, there were a lot of changes in France.*

	present	past
1.		✓
2.		
3.		
4.		
5.		
6.		
7.		
8.		

D Identifying vowel sounds

Look at the phrases below.

1. How do you say *a* in each underlined word?

   a. Do you all <u>have</u> a book?
   b. Let me <u>start</u> with …
   c. It's an important <u>part</u> of the topic.
   d. He's called 'The <u>Father</u> of Sociology'.
   e. He <u>began</u> writing in 1957.
   f. It's important to <u>understand</u> this.

2. Read the Pronunciation Check.
3. 🔊 2.6 Listen and check your answers.

a.	✓	sociology		sociologists
b.		man		human
c.		behave		behaviour
d.		friends		friendship
e.		safe		safety
f.		study		student
g.		aims		names
h.		pupils		people
i.		rights		right
j.		most		must

Skills Check

Recognizing time signposts

Time expressions help you understand a lecture. You can predict the tense of the sentence.

At that time	the sentence = past
These days	the sentence = present

Learn to recognize past-time expressions in speech.

Past

	1984, …	dates
In	the 14ᵗʰ century, …	centuries
	the 1960s, …	time periods
In	those days, …	
	the past, …	
At	that time, …	expressions
	one time, …	
	Many years later, …	

Present

At	the present time, …	
	Today, …	
	Now(adays), …	expressions
	These days, …	

Pronunciation Check

Hearing vowels: /æ/ and /ɑː/

The letter *a* has two common sounds:
1. the short sound in *have* – /æ/.
2. the long sound in *half* – /ɑː/.

The difference is very important for meaning in English, so you must learn to hear it.

Note: The letter *a* can make other sounds.

Examples: *all, what, name, many*

⑩

present time	past time
1. Sociology is about human behaviour in groups.	There was a lot of unrest.
2. Groups are like animals.	Poor people were unhappy.
3. Sociology has three main aims.	Plato had ideas about people and groups.
4. Giddens writes about modern groups.	Marx wrote a famous book.
5. They start to fight for their rights.	They started to fight for their rights.
6. Good teachers treat children well.	The teacher treated the children well.
7. Lectures last one hour.	The lecture lasted one hour.
8. They want to go home.	They wanted to go home.
9. We try to understand all the time.	We tried to understand during the lecture.
10. They work for a bank at the moment.	They worked for a bank at that time.
11. I live there now.	I lived there for years.
12. Groups sometimes behave badly.	The group behaved badly later in the evening.

Sentences 1–4: It is easy to recognize past-time sentences with **irregular past tense verbs**. You can hear the different words.

Sentences 5–8: It is difficult to recognize past-time sentences with **regular verbs ending in *t* or *d*** but you can sometimes hear the extra /ɪd/ sound.

Sentences 9–12: It is often impossible to recognize past-time sentences with **other regular verbs**. You must listen for time expressions in the sentence.

A Recognizing time from verb form (1)

1. 🔊 2.7 Listen to some verbs. Say *present* or *past* in each case.
2. 🔊 2.8 Listen to some sentences. Say *present* or *past* in each case.

B Recognizing time from verb form (2)

1. 🔊 2.9 Listen to some verbs. Say *present* or *past* in each case.
2. 🔊 2.10 Listen to the same verbs in sentences. Say *present* or *past* in each case.

C Recognizing time from time expressions

1. 🔊 2.11 Listen to some sentences. Say *present* or *past* or *I don't know* in each case.
2. 🔊 2.12 Listen to the same sentences with time expressions. Say *present* or *past* or *I don't know* in each case.

A   Reviewing vocabulary

2.13 Listen and complete the phrases.

1. human   _behaviour_   5. main   ....
2. modern   ....   6. famous   ....
3. important   ....   7. people in   ....
4. twentieth   ....   8. in the   ....

B   Activating knowledge

Look at the poster for a talk on the right.

1. Discuss the questions on the poster.

2. 2.14 DVD 2.B Watch the first part of the talk. Complete the sentences in your own words.

Psych. = ...
Psych. ≠ ...
Psych. = understand:
the way ...
the things ...
the things ...

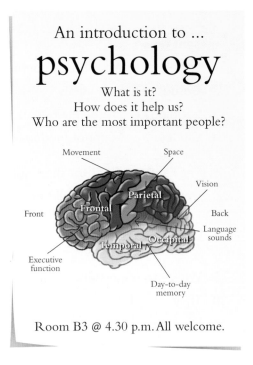

An introduction to ...

psychology

What is it?
How does it help us?
Who are the most important people?

Movement   Space
Vision
Parietal
Frontal
Front   Back
Language sounds
Temporal   Occipital
Executive function
Day-to-day memory

Room B3 @ 4.30 p.m. All welcome.

C   Applying a key skill

1. 2.15 DVD 2.C Watch the second part of the talk. The events are in order. Add a time expression to each one.

A long time ago ...	Aristotle – first book: _Para Psyche_
	Locke + Descartes – 'mind and body?'
	Wundt – psychology school
	Pavlov – 'How do people learn?'
	Sigmund Freud – dreams
	Watson – 'only study behaviour'
	Neisser – 'must study mind' = cognitive psychology

2. 2.16 DVD 2.D Watch the third part of the talk. Circle the correct verb form below.

Elizabeth Loftus

She is / (was) interested in learning.

She **works** / **worked** with the police.

Steven Pinker

He **is** / **was** a psychology teacher.

He **does** / **did** research into language and the mind.

Elizabeth Spelke

She **described** / **describes** new ideas about babies.

She **teaches** / **taught** psychology in the USA.

Speaking: Human behaviour

2.6 Vocabulary for speaking Personality

A Reviewing vocabulary

Label the diagram, using the expressions in the box.

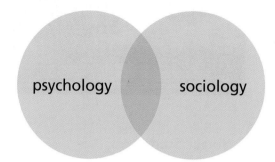

predicts group behaviour

both predict human behaviour

predicts individual behaviour

personal identity

group identity

B Understanding new vocabulary

1 A: Do you like being on your _____?

   B: It _____. Sometimes I like being with other people.

2 A: Is _____ the same as behaviour?

   B: Well, I think it _____ behaviour.

3 A: What is _____?

   B: I think it's _____ behaviour.

4 A: Can people _____ their behaviour?

   B: Yes, but they can't change _____.

1. 🔊 2.17 Listen and complete the conversations with words from the list on the right.
2. Practise the conversations in pairs.
3. Add more lines to each conversation.

C Practising new vocabulary

Discuss these questions.

1. When do you like being on your own?
2. When do you like being with other people?
3. Can you predict your friends' behaviour in different situations?
4. Which is the bigger influence on your personality – your family or your friends?
5. Has your personality changed in the last two or three years? If so, how?

D Learning new vocabulary

1. Tick the words used in this lesson in the list on the right.
2. Say each word ten times.
3. Try to use each word in a sentence in the next week.

aggressive (*adj*)
and so on
behaviour (*n*)
change (*v*)
clear (*adj*)
completely (*adv*)
depend (*v*) [on]
difference (*n*)
discuss (*v*)
excuse me
friendly (*adj*)
human (*adj* and *n*)
identity (*n*)
influence (*n* and *v*)
mind (*n*)
other (*adj*)
own (*pron*)
personality (*n*)
predict (*v*)
psychologist (*n*)
psychology (*n*)
quote (*n*)
similar (*adj*) [to]
situation (*n*)
smile (*n* and *v*)
society (*n*)
sociologist (*n*)
sociology (*n*)
together (*adv*)
useful (*adj*)

A Previewing vocabulary

1. 🔊 2.18 Listen and mark the stress on these words.

   a. be'haviour   f. f r i e n d l y
   b. c h a n g e s   g. i m p o r t a n t
   c. c o m p l e t e l y   h. i n f l u e n c e s
   d. d e p e n d   i. p e r s o n a l i t y
   e. d i f f e r e n c e   j. s i t u a t i o n

2. 🔊 2.19 Listen again and repeat the words.

B Studying a model

You are going to watch a group of students.

1. Look at the assignment title on the right. What is the group going to do?

2. 🔊 2.20 DVD 2.E Watch the discussion. Match the students, 1–4, with the opinions below.

Behaviour is more important than personality.	4
Personality is more important than behaviour.	
Personality and behaviour are the same.	
Personality and behaviour are different.	

C Practising a model

1. Look at the sentences in the box on the right. Put a line / between each group of words.

2. Say the sentences. Pause after each group of words.

D Speaking accurately

1. Three of the sentences below are grammatically incorrect. Find them and correct them.

   a. Sociology is a newer subject than psychology.
   b. Psychology and sociology they both predict human behaviour.
   c. Bad teachers are more sarcastic than good teachers.
   d. My friend and I are studying the same subject.
   e. An aggressive person acts in a different way from a friendly person.
   f. Your happiness partly depends with your family.
   g. My mother doesn't like be on her own.

2. Make sentences using *both, the same, different from, no difference between.*

E Developing critical thinking

Which opinion in the study group do you agree with? Why?

Social Studies
(Module SSU24)

Assignment

Behaviour and personality:
are they the same or different?

BEHAVIOUR   PERSONALITY

---

a. An aggressive person / acts / in one way.

b. There is no difference between personality and behaviour.

c. Behaviour changes for each situation.

d. In the same situation, a friendly person acts in a different way from an aggressive person.

e. You learn good behaviour when you're a child.

f. Your personality depends on your friends, the places you go, and so on.

A Activating ideas

Study the words and phrases in the box. Which are connected with a library? Which are connected with a bookshop?

student discount   author   title   borrow   lend   buy   price   in stock   out
deposit   card   form   passport photo   assistant   librarian   cashier   copy

B Understanding conversations

Cover the conversations in Exercise C.

1. Look at the first line of each conversation on the right. How could each conversation continue?

2. 🔊 2.21 Listen to the conversations. Number the sentences on the right in the correct order.

	Is this the way to the bookshop?
	Excuse me. Where's the library?
	How do you reserve a book?
	Do you give a student discount?
	How much does this book cost?
	When does the library tour start?

C Practising conversations

Practise the conversations in pairs.

1
A: Excuse me. Where's the library?
B: It's in the other building.
A: Thanks. Which floor is it on?
B: The second.

4
A: Is this the way to the bookshop?
B: Yes. I'm going that way too.
A: Do you mind if I go with you?
B: No, not at all.

2
A: When does the library tour start?
B: Ten o'clock, I think.
A: How long does it last?
B: An hour.

5
A: How much does this book cost?
B: It's on the back.
A: Oh, yes. Thank you.
B: No problem.

3
A: How do you reserve a book?
B: You have to fill in a form.
A: OK. Sorry. Where are the forms?
B: They're next to the index.

6
A: Do you give a student discount?
B: Yes, with a student ID card. It's 10 per cent.
A: Oh, great. Can I pay for these books then?
B: Certainly.

D Real-time speaking

Choose three or four of the real-life situations below. Role-play a conversation in each case. Use expressions from the conversations above.

You want to know:

- how you get ... *computer access / a parking permit / a safety certificate.*
- the way to ... *the Resource Centre / your tutor's office / the lifts.*
- the time of ... *a film in the Students' Union / a meeting / lunch in the canteen.*
- the location of ... *the gym / Seminar Room E105 / the toilet.*

A Saying consonants

1. Read Pronunciation Check 1. Say the sets of words below.

	A	B	C
1.	thin	think	thing
2.	sin	sink	sing
3.	sun	sunk	sung
4.	ran	rank	rang
5.	win	wink	wing

2. Circle one word in each set. Don't show your partner.

3. Say the word that you circled. Tick the word you hear.

B Saying vowels

1. Read Pronunciation Check 2.

2. Circle one word in each set below. Don't show your partner.

3. Say the word that you circled. Tick the word you hear.

	A	B
	A	**B**
a.	☐ hat	☐ heart
b.	☐ pat	☐ part
c.	☐ cat	☐ cart
d.	☐ had	☐ hard
e.	☐ pack	☐ park

C Identifying a new skill (1)

1. Read Skills Check 1. How can you start your turn?

2. 🔊 2.22 Listen. Complete the sentences.

   a. I found a good article in the library.
   b. _____ we should discuss sociology first.
   c. _____, what is the difference between them?
   d. _____ a lot of psychologists are women.
   e. _____, and what about old people?
   f. _____ a quote about that on the Internet.
   g. _____ that's not a new idea.
   h. _____ it's an interesting website.

D Identifying a new skill (2)

1. Read Skills Check 2. How can you recognize the end of a turn?

2. 🔊 2.23 Listen. Are these examples of good or bad turn-taking?

Pronunciation Check 1

Saying consonants: /n/, /ŋ/ and /ŋk/

The letter *n* is often followed by *k* or *g*.
1. The letters *nk* make the sound /ŋ k/.
   Examples: *think, thank*
2. The letters *ng* make the sound /ŋ/.
   Examples: *writing, thing, studying*

These sounds often come at the end of words.

Pronunciation Check 2

Saying vowels: /æ/ and /ɑː/

These two sounds are similar:
/æ/ is short, /ɑː/ is long.

When the letter *a* is stressed, it often makes the sound /æ/.

Examples: *man, bad, understand, began*

The letters *ar* often make the sound /ɑː/.

Examples: *part, start, hard*

Skills Check 1

Taking turns: starting a turn

In English-speaking cultures, people speak in turn. I wait for another person to finish. Then it is my turn to speak.

Begin a turn with a very short introduction.

Examples:

OK, ...
Right, ...
Well, ...
I think ...
I heard / read that ...

Skills Check 2

Taking turns: recognizing the end of a turn

You know that a person has finished speaking when the voice goes down.

Examples:

You like some things and you don't like other things.

Your personality depends on your friends, the places you go, and so on.

We use modals to talk about things like possibility and orders. ⑪

subject	modal	verb	extra information	
Behaviour		changes	in different situations.	= *fact*
People	can	change	their behaviour.	= *possibility*
Personality		doesn't change	very often.	= *fact*
People	can't	change	their personality easily.	= *possibility*

Look at the word order in *Yes / No* questions.

modal	subject	verb	extra information			
Can	psychologists	predict	behaviour?	Yes,	they	can.

Look at the word order in information questions.

question word	modal	subject	verb	extra information
How	can	psychologists	predict	behaviour?

A Talking about possibility

Make a sentence with *can* or *can't* from each set of words.

1. psychologists / predict / individual behaviour ⟶ <u>Psychologists can predict individual behaviour.</u>
2. sociologists / predict / group behaviour
3. leave school / Britain / 16
4. babies / talk / three years old
5. drive / Britain / 17

B Asking about possibility

Work in pairs.

Student A: Ask about each point in Exercise A above.

Student B: Give the correct short answer.

> *Can psychologists predict individual behaviour?*

> *Yes, they can.*

C Consolidation

Write the words in the correct order.

1. me   you   can   a   pen   lend
   <u>Can you lend me a pen?</u>

2. a   I   can   pen   from   borrow   you

3. me   you   the   gym   can   the   way   show   to

4. join   can   how   the   sports   I   centre

5. can   many   the   library   how   you   borrow   books   from

6. learn   can   where   to   speak   I   Spanish

A Reviewing sounds

    1. What is the sound of the underlined letters?

       a. An aggressive person <u>a</u>cts in one way.

       b. It's h<u>ar</u>d to understand the mind.

       c. Your person<u>a</u>lity depends on many things.

       d. How long does this lecture l<u>a</u>st?

       e. The question h<u>a</u>s two p<u>ar</u>ts.

    2. Say the sentences above.

B Reviewing vocabulary

    1. Copy the words from the box into the correct columns below.

human	individual	together	between	behaviour
	psychology	understand	knowledge	

2 syllables	3 syllables	4 syllables
'useful	im'portant	psy'chologist

    2. Mark the stressed syllable in each word.

C Researching information

    1. Read the note on the right. What is the study group going to do?

    2. Work in four groups.

       Group A: Read the text on page 175.

       Group B: Read the text on page 176.

       Group C: Read the text on page 172.

       Group D: Read the text on page 179.

    3. Look at your information.

    4. Add your own ideas.

Don't forget!
STUDY GROUP

DISCUSS Week 2 assignment —
Do psychologists and sociologists help us?
Meet in Common Room Tue 2.00 p.m.
(Room G201)
See you there! ☺

D Using a key skill

    1. Prepare your turn for the discussion. Remember:

       • how do you begin your turn?
       • how do you end your turn?

    2. Practise your turns in your group.

    3. Make a study group. The group must have students from groups A, B, C and D. Discuss the question.

E Developing critical thinking

Do sociologists and psychologists help us?
What do you think?

Reading: Personality and behaviour

2.11 Vocabulary for reading — Describing personality

A Reviewing vocabulary

All the words below are connected with sociology or psychology.
Complete and say each word.

1. al*on*e
2. hu_____n
3. fa_____ly
4. be_____ng
5. col_____ue
6. beh_____ur
7. re_____on
8. ind_____al
9. rel_____ip
10. nei_____od

B Recognizing patterns

1. What kind of word can come in each space below?

   a. They are _plural noun_ .
   b. She is _____ happy.
   c. _____ came late.
   d. He is a very _____ person.
   e. What is your _____ ?
   f. Do you _____ a lot?

2. Find words in the list on the right for each space in the sentences below. Make any necessary changes.

   a. They are _teenagers / kind_ .
   b. She is _____ happy.
   c. _____ came late.
   d. He is a very _____ person.
   e. What is your _____ ?
   f. Do you _____ a lot?

C Developing vocabulary

What is the connection between each pair of words?

1. kind   unkind   _opposites_
2. always   never   _____
3. usually   often   _____
4. everybody   no one   _____
5. everyone   everybody   _____
6. height   weight   _____
7. physically   mentally   _____

always (*adv*)
background (*n*)
  [= upbringing]
body (*n*)
bully (*n* and *v*)
combination (*n*)
concerned (*adj*)
everybody (*n*)
everyone (*n*)
face (*n*)
height (*n*)
kind (*adj* and *n*)
make fun of
mentally (*adv*)
miserable (*adj*)
never (*adv*)
nobody (*n*)
no one (*n*)
normal (*adj*)
often (*adv*)
physically (*adv*)
race (*n*) [= ethnic]
rarely (*adv*)
rude (*adj*)
sometimes (*adv*)
stupid (*adj*)
teenager (*n*)
unkind (*adj*)
usually (*adv*)
weight (*n*)
worry (*v*)

A   Activating ideas

You are going to read the article on the opposite page.

1. Read the heading. Answer the question in the heading.
2. What sort of information do you expect to find in the article? Tick one or more.

    ☐ facts

    ☐ ideas

    ☐ opinions

    ☐ advice

    ☐ rules

    ☐ jokes

3. What tenses will be in the text? Why?

B   Making and checking hypotheses

1. Read the first paragraph. What question will the article answer?
2. What is *your* answer to the question?
3. Read the rest of the article.

    According to the text, …

    a. which part of a person is the most important?

    b. what do people often *say about themselves*?

    c. what do people often *think about other people*?

C   Understanding vocabulary in context

Find the words below in the text. Match each word to a definition.

1. personality   ☐ not intelligent
2. normal   ☐ there are other examples
3. combination   ☐ not very often
4. worry   ☐ usual, happening all the time
5. like   ☐ for example / opposite of *hate*
6. etc.   ☐ joining together
7. stupid   ☐ the things you do all the time
8. behaviour   ☐ most of the time
9. rarely   ☐1☐ the way you look at life
10. usually   ☐ think about in a bad way

D   Developing critical thinking

1. Cover the diagram in the article. Draw the diagram.
2. Explain the diagram.

Why do people like YOU?

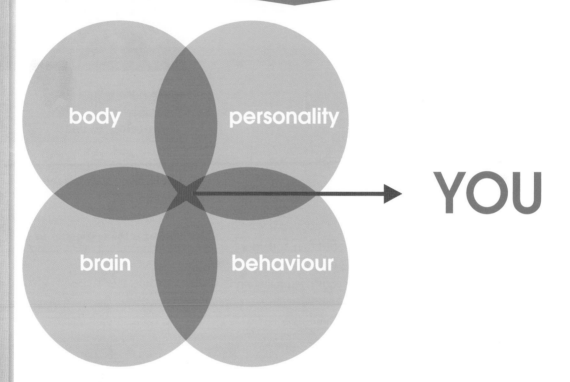

body

personality

brain

behaviour

YOU

What is a person? Everyone is a body with a face. Everyone has a brain. Everyone has a personality. Everyone has normal behaviour, things they do or say all the time. So everyone is a combination of four things. Which part of a person is the most important?

People often think: 'My body is the most important thing.' They worry about their weight or their height. They say things like: 'I don't like my hair (or my mouth, or my ears, etc.).' People sometimes worry about their brains. They say things like: 'I'm stupid because I can't do maths (or remember names, or understand science, etc.).' People do not often think about their personality or their behaviour. So, when people think about *themselves,* they usually think about the body and the brain.

However, most people rarely think about *other* people in that way. When people think about other people, they usually think about their personality and behaviour. When they like someone, they often think things like: 'He is a kind person. She is always happy. He often helps people. She never says bad things about people.' When they don't like someone, they say things like: 'He is unkind. She is always depressed. He never helps people. She always says bad things about people.'

Remember: when people think about *you,* they don't think about your body or your brain. They think about your personality and your behaviour. Don't worry about your body or your brain. If you want people to like you, perhaps you need to change your personality and your behaviour.

A Reviewing key vocabulary

Complete these words from the article in Lesson 2.12.

1. pers on/onality
2. beha
3. norm
4. usu
5. combi
6. wor
7. wei
8. hei
9. some
10. rar

B Identifying a new skill

1. Read the Skills Check.
2. Study the illustration in the article in Lesson 2.12.
   Tick the true sentences.

   a. ☐ You have a body, a personality, a brain and behaviour.

   b. ☐ There is a link between your body and your brain.

   c. ☐ There is a link between your brain and your personality.

   d. ☐ There is no link between your personality and your behaviour.

   e. ☐ You are a combination of three things.

Skills Check

Preparing to read

Always look at any illustrations – photographs, drawings, graphs – **before** you start to read a text.

Think:

What does this illustration show?

What is the text going to say?

C Using a new skill

1. Study each figure on the right. What will each text be about?
2. Read each sentence below. Which text does it come from? Write *1*, *2* or *3*.

   a. ...... People behave in a certain way because they have a particular personality.

   b. ...... You are at the centre of a set of primary groups.

   c. ...... Some friends are also colleagues.

   d. ...... It is a combination of two things.

   e. ...... Your local area includes you, your family and your neighbours.

   f. ...... Most of your neighbours are not your friends.

   g. ...... There is a link between the two things.

Figure from Text 1

Figure from Text 2

Figure from Text 3

We can change the meaning of a sentence with a frequency adverb.

There are six common frequency adverbs.

Look for frequency adverbs:

- **after** the verb *be*.
- **before** other verbs.

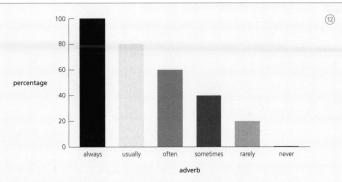

subject	verb	adverb	complement
I	am	usually	on time.
She	is	always	happy.
They	are	often	sad.

subject	adverb	verb	extra information
I	rarely	come	on time.
She	never	says	bad things about people.
They	sometimes	help	people.

The adverb *sometimes* can also come at the beginning or the end of a sentence.
Sometimes he is unkind to people. He is unkind to people sometimes.

A Recognizing the effect of frequency adverbs (1)

What is the difference between each pair of sentences below?

1. I am never late.   I am always late.
2. She is kind.   She is usually kind.
3. He sometimes helps people.   He often helps people.
4. I often go out in the evenings.   I rarely go out in the evenings.
5. They say bad things about people.   They say bad things about people sometimes.
6. Sometimes I forget names.   I always forget names.

B Recognizing the effect of frequency adverbs (2)

Study the sentences on the left. Are the sentences on the right true (T) or false (F)?

1. I am never late.   .... I am always on time.
2. Sometimes I don't like my hair.   .... I sometimes like my hair.
3. I often go out in the evenings.   .... I never stay at home in the evenings.
4. They never say good things about people. .... They sometimes say bad things about people.
5. I rarely forget names.   .... I usually remember names.
6. People usually think about their   .... People do not often think about their
   bodies and their brains.   bodies and their brains.
7. People do not often think about their own .... People rarely think about their own personality
   personality or behaviour.   or behaviour.
8. She often eats in a restaurant.   .... She eats in a restaurant once or twice a week.

C Consolidation

Write one true sentence about yourself or your country with each of the frequency adverbs in the tables above.

A   Reviewing vocabulary

Read each noun. Say three more words that are linked.

1. height … *tall, short, medium*
2. weight …
3. personality …
4. body …
5. behaviour …
6. brain …

B   Applying a new skill (1)

You are going to read another article from a magazine, on the page opposite.
Read the title and look at the diagram.

1. Cover the text. Describe the diagram.
2. What are *social groups*?
3. What does *background* mean?
4. Which of these sentences are true from the illustration?
    a. ☐ You are a combination of four things.
    b. ☐ They are the same four things that make people like you (Lesson 2.12).
    c. ☐ Three of the four things are linked.
    d. ☐ All four things contribute to a person.

C   Applying a new skill (2)

Read the first paragraph.

Which of the following sentences will you find in the text?

1. ☐ Children often call friends 'stupid' if they forget something.
2. ☐ Don't make jokes about someone's body.
3. ☐ Parents are often very proud of their children.
4. ☐ Teenagers often make jokes about poor people.
5. ☐ People sometimes move to a different town.
6. ☐ Young children sometimes make fun of people because they are short.
7. ☐ Some children are very clever.
8. ☐ Teenagers sometimes use a rude word about someone's race.

D   Showing comprehension

Read the text. What does the text say about the following people?

1. Young children
    a. What do they sometimes do?
    b. What do they often call other children?
    c. Why do they behave like this?

2. Teenagers
    a. What do they sometimes do?
    b. What do they sometimes make jokes about?
    c. Why do they behave like this?

3. Bullies
    a. What are the two kinds of bullying?
    b. What does the first kind of bully do?
    c. What about the second kind?

E   Developing critical thinking

Discuss in groups.

1. Have you learnt anything new in this theme?
2. Will you change your behaviour in any way?

You can't change YOU!

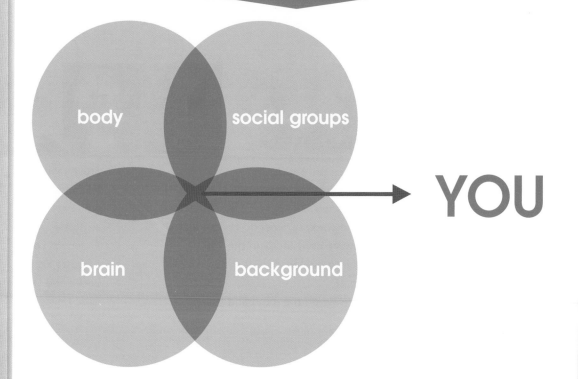

You can change your behaviour. Perhaps you can change your personality. But you cannot change some things. You can hardly change your body. You cannot change your brain at all. You cannot change your social groups – race, religion, nationality. Nobody can change their background, their family and their hometown.

Young children are very concerned with bodies and brains. They sometimes make fun of people because they are tall or short, or because they wear glasses. They often call other children 'Fatty' or 'Shorty' or 'Four Eyes'. Children often call friends 'stupid' if they forget something or do something wrong. But we cannot change our bodies or our brains.

Teenagers are often very concerned about social groups and background. They sometimes use a rude word about someone's race or the colour of their skin. They sometimes comment on their religion or nationality. They often make jokes about poor people, or about people from a particular town or village. But we cannot change our social groups or our background.

Everyone knows that hitting someone is bullying. It is physical bullying. But hurting someone mentally is also bullying. Don't make jokes about someone's body or someone's brain. Don't make fun of someone's social groups or someone's background. If you make jokes about things a person cannot change, you are a kind of bully.

How much have you learnt about sociology and psychology in Theme 2 so far?

Test your knowledge and your partner's knowledge.

1   Answer the questions in your own words.

a. What do psychologists study?

b. What do sociologists study?

c. What is bullying?

d. What is the difference between behaviour and personality?

2   Find the correct person in each case.

a. Who wrote *Para Psyche* in the 4th century BCE?   ☐ Steven Pinker

b. Who is sometimes called the 'Father of Sociology'?   ☐ Wilhelm Wundt

c. Who opened the first psychology school?   ☐ Ivan Pavlov

d. Who, at the end of the 19th century, asked: 'How do people learn?' ☐ Aristotle

e. Who started the science of cognitive psychology in the 1960s? ☐ Elizabeth Loftus

f. Who is well known for research into human memory?   ☐ Auguste Comte

g. Who wrote *The Language Instinct*?   ☐ Locke and Descartes

h. Who, in the 17th century, asked: 'How do the mind and the   ☐ Ulric Neisser
    body work together?'

3   Find the correct speaker in each case.

a. 'There are three important things for groups.   ☐ Ibn Khaldun
    They are religion, work and money.'

b. 'People make society ... then society makes people.' ☐ Max Weber

c. 'People from different groups must fight each other.' ☐ Karl Marx

d. 'Groups are like animals. They are born, they grow and then they die.' ☐ Plato

e. 'Groups must have rules of behaviour.'   ☐ Anthony Giddens

4   Draw a diagram of one of the following:

• your primary groups.

• the relationship between psychology and sociology.

• what makes you the person you are.

Writing: Extroverts and introverts

2.16 Vocabulary for writing Personality types

A Reviewing vocabulary

Rewrite these words from Themes 1 and 2. Which letters are doubled in each word?

1. usualy   <u>usually</u>
2. coleague   ....
3. agresive   ....
4. acomodation   ....
5. degre   ....
6. curiculum   ....
7. profesor   ....
8. posesion   ....

B Recognizing paragraph structure

The text below is not complete. Rewrite the text. Add the sentences from the box underneath the text. Choose the best place for each sentence.

According to the Swiss psychiatrist, Carl Jung, there are two basic personality types. The words mean 'turn inside' and 'turn outside'. Introverts look inside themselves and get energy from their own thoughts. However, very few people are complete introverts or extroverts. Most people are a mixture of the two extremes. In addition, some people change from one personality type to another in different situations. For example, you may be an extrovert with your family but an introvert with a group of strangers. The American sociologist, Timothy Leary, put personality types in a circle. People can be strong or weak. They can also be sociable or aggressive. A sociable, weak person is warm or polite.

Figure 1: *Jung's personality extremes*

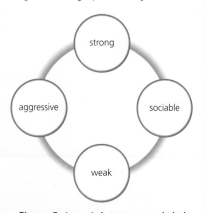

Figure 2: *Leary's interpersonal circle*

An unfriendly, strong person is cold or competitive.
Extroverts look outside themselves and get energy from other people.
The two types are *introvert* and *extrovert*.
This is similar to *extrovert* and *introvert*.
Where do you fit on the line (Figure 1)?
An aggressive, strong person is cold or competitive.

C Understanding vocabulary in context

Find 12 words in your rewritten text from the list on the right. Underline them. Try to work out the meanings, then check your ideas in a dictionary.

D Developing vocabulary

1. Look at the words in the table. What do they mean in everyday English?
2. What do they mean when they describe a personality?
3. Write a sentence for some of the words.

adjectives	warm cold strong weak
verbs	act hide lose show stand

act on impulse
aggressive (*adj*)
attitude (*n*)
basic (*adj*)
calm (*adj*)
centre of attention
cold (*adj*)
competitive (*adj*)
confident (*adj*)
easily (*adv*)
energy (*n*)
excitement (*n*)
extreme (*adj* and *n*)
extrovert (*n*)
fit (*v*)
friendly (*adj*)
hide [one's] feelings
interact (*v*)
introvert (*n*)
lose [one's] temper
mixture (*n*)
optimistic (*adj*)
pessimistic (*adj*)
polite (*adj*)
prefer (*v*)
psychiatrist (*n*)
show [one's] feelings
shy (*adj*)
similar (*adj*)
sociable (*adj*)
sociologist (*n*)
stand out (*v*)
stranger (*n*)
strong (*adj*)
trust (*n* and *v*)
unfriendly (*adj*)
unsociable (*adj*)
warm (*adj*)
weak (*adj*)

A Activating ideas

Answer these questions about extroverts from your own knowledge. Write full sentences.

1. Do extroverts prefer to be alone or in groups?

   Extroverts prefer to be in groups.

2. Do extroverts have many friends?

3. Do extroverts like reading?

4. Are extroverts good learners?

5. What sort of sports do extroverts like?

6. How do extroverts often behave?

7. What attitude do extroverts have to the future?

8. What jobs do extroverts often have?

B Understanding a type of text (1)

Study the spidergram on the opposite page. Check your answers to the questions in Exercise A.

C Understanding a type of text (2)

Study the section of an essay about personality types on the opposite page. Complete the section with information from the spidergram.

D Producing key patterns

Tick the sentences which are true about you. Rewrite the sentences which are not true about you.

1. I prefer to be alone.   ✓
2. I have many friends.   ✗   _I don't have many friends. OR I have a few friends._
3. I like exciting sports.
4. I don't like reading.
5. I am sociable.
6. I don't talk to people easily.
7. I don't like going to parties.
8. I am very optimistic about the future.
9. I often lose my temper.
10. I learn things quickly.

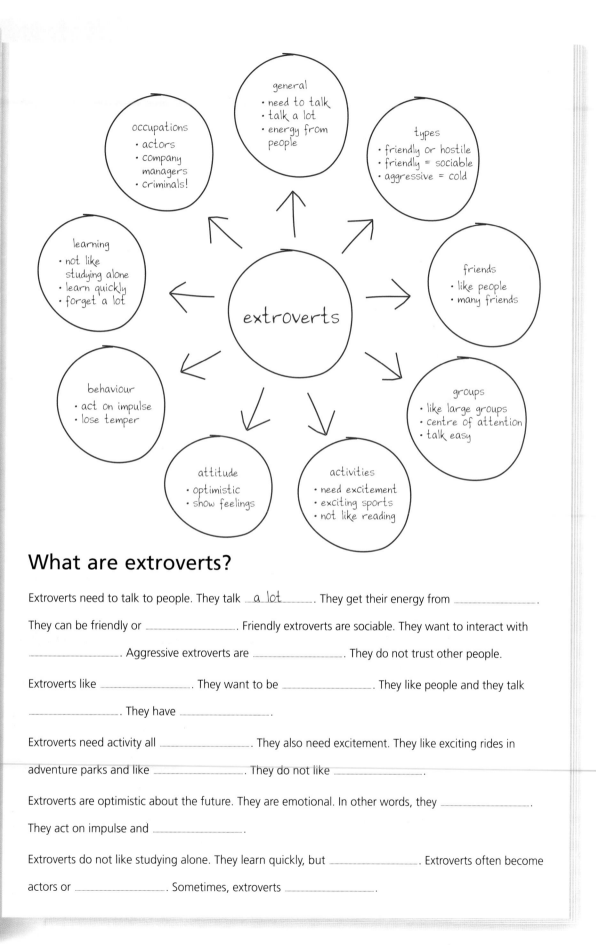

occupations
• actors
• company managers
• criminals!

general
• need to talk
• talk a lot
• energy from people

types
• friendly or hostile
• friendly = sociable
• aggressive = cold

learning
• not like studying alone
• learn quickly
• forget a lot

extroverts

friends
• like people
• many friends

behaviour
• act on impulse
• lose temper

groups
• like large groups
• centre of attention
• talk easy

attitude
• optimistic
• show feelings

activities
• need excitement
• exciting sports
• not like reading

What are extroverts?

Extroverts need to talk to people. They talk _a lot_. They get their energy from _____ .

They can be friendly or _____ . Friendly extroverts are sociable. They want to interact with

_____ . Aggressive extroverts are _____ . They do not trust other people.

Extroverts like _____ . They want to be _____ . They like people and they talk

_____ . They have _____ .

Extroverts need activity all _____ . They also need excitement. They like exciting rides in

adventure parks and like _____ . They do not like _____ .

Extroverts are optimistic about the future. They are emotional. In other words, they _____ .

They act on impulse and _____ .

Extroverts do not like studying alone. They learn quickly, but _____ . Extroverts often become

actors or _____ . Sometimes, extroverts _____ .

A Developing vocabulary

All these words from the course so far have the same vowel sound. What is the sound? What is the correct spelling?

1. Write one or two letters in each space.

a. _ar_ ticle   f. ....sk

b. m........k   g. ....nswer

c. p........ss   h. p........st

d. p........t   i. l........st

e. h........d   j. cl........ss

2. Read the Pronunciation Check and check your answers.

3. Write some more words with the /ɑː/ sound.

B Identifying a new skill

1. Read Skills Check 1 and Skills Check 2.

2. Study the essay section about extroverts in Lesson 2.17. Find the sub-topic(s) in each paragraph.

C Practising a new skill

1. Think again about the sub-topics in a Personal Statement (Theme 1). Complete the spidergram below.

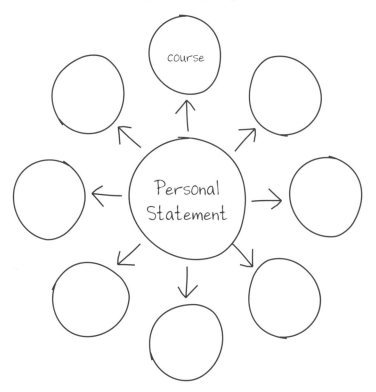

2. Make a spidergram about sociology (Lesson 2.2). Add bullet points to each sub-topic.

Pronunciation Check

Spelling the /ɑː/ sound

Some words with the /ɑː/ sound are spelt with the letter *a* alone.

Examples: *pass, answer, last*

Some words with the /ɑː/ sound are spelt with *ar*.

Examples: *article, mark, hard*

Skills Check 1

Gathering and recording information

You must gather information for an essay. You can record information in a spidergram.

• Write the topic of the essay in the centre of the page.

• Write the sub-topics around the topic.

• Add bullet points or extra branches to each sub-topic.

Skills Check 2

Organizing information into paragraphs

Make one **paragraph** from the information for each sub-topic.

Sometimes, you can **combine** two or three sub-topics into one paragraph.

Decide on the **best order** for the paragraphs.

We use the **present simple** to write about **general facts**. We also use the present simple with the ⑬
verbs *like*, *want* and *need*.

subject	verb *be*	complement
Extroverts	are	optimistic.
		sociable.
		often actors.
They	are not	shy.
		anxious.

subject	other verbs	extra information
Extroverts	talk	a lot.
	interact	with people.
	need to talk	to people.
They	do not want	to be alone.
	do not like	reading.

A   Describing people (1)

Study the example sentences in the tables above. Complete each sentence below with a verb from the box in the correct form. You can use some verbs more than once.

be   give   have   keep   like   make   treat   want

1. Good teachers _are_ interested in their subjects.
2. They _____ enthusiastic about teaching.
3. They _____ the children as individuals.
4. They _____ excited about teaching.
5. They _____ order in the classroom.
6. They _____ fun of children.
7. They _____ rewards to the right children.
8. They _____ a good sense of humour.
9. They _____ teaching.
10. They _____ to know about the children.

B   Describing people (2)

Study the sentences about good teachers in Exercise A. Write sentences about bad teachers.

1. Bad teachers are not interested in their subjects.

We can join sentences with the same subject with *and*. We can delete the subject of the second sentence. ⑭
Extroverts are sociable. They love large groups. ⟶ Extroverts are sociable and ~~they~~ love large groups.
Extroverts like people. They talk to them easily. ⟶ Extroverts like people and ~~they~~ talk to them easily.

C   Producing sentences with *and*

1. Study the examples in the box above.
2. Find pairs of sentences below. Join them. Delete the subject of the second sentence.

Bad teachers are sarcastic.	They are excited about teaching it.
Bad teachers are unfair.	They give punishments to the wrong children.
Good teachers have a sense of humour.	They know personal facts about them.
Good teachers know the names of their students.	They make fun of children.
Good teachers like their subject.	They make jokes.

A Reviewing vocabulary

1. What word or phrase can follow each verb? All the phrases are in the explanation of extroverts (Lesson 2.17).

a. show   *your feelings*

b. lose

c. study

d. learn

e. have

f. need

g. interact

h. act

i. get

2. What is the opposite of each phrase?

a. hide your feelings

B Thinking

You are going to write about introverts.
Work in groups.

1. What sub-topics must you talk about? Draw a spidergram.

2. Read the information that you receive. Share your information with the other people in your group. Complete bullet points on your spidergram.

C Organizing

Decide on the best order for the sub-topics. Combine two or three sub-topics if possible.

D Writing

Write an explanation of introverts. Remember to:

• use verbs in the present simple.

• join related sentences with the same subject with *and*.

E Editing

Exchange explanations with a partner. Read and mark his/her explanation with *?, S, G* or *P*.

F Rewriting

Read your explanation again. Look at the marks on your first draft. Write the explanation again.

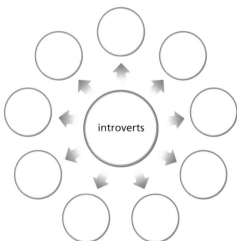

A   Activating schemata

How many personality words do you know in English? Can you think of one word for each letter of the alphabet?

a. _amusing, ambitious_

b. _____

c. _____

d. _____

e. _____

f. _____

g. _____

h. _____

i. _____

j. _____

k. _____

l. _____

m. _____

n. _____

o. _____

p. _____

q. _____

r. _____

s. _____

t. _____

u. _____

v. _____

w. _____

x. _____

y. _____

z. _____

B   Gathering information

1. Do the personality quiz on pages 70–71. Answer truthfully. Check vocabulary with other people.
2. Score your answers using pages 170–171. (The teacher will explain how.)
3. Read the interpretation of scores on page 71. What kind of person are you, according to other people?

C   Writing about personality

What kind of person are you, according to you?

Write one paragraph about your personality.

Personality quiz

Tick the best way to complete each sentence for you.

1 I feel best ...

a. in the morning.
b. at lunchtime.
c. during the afternoon.
d. in the early evening.
e. late at night.

2 I usually walk ...

a. fast, with long steps.
b. fast, with short steps.
c. quite fast, with my head up.
d. quite fast, with my head down.
e. slowly.

3 When I talk to someone, I ...

a. stand with my arms folded.
b. clasp my hands behind my back.
c. have one or both of my hands on my hips.
d. touch the arm of the other person.
e. play with my hair or touch my face.

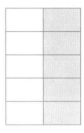

4 When I relax, I sit ...

a. with my legs side by side.
b. with my legs crossed.
c. with my legs out straight.
d. with one leg under the other leg.
e. on the floor.

5 When I find something funny, I ...

a. laugh loudly.
b. laugh quietly.
c. smile broadly.
d. smile slightly.
e. smile to myself.

6 When I go to a party, I ...

a. make sure everyone notices me.
b. look for a new person to speak to.
c. look for a friend to speak to.
d. enter quietly and speak to the host.
e. enter quietly and do not speak to anyone.

7 When I am working and someone interrupts me, I ...

   a. am always happy to stop.
   b. always get angry, but do not show my feelings.
   c. always get angry and show my feelings.
   d. sometimes get angry, sometimes not.
   e. carry on working.

8 My favourite colour is ...

   a. red or orange.
   b. black.
   c. yellow, light blue or green.
   d. dark blue or purple.
   e. white, brown or grey.

9 When I am going to sleep, I lie ...

   a. on my back.
   b. on my front.
   c. on my side.
   d. with my head on one arm.
   e. with my head under the sheet.

10 I often dream about ...

   a. falling.
   b. fighting.
   c. searching for something or somebody.
   d. flying.
   e. running away from something or somebody.

Interpretation

This interpretation of your score answers the question: *How do people see you?*
Do you agree with this interpretation?

Over 60 points:
You are very dominant. You are self-centred. Some people admire you. Some people are afraid of you.

51–60 points:
You are an exciting person. You are impulsive. You take chances. You are a natural leader.

41–50 points:
You are lively. You are funny. You always have something interesting to say. You are kind and considerate.

31–40 points:
You are a sensible person. You are cautious. You are practical. You are clever but modest. You are loyal to your friends.

21–30 points:
You are very cautious. You take a long time to make decisions. You do not like doing new things.

Under 21 points:
You are very introvert. You are shy. You find it very difficult to make decisions. You worry a lot. You prefer being on your own.

Theme 3

Work and business

- How to be a good employee

- Summer jobs

- Choosing a career

- The interview process

Listening: How to be a good employee

3.1 Vocabulary for listening   Responsibilities at work

A Activating knowledge

1. Look at the pictures above. What jobs are people doing? What are the responsibilities of each person?
2. 🔊 3.1 Listen to descriptions of the jobs above. Number the pictures in order.

B Understanding vocabulary in context

1. 🔊 3.2 Listen. The people in the pictures above are talking about their jobs. You will hear two of the words or phrases below in each description. Number the words.

> I'm responsible for the **equipment** in the hospital. My job is to clean it and keep it **in order**.

	colleagues		projects
	customers		punctual
1	e'quipment		respect
	finish		satisfied
	money		systems
	in order		workspace

2. Mark the stressed syllable in each word or phrase above.

C Developing critical thinking

Study the photographs above. Discuss these questions.

1. Which jobs involve managing people?
2. Which jobs involve managing things?
3. Which jobs produce things?
4. Which jobs provide a service?
5. Which jobs are well paid?
6. Which jobs are interesting?
7. Which jobs are dangerous?
8. Which jobs require high-level qualifications?

alphabetical order
businessperson (n)
chronologically (adv)
comfortable (adj)
customer (n)
description (n)
employee (n)
employer (n)
equipment (n)
expect (v)
file (n and v)
ill (adj)
in order (adv and n)
involve (v)
manager (n)
meeting (n)
mess (n)
money (n)
on time (adv)
organize (v)
personal (adj)
punctual (adj)
quality (n)
reason (n)
rely on (v)
respect (n and v)
responsibility (n)
satisfied (adj)
sensibly (adv)
shelf / shelves (n)
sick (adj)
spend (v)
system (n)
task (n)
tidy (adj)
wages (n pl)
waste (v)
workspace (n)

A Activating ideas

Discuss these questions.

1. What are the main differences between having a job and going to university?
2. What are the main similarities between the two?

B Predicting content

You are going to watch the first part of a talk by a visiting local businessperson. It is called *How to be a good employee*.

1. Look at the pictures opposite. Think of ten words you expect to hear in the talk.
2. What kind of information are you going to hear? Tick one or more.

   ☐ jokes
   ☐ stories
   ☐ advice
   ☐ names and dates

C Showing comprehension

1. 🔊 3.3 DVD 3.A Watch the talk. What does the speaker say about each point? Write some words under each picture.
2. The words below are in the talk. How does the speaker define each word?

   a. punctual _always on time_
   b. manager ....
   c. colleagues ....
   d. customers ....
   e. tasks ....
   f. quality ....
   g. equipment ....
   h. workspace ....
   i. chronologically ....

D Making notes of the main points

1. Complete the notes below with a verb in each space.
2. DVD 3.A Watch the talk again and check your notes.

   How to be a good employee
   You must:

   1. _____ to work every day.
   2. _____ punctual.
   3. _____ colleagues and customers.
   4. _____ all tasks on time.
   5. _____ all tasks well.
   6. not _____ computers for personal things.
   7. _____ your workspace tidy.
   8. _____ files sensibly.

E Listening and reacting

Discuss these questions.

1. Which points in the talk are new to you?
2. Which points must you change in your university life?

1 every day / phone / sick

2

3

4

5

6

7

8

A Reviewing key words

🔊 3.4 Listen to the sentences. What is the next word?

> Always arrive on time. It's important to be …

> punctual!

B Identifying a new skill

1. Read Skills Check 1. When you listen, how do you know which words are important?

2. Look at the sentences from another lecture. Which words will be stressed?

   a. Companies want college or university graduates.

   b. All employers want critical thinking.

   c. 'But how can I get work skills?' you might ask.

   d. You can learn management skills in university clubs.

   e. You must show that you want to learn.

   f. You must take responsibility for your mistakes.

3. 🔊 3.5 Listen. Underline the stressed words.

C Making notes

1. Read Skills Check 2. Which words do you write in your notes?

2. 🔊 3.6 Listen and note the key words in each sentence.

Skills Check 1

Hearing important words

When a speaker gets to an important word in a sentence, he/she often says it **more loudly**. That is, the word is **stressed**. Listen for the loud words in each sentence.

Examples:

You must **go** to work **every day**.
You **can't** wear **jeans** in the **office**.

Skills Check 2

Noting key words

The loud words are the important words for you to write down in your notes.

the speaker says ...	you write ...
You must **go** to work **every day**.	go every day
You must be **punctual**.	punctual
You must **respect** your **manager** and your **colleagues**.	respect manager & colleagues

---

D Identifying consonant sounds

1. Tick the correct column for each word according to the underlined sound.

2. Read the Pronunciation Check.

	/g/		/ʝ/
	good	*manager*	*you*
chan**g**e		✓	
be**g**in			
get			
job			
university			
young			
wa**g**e			

Pronunciation Check

Hearing consonants: /g/, /dʒ/ and /ʝ/

1. The sound /g/ is the sound of a written letter *g* or double *gg*.

   Examples: *good, colleague, bigger*

2. The sound /dʒ/ is the sound of the letters *ge* and *j*.

   Examples: *manager, job, college*

3. The sound /ʝ/ is the sound of the letters *y* or *u*.

   Examples: *yes, usually, you*

3. 🔊 3.7 Listen and check your answers.

It is easy to hear a negative verb with some structures. There is an **extra word** or a **different word**. ⑮

positive			negative		
The company	**wants**	good workers.	It	**doesn't** want	bad workers.
You	**went**	yesterday.	You	**didn't** go	the day before.
The manager	**'ll ask**	about it.	You	**won't** get	a good job.
I	**'d like**	that.	I	**wouldn't** do	that.

Which word is stressed in each positive sentence? What about each negative sentence?

A Recognizing negatives from verb form (1)

1. 🎧 3.8 Listen to some verbs. Say *positive* or *negative* in each case.
2. 🎧 3.9 Listen to some sentences. Say *positive* or *negative* in each case.

It is difficult to hear a negative verb with some structures. ⑯

positive			negative		
It	**'s**	important ...	It	**isn't**	important ...
You	**'re**	responsible ...	You	**aren't**	punctual.
They	**were**	on time.	They	**weren't**	ready.
You	**can get**	work skills.	You	**can't** be	late.
You	**must respect**	the customers.	You	**must**n't be	rude.

Which word is stressed in each positive sentence? What about each negative sentence?

B Recognizing negatives from verb form (2)

1. 🎧 3.10 Listen to some verbs. Say *positive* or *negative* in each case.
2. 🎧 3.11 Listen to some sentences. Say *positive* or *negative* in each case.

Speakers often follow an **obligation** with a **reason**. We can link the obligation and the reason in several ⑰ ways. But be careful! Sometimes the next sentence is a **new point**.

first sentence	second sentence		
	because	It makes people angry.	*reason*
Managers mustn't behave rudely	Why? Because		
	(pause)		
		They mustn't get angry.	*new point*

C Recognizing reasons

1. 🎧 3.12 Listen to some sentences. Does the speaker give a reason? Say *Yes* or *No*.
2. 🎧 3.13 Listen. Is the second sentence a reason or a new point?
3. 🎧 3.14 Listen. The speaker gives a silly reason! Correct the reason in each case.

A   Reviewing vocabulary

1. Cover the second and third columns below. How can you complete the phrases?

a. If you are ill and can't work,	✓ stay in bed, but phone.	☐ do your work at home.
b. The company doesn't want to	☐ lose money.	☐ waste money.
c. It's important to respect your	☐ managers and colleagues.	☐ colleagues and customers.
d. You're responsible for	☐ your office equipment.	☐ the quality of your work.
e. Organize your files in	☐ alphabetical order.	☐ chronological order.
f. Make sure your workspace is	☐ tidy and comfortable.	☐ organized.

2. Uncover the columns. 🎧 3.15 Listen and tick the phrase you hear.

B   Predicting content

You are going to watch the second part of the talk.

1. What is the speaker going to talk about? (He said it at the end of the first part.)
2. Study the notes below. Think of a reason for each point.

C   Practising a key skill

🎧 3.16 DVD 3.B Watch the talk. Complete the *Why?* column in the table below. Write two or three stressed words for each point.

> You must go to work every day, because people rely on you to go.

You must ...	Why?
1. go to work every day	rely on you
2. be punctual	
3. respect colleagues and customers	
4. do all tasks on time	
5. do all tasks well	
6. not use computers for personal things	
7. keep your workspace tidy	
8. organize files sensibly	

D   Developing critical thinking

Discuss these questions.

1. Which work skills do you think you have?
2. Which work skills do you need to work on?
3. How can you develop your own work skills?

Speaking: Summer jobs

3.6 Vocabulary for speaking Employment

A Reviewing vocabulary

Think of adjectives to complete each sentence.

1. A good employee is _reliable and responsible_ .
2. A good employer is ....
3. A successful businessperson is ....
4. A helpful colleague is ....

B Practising new vocabulary

Study the conversations below.

1. Complete each conversation with words from the list on the right.
   🔊 3.17 Listen and check.

2. Practise the conversations in pairs.

1
A: You look _smart_ !
B: Thanks. I'm on my way to a .... agency.
A: Oh, what for?
B: I've got an .... for a summer job.
A: Well, good luck!

2
A: Could you put an .... in the paper for a summer job?
B: Yes, of course. What's the exact job ....?
A: Um. Sales ...., I think.
B: Full-time or ....?
A: Part-time.

3
A: Did you have a good summer?
B: Not really. I was working for a building ....
A: In the office?
B: No, I wasn't doing .... work. I was ....
A: So .... work, then.
B: That's right. It was hard work, but the .... was good.

C Extending new vocabulary

1. Look at these nouns. Check any meanings you are not sure of in a dictionary.

nouns	verbs
a d ' v e r t i s e m e n t	advertize
a d v i s o r	
i m p r e s s i o n	
o r g a n i z a t i o n	
p r e p a r a t i o n	
r e c r u i t m e n t	

2. Complete the table.
3. Mark the stress in all the words in the table.
4. 🔊 3.18 Listen to some sentences and check your ideas.

---

abroad (*adj*)
ad (*n*)
advert (*n*)
advertisement (*n*)
advisor (*n*)
assistant (*n*)
body language (*n*)
career (*n*)
careers advisor
clerical (*adj*)
company (*n*)
counsellor (*n*)
creative (*adj*)
department (*n*)
eye contact (*n*)
full-time (*adj*)
honest (*adj*)
impolite (*adj*)
impression (*n*)
interview (*n*)
interviewee (*n*)
interviewer (*n*)
job title (*n*)
lazy (*adj*)
look (*v*) [= appear]
manual (*adj*)
organization (*n*)
outgoing (*adj*)
outside (*adj*)
part-time (*adj*)
pay (*n* and *v*)
recruitment (*n*)
retail (*adj*)
rude (*adj*)
salary (*n*)
self-motivated (*adj*)
shy (*adj*)
smart (*adj*)
sound (*n* and *v*)
vacation (*n*)

A Developing independent learning

1. Read the Pronunciation Check. What sound does the symbol /g/ represent? What about /dʒ/?

2. Use a dictionary to check the pronunciation of the letter *g* in the words below. Tick the correct column.

	/g/	/dʒ/
agitate		
catalogue		
gesture		
regular		

B Understanding a situation

Julia Greco is at university. She wants to get a job during the summer vacation. She has filled in a form on a website.

1. Read the form. What kind of job would she like?

2. What does the computer suggest?

C Understanding a model

🔊 3.19 Listen. Julia is talking to her friend, Carla. Fill in the form below for Carla.

☐ in my own country   ☐ abroad
☐ alone   ☐ with other people
☐ inside   ☐ outside

A good job for you is:

D Studying a model

🔊 3.20 Listen. Write one or two words in each space.

C: Are you going to ...get... a job in the university holidays?

J: I'd like to. What about you?

C: Yes, I _____ so.

J: What do you want _____?

C: I'm not sure.

J: Would you _____ to work abroad?

C: Yes, I _____. I'd love to work in another country.

J: Do you like _____ alone or with other people?

C: With other people, definitely. I don't _____ working alone. But I would prefer to do something with adults because I _____ no experience with children.

J: _____ you like working inside or outside?

C: Mm. Let me think. Inside. No, I'll change that. Outside.

E Practising a model

1. Practise the conversation between Carla and Julia.

2. Practise the conversation again. Give true answers for yourself. Give full answers.

File Edit View Favorites Tools Help

http://www.find-a-job.com

find-a-job.com
The summer job finder for students
Find Jobs | About Us | Contact
How to get a holiday job

Do you want a summer job?
What kind of job would you like?
Answer the questions, press **FIND** and
Find-a-job.com will do the rest!

I live in [-- All --]

I would like a summer job:

☑ in my own country   ☐ abroad
☐ alone   ☑ with other people
☑ inside   ☐ outside

(FIND)

A good job for you is:
nursery school assistant
shop assistant

Talking about days and times

1. .... 2. .... 3. .... 4. ....

A Activating ideas

1. Cover the conversations below. Which picture above does each sentence go with?

   a. Let me check. The ninth.   c. We're late!

   b. What day is our test?   d. Yes. It's just after three forty.

2. ⓢ 3.21 Listen and match a conversation with each picture.

B Practising conversations (1)

Uncover the conversations. Practise in pairs.

1
A: Excuse me. Have you got the time?
B: Yes, it's just after three forty.
A: Thank you.
B: That's OK.

3
A: What's the date today?
B: Let me check. The ninth.
A: So what's the date next Wednesday?
B: The fifteenth.

2
A: Excuse me. What day is our test?
B: Next Monday.
A: What time does it start?
B: At nine thirty.

4
A: Hurry up! We're late!
B: What time is it?
A: It's nearly eight fifteen. The bus is at half past.
B: OK. I'll be as quick as I can.

C Practising conversations (2)

There are two conversations below.

1. Find the sentences for each conversation. Number the sentences in a logical order.

   .... A: Is it the same every day?   .... B: Seven till nine.

   .... A: What are the working hours?   .... B: Three o'clock.

   .... A: What time is your interview?   .... B: About 15 minutes, I think.

   .... A: How long will it last?   .... B: Every weekday, yes.

2. Practise the conversations in pairs.

D Real-time speaking

Work in pairs. Role-play conversations. Use expressions from the conversations above.

Student A

Ask your partner about ...

• the time of the next lecture.

• how long it is before the end of the lesson.

• the time now.

• the date of the end of the semester.

Student B

Ask your partner about ...

• the day of the last English lesson.

• how long it is before the end of the day.

• when the lesson starts and ends.

• the dates of next semester.

A Saying consonants

Look at these phrases and sentences from Lesson 3.7.

1. What is the sound of the underlined letters?

a. I'm <u>u</u>sing this webpage.

b. Are <u>y</u>ou going to get a job?

c. What <u>do y</u>ou want to do?

d. What does the computer sug<u>g</u>est?

e. A good job for <u>y</u>ou is camp counsellor.

f. Woul<u>d y</u>ou like to work abroad?

2. Practise saying the phrases and sentences.

B Identifying a key skill (1)

1. 🔊 3.22 DVD 3.C Watch an interview between a careers advisor and a student. Does the interviewee make a good impression? Why (not)?

2. 🔊 3.23 DVD 3.D Watch another interview. Does the interviewee make a good impression? Why (not)?

3. Read Skills Check 1. What good things does the interviewee do in the second interview? Tick points in Skills Check 1.

C Identifying a key skill (2)

1. Study this section from an interview. How could the interviewee improve the answers?

> What sort of summer job would you like?

> With people.

> Would you like to go abroad?

> No.

2. Read Skills Check 2. Check your ideas.

D Practising a key skill

Study each pattern below. Think of true information for each space.

1. I'm studying ... and I ...

2. I want to be a/an ... because ...

3. I enjoy ..., so ...

4. I'm interested in ... That's why ...

5. I'd like to work in ... because ...

Skills Check 1

How to make a good impression

You must make a good impression at an interview.

1. Preparing

Think about the interview before it starts.

- What questions will the interviewer ask?
- Think of a good, truthful answer in each case.

2. During the interview

You must have the correct body language.

- Sit up straight.
- Put your hands in your lap or on the table.
- Look at the interviewer.
- Smile!

Skills Check 2

Extending a turn

How can you make a good impression when it is your turn to speak?

One way is to extend the turn.

Examples:

What are you studying?

Education. → *Education, and I really like it.*

What do you want to be?

I want to be a primary teacher. → *I want to be a primary teacher because I love working with children.*

The start of *Yes / No* questions is very important.
In most cases you can use the first word in your *Yes / No* answer.   ⑱

start	Yes	No	start	Yes	No
Are you ...	Yes, I am.	No, I'm not.	Do you ...	Yes, I do.	No, I don't.
Are they ...	Yes, they are.	No, they aren't.	Have you ...	Yes, I have.	No, I haven't.
Is he ...	Yes, he is.	No, he isn't.	Can you ...	Yes, I can.	No, I can't.
Were you ...	Yes, I was.	No, I wasn't.	Would you ...	Yes, I would.	No, I wouldn't.
Was she ...	Yes, she was.	No, she wasn't.	Did you ...	Yes, I did.	No, I didn't.

A   Answering closed questions

🔊 3.24 Listen and give true answers with *Yes, + ...* or *No, + ...*

> *Do you go to university?*   *Yes, I do.*   *No, I don't.*

Sometimes, closed questions offer a choice. You cannot answer with *Yes / No*.   ⑲

	choice 1		choice 2	answer
Would you like to have	tea	or	coffee?	Tea, please.

B   Answering closed questions with a choice

🔊 3.25 Listen and give true answers. Select the first choice or the second choice.

> *Would you like to visit Russia or America?*   *Russia.*   *America.*

C   Answering mixed questions

Ask and answer in pairs. Use question types from Exercise A and Exercise B.
Find a good summer job for your partner.

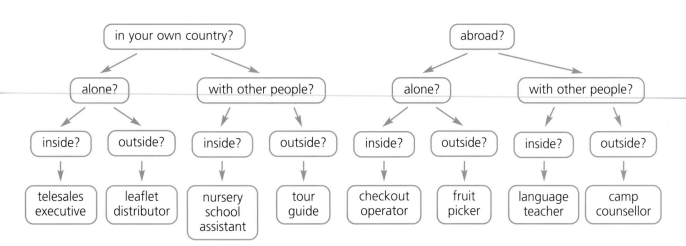

A Reviewing sounds

Say each pair of words below. Make sure your partner can hear the difference.

	A	B
1.	go	joe
2.	get	jet
3.	ago	age
4.	wag	wage
5.	colleague	college
6.	gust	just
7.	use (n)	juice
8.	leg	ledge
9.	angle	angel
10.	you'll	jewel

B Researching information (1)

1. Study the information from a recruitment website on the right.

2. Cover the information. What must you do before you go for a job interview?

File   Edit   View   Favorites   Tools   Help

http://www.find-a-job.com

find-a-job.com
The summer job finder for students
Find Jobs   About Us   Contact
How to get a holiday job

How to get a holiday job

1. **Read** the **job advertisement** carefully. Do you have the skills for this job?

2. **Research** the **company**. Why? Because you cannot give good answers to questions in the interview if you don't know anything about the company.

3. **Prepare** an answer for the **first part** of the interview. Why? Because first impressions are very important. The interviewer often says: *Tell me about yourself.*

4. **Prepare** an answer for **other common questions**. Why? Because the interviewer is probably going to interview several people. You must stand out from the other interviewees. Other common questions are: *Why do you want to work here? Why should we hire you?*

C Researching information (2)

Study the information below. Job adverts are on the left and company research information is on the right. Which job(s) could you do? Which job would you like to do most?

SALES ASSISTANT required. FRESH FOODS in Winton. Daily 3 hours. No weekends. Includes stacking shelves and checkout work. Must be smart, with good maths skills. For more information, call …

FRESH FOODS

Small, family-run company in the centre of Winton. Sells fresh food – fruit, vegetables, bread, dairy products. Established in 1975. Working hours: Mon–Sat 8.30–5.30. Closed Sundays.

HOME-BASED Typist/Data Entry Processor required. INTERMAIL are looking for honest, self-motivated people. Work from your own home. Applicants should have Internet access. Must have basic computer and typing skills. Please call …

INTERMAIL

New company (est. 2008). Only employs home-workers. Pays good piecework rate for typing work in Word and data entry into Excel spreadsheets.

TOUR GUIDE required. BIG CITY TOUR Co. is looking for smart, extrovert people to act as tour guides on their buses this summer. Full training supplied. Do one or two tours per day (1½ hours per tour). Must know local area. Phone …

BIG CITY TOUR CO.

Franchise company – more than 150 branches in all major cities. Won Tour Guide Company of the Year (2007). Also won Investors in People award for in-company training.

D Using a new skill

Work in pairs.

Student A

Choose one of the jobs in Exercise C. Make a good impression at your interview.

Student B

Interview A. Are you going to give A the job?

Reading: Choosing a career

3.11 Vocabulary for reading   Word building

A **Predicting the next word**

Study the sentences and the dictionary extracts below. What part of speech is the missing word in each case?

1. A good _employer_ looks after all the people in the company. _noun_
2. The company has 200 _____ in its main office. _____
3. We would like to _____ you to work as a teacher. _____
4. What is the length of _____ in this job? I mean, how long do you want me for? _____
5. If you learn many skills at college, you will be _____ when you leave. _____

> **employ** (*v*) to pay someone to do a job
> **employable** (*adj*) easy to employ; *an ~ person has a lot of useful skills for an employer*
> **employee** (*n*) a person who is paid to do a job
> **employer** (*n*) a person or company who pays someone to do a job
> **employment** (*n*) 1 employing or being employed 2 a person's job

B **Building vocabulary**

1. What part of speech are the following words?

   > ability   business   counsellor   experience   worker
   > impressions   journalist   recruitment   trainee

2. Read the information below and check your ideas.

   Noun endings

   Sometimes, the end of a word helps you decide the part of speech. Here are the most common noun endings.

~tion/~sion	~ity	~er/~or	~ist/~ian
~ment	~ness	~ance/~ence/~ency	~ee

3. Find one example of each noun ending from the word lists in Themes 1, 2 and 3.

4. What is the base word for each of the following nouns?

   a. advisor _advice_   e. responsibility _____
   b. manager _____   f. payee _____
   c. deletion _____   g. kindness _____
   d. efficiency _____   h. requirement _____

---

ability (*n*)
appropriate (*adj*)
architect (*n*)
architecture (*n*)
area (*n*) [= of work]
benefit (*n* and *v*)
career-entry (*adj*)
contribute (*v*)
counsellor (*n*)
deadline (*n*)
deletion (*n*)
design (*n* and *v*)
employ (*v*)
employable (*adj*)
experience (*n* and *v*)
freelance (*adj* and *n*)
impression (*n*)
journalist (*n*)
kindness (*n*)
(the) mass media (*n*)
meet a deadline
motivate (*v*)
overtime (*n*)
part of speech
perk (*n*) [= work benefit]
personal qualities
qualifications (*n*)
recruitment (*n*)
reliability (*n*)
requirement (*n*)
research (*v*)
responsibility (*n*)
rise (*n* and *v*)
shift (*n*) [= work period]
technology (*n*)
trainee (*n*)
unemployment (*n*)
unpaid (*adj*)
worker (*n*)
working hours (*n*)
workplace (*n*)

A Activating ideas

Think of a job you would like to do when you finish your education. Answer these questions.

1. What qualifications do you need?
2. What experience do you need?
3. What personality do you need?
4. What abilities do you need?
5. What is the location of this job?
6. What are the working hours?

B Preparing to read

1. What should you look at before you read a text?

2. Read the questions below. Then look quickly at the text opposite and answer them.

   a. Where does this text come from? ....

   b. What kind of text is it? ....

   c. What is it about? ....

3. Cover the page opposite. Look at the section headings on the left below. Find one sentence on the right from each section.

a	**Personal qualities and abilities**		Employers look for people who have contributed to school newspapers or club newsletters.
b	**Working hours**		Career-entry jobs are low-paid.
c	**Workplace**	a	Journalists must be articulate ...
d	**Qualifications**		You need a degree in journalism ...
e	**Experience**		There is a lot of weekend work ...
f	**Salary and benefits**		Some journalists travel all over the world.

C Selecting the correct meaning

Read the job description opposite. Find the words below in the text. Both meanings are possible. Tick the best meaning for each word in context.

1. articulate ☐ (v) move ☑ (adj) able to put words together well
2. issues ☐ (n) important points ☐ (v) sends out
3. shifts ☐ (n) working periods ☐ (v) moves
4. freelance ☐ (n) a person who works for him/herself ☐ (adj) not employed by one company
5. mass ☐ (adj) going to a large number of people ☐ (n) large number
6. field ☐ (n) place for animals or crops ☐ (n) area, e.g., of work, study
7. contribute ☐ (v) give money to ☐ (v) give items to
8. cub ☐ (n) junior employee ☐ (n) small animal
9. rise ☐ (n) increase ☐ (v) increase
10. perks ☐ (v) gets more active ☐ (n) extra benefits

D Reading and reacting

Answer the questions below. Explain your answers.

1. Do you have the personality to be a journalist?
2. Do you have the abilities to be a journalist?
3. Would you like the working hours of a newspaper journalist?
4. Do you have the right sort of experience to be a journalist?
5. How do you feel about the salary and benefits?

File　Edit　View　Favorites　Tools　Help

http://www.choose-a-career.com/journalist

choose-a-career.com

The website that helps you find the right career for you.

So you want to be a …

journalist

We all read newspapers and magazines. We all watch the news on television or listen to it on the radio. Perhaps you even read the news on a website. But would you like to write the news? If so, think about a career in journalism.

a Personal qualities and abilities

Journalists must be articulate in speech and writing. They must be outgoing and like meeting new people. They must be interested in issues like pollution and climate change. They must also be able to type and use information technology.

b Working hours

Magazine journalists work from 9 a.m. to 5 p.m., Mondays to Fridays, but newspaper journalists sometimes work shifts. There is a lot of weekend work and unpaid overtime as well. The news never stops!

c Workplace

Journalists usually work in a newspaper or magazine office, but freelance journalists work from home. Some journalists travel all over the world.

d Qualifications

You need a degree for most jobs in this field. Employers prefer candidates with a degree in journalism or media studies. Media studies courses look at communication in the mass media.

e Experience

Employers look for people who have contributed to school newspapers or club newsletters.

f Salary and benefits

Career-entry jobs are low-paid. The starting salary for a cub reporter on a local newspaper is about £10,000 per year, but this can rise quite quickly. There are very few perks except, perhaps, a company car.

A Reviewing vocabulary

Match words to make a phrase.

1. freelance .... technology
2. mass .... studies
3. media .... overtime
4. company .... salary
5. starting ...1... journalist
6. unpaid .... job
7. information .... car
8. career-entry .... media

B Identifying a new skill (1)

1. Study the sentences below. Do you know the underlined words?

   a. Employers look for <u>conscientious</u> people who work hard all the time.

   b. You must <u>motivate</u> yourself to do boring work and find something interesting in each job.

   c. <u>Reliability</u> is very important, because your colleagues need your work on time.

   d. I work for a <u>multinational</u> company with offices all over the world.

   e. Always ask your <u>line</u> manager if you have a problem.

2. Read Skills Check 1.

3. Read the sentences above again. Follow the advice in Skills Check 1. Do you understand the sentences?

C Identifying a new skill (2)

1. Read Skills Check 2. What is a section?
   Study the section headings below from an article:

   Get a good job … and keep it.

2. Find two sentences on the right which might appear in each section.

Skills Check 1

Dealing with new words

When you find a new word, think:

Can I understand this sentence without the new word?

Example:

Journalists must be <u>outgoing</u> and like meeting new people.

Perhaps you don't know the word *outgoing*. Cross out the word.

Journalists must be ~~outgoing~~ and like meeting new people.

Can you understand the sentence from the other words?

Skills Check 2

Preparing to read: section headings

Many texts have section headings. A **section heading** is a title for one part of the text.

Always read the section headings **before** you read the section. Think …

What question(s) will this section answer?

1 **Choose the right career for you**	Always get to work on time.
	Do summer jobs during your time at university.
	Find out the requirements for a career-entry job.
2 **Get the right qualifications**	Join university clubs and help to organize events.
	Meet all the work deadlines.
3 **Get useful work experience**	Research the universities which offer the appropriate degree or diploma courses.
	Think about your hobbies and interests.
4 **Getting your first job**	Wear smart clothes and give interesting answers to all the questions.
5 **Being a good employee**	You must be interested in the field.
	You must sell yourself at the interview.

There are three main kinds of word.   ⑳

nouns (*n*)	verbs (*v*)	adjectives (*adj*)
man, career, idea	be, go, walked, can do	good, intelligent, three, green

A new word in a text will probably be a noun, a verb or an adjective, but there are also pronouns (*pron*), prepositions (*prep*), and adverbs (*adv*). When you find a new word in a text, think: *Is this word a noun, a verb or an adjective?*

A   Identifying parts of speech

Read the text below. Box the nouns. Underline the verbs. Circle the adjectives.

The world of work is changing. At one time, most people got a job and they stayed in that job for the whole of their life. Employers paid employees for their time. But in the modern world, you cannot expect to get a job for life when you finish your full-time education. You will probably have many different jobs in your lifetime. Now, employers pay people for useful skills.

English is an SV(O) language. This means the **basic** sentence pattern in English is: subject–verb–(object).   ㉑

subject (S)	verb (V)
The woman	listened.
He	left.

subject (S)	verb (V)	object (O)
The company	has	two hundred employees.
You	need	a degree.

However, there are other common patterns.

S	V	complement (C)
The job	is	interesting.
They	are	journalists.

S	V	adverbial (A)
Some journalists	work	from home.
We	travel	all over the world.

The pattern of the sentence will help you understand the meaning. It will also help you work out the meaning of new words.

B   Identifying sentence patterns

Read the sentences below.

1. Divide each sentence into parts with /. Label the parts of each sentence.

S   V
Employment / is declining. Unemployment is rising. Many young people are out of work.
Good jobs are scarce. Most employers want skilled workers. Unskilled workers cannot get
full-time positions. They work now and then. They don't earn every week.

2. Work out the meaning of the underlined word or phrase in each sentence.

A Reviewing key skills

You are going to read about another job.

1. What should you look at before you read the text? Make a list of items to look at.

2. Find all the items in the text opposite.

B Predicting content from section headings

Look at the section headings. Which section will answer each question?

1. What can I earn?   _f_
2. What examinations must I pass?   ....
3. What must I be able to do?   ....
4. What sort of personality must I have?   ....

5. What work skills must I have?   ....
6. When must I work?   ....
7. Where must I work?   ....

C Checking predictions

Read the text opposite. Find one answer to each question in Exercise B. Go straight to the correct section.

*What can I earn? = Go to **Salary and benefits** = £25,000 per year*

D Dealing with words in context

The words and phrases below are in the text.

	words	part	How do you know?	meaning in context
1.	centres	n	*There are + noun phrase*	*places with a lot of shops*
2.	draw			
3.	complex			
4.	carry on			
5.	practice			
6.	cover			
7.	background			
8.	packages			

1. Find each word in the text and underline it. Is it a noun, a verb or an adjective? Write the part of speech in the second column.

2. How do you know the part of speech? Write the pattern in the 'How do you know?' column.

3. What does each word mean in context?

E Developing critical thinking

Think about the two jobs discussed in this section.

1. Find two similarities.
2. Which job:
   a. has the higher salary?
   b. is the harder?
   c. is the more interesting?
3. Which job would you like to do most?

File　Edit　View　Favorites　Tools　Help

http://www.choose-a-career.com/architect

choose-a-career.com
The website that helps you find the right career for you.

So you want to be an …

architect

The world around us is changing. There are new buildings everywhere. There are new shopping centres, new houses and flats, new factories. Would you like to design new buildings, to make them safe, comfortable and beautiful? If so, think about a career in architecture.

a Personal qualities and abilities

Architects must be good at mathematics. They must also be able to draw well. They must be able to listen to clients, to find out their wants and needs. They must also be able to use complex programs for drawing on a computer.

b Working hours

Architects work from 9 a.m. to 5 p.m., Mondays to Fridays, but they often do lots of overtime to meet a deadline. If the deadline is tomorrow, and you haven't finished by 5 p.m., you must carry on working through the night! Of course, this overtime is usually unpaid.

c Workplace

Architects often work for large companies like banks or supermarkets. When you have a lot of experience, you can start a practice of your own.

d Qualifications

You need a degree in architecture. Some degree courses take five years or more. They cover engineering principles and town planning laws as well as design.

e Experience

Employers look for people with a background in design.

f Salary and benefits

The starting salary for an architect is high. You earn about £25,000 per year. But remember! You will be 24 or 25 before you start earning. There are no perks, except perhaps free use of expensive packages for the computer.

Knowledge quiz   Review

1   Match the questions and answers. All the words are from Themes 1, 2 or 3.

a.	What is a *campus*?	.... They are people you work or study with.
b.	What is a *graduate*?	.... People who make fun of something you can't change.
c.	What is *plagiarism*?	.... Using someone else's work without naming them.
d.	What is a *tutorial*?	.... The human brain and individual behaviour.
e.	What is an *assignment*?	.... People who show their feelings.
f.	What does a *psychologist* study?	.... The third stage, after secondary.
g.	What does a *sociologist* study?	.... Employing someone for a job.
h.	What is *tertiary* education?	.... A person who writes for a newspaper or a magazine.
i.	What are *bullies*?	.... A person who designs buildings.
j.	What are *colleagues*?	.... Payments for work.
k.	What are *emotional* people?	.... The behaviour of people in groups.
l.	What are *wages* and *salary*?	.... A piece of written work, usually homework.
m.	What is *recruitment*?	.... A discussion in a small group with a tutor about a topic.
n.	What is a *journalist*?	...a... All the buildings of a university or college.
o.	What is an *architect*?	.... A person with a degree.

2   Match the opposites.

a.	dominant	.... in your own country
b.	mentally	.... dissatisfied
c.	optimistic	.... with other people
d.	punishment	.... chronological
e.	satisfied	.... clerical
f.	alone	.... part-time
g.	alphabetical	.... physically
h.	abroad	.... reward
i.	full-time	...a... submissive
j.	manual	.... pessimistic

3   Match the words with similar meanings.

a.	hire	.... need
b.	punctual	.... outgoing
c.	hostile	.... old
d.	ancient	.... organization
e.	behave	.... mind
f.	company	.... on time
g.	extrovert	.... sick
h.	brain	...a... employ
i.	require	.... act
j.	ill	.... aggressive

Writing: The interview process

3.16 Vocabulary for writing   Selecting people for jobs

A   Building knowledge

1. Read the text below about the selection process. Divide the text into four paragraphs.
2. Find and underline words in the text from the list on the right. Try to work out the meaning of the words from context.

Selecting a new member of staff is not easy. Many companies have a long selection process with many stages. The aim is to get a large number of candidates for a job and then to choose the best one. The process begins with a job description and ends with the appointment of one person. The process often includes references and interviews. Acme Engineering does not have a good selection process. When there is a vacancy in any department, the manager puts an advertisement in the local paper. Candidates are asked to write a letter with information about their qualifications and experience. The manager does not take up references from previous employers. She does not conduct interviews. As a result, Acme Engineering has appointed many unsuitable people in the past few years. The manager of Acme Engineering has asked a management consultant to design a good selection process for the company. The management consultant has suggested writing a person description for each vacancy. One way to write a person description is the Munroe-Fraser Plan (see Table 1).

B   Understanding new vocabulary

Match each point from the Munroe-Fraser Plan with an example.

Table 1: *The Munroe-Fraser Plan*

1.	qualifications		wants to become a manager; willing to work long hours to solve problems
2.	experience		able to manage a team of people, including some older engineers
3.	appearance		at least two years' work in a maintenance department
4.	attitude		able to learn about new products quickly; able to find solutions to problems
5.	intelligence		friendly, helpful
6.	motivation		smart
7.	interpersonal skills	1	degree in Engineering

C   Developing critical thinking

Study each point in the plan again.

1. Give another example for each point.
2. How can a manager check each point during a selection process?

1. Qualifications
    A manager can check qualifications on the application form.
    A manager can also check original documents at the interview.

appearance (n)
appoint (v)
appointment (n)
arrow (n)
attitude (n)
candidate (n)
conduct (n and v)
consultant (n)
contact (v)
department (n)
description (n)
design (n and v)
executive (n)
experience (n)
flow chart
intelligence (n)
interpersonal (adj)
interview (n and v)
member (n)
motivation (n)
original (adj)
petroleum engineer
process (n)
put in (v)
referee (n)
reference (n)
selection (n)
short list (n)
staff (n)
stage (n)
successful (adj)
take up (v)
unsuccessful (adj)
unsuitable (adj)
vacancy (n)

A Reviewing vocabulary

Complete each phrase with a suitable verb.

1. _write_ a job description
2. _____ an advertisement
3. _____ an application form
4. _____ a short list
5. _____ references
6. _____ interviews
7. _____ candidates
8. _____ the best candidate

B Understanding a discourse structure (1)

Study the flow chart on the opposite page. Discuss these questions.

1. How many stages are there in this selection process?
2. What is the first stage?
3. What is the final stage?
4. Why does **Job description** come before **Person description**?
5. Why does **References** come after **Short list**?

C Understanding a discourse structure (2)

1. Read the assignment for the Business Studies Faculty.
2. Study the essay about the selection process under the flow chart opposite. Complete the essay with information from the flow chart.
3. Cover the flow chart. Try to draw the flow chart from the information in the essay.

D Developing critical thinking

The writer of the essay on the opposite page has not given the reason for some of the stages.

Write the reason for these stages in the correct place.

1. The manager makes a short list.
2. The manager telephones the referees.
3. The manager interviews some of the candidates.

Business Studies Faculty
Human resource management: selecting people
Assignment 2

- Draw a flow chart of a good selection process.
- Write a description of the process. Explain the reason for stages of the process if necessary.

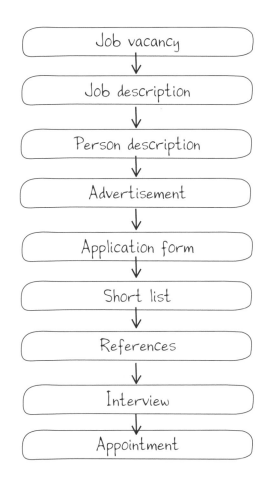

A selection process

Firstly, ‥‥‥‥ the manager writes a job description ‥‥‥‥ . The job description gives full details of

the job. Then, ‥‥‥‥‥‥‥‥‥‥‥‥‥‥‥‥‥ . The person description describes the

best person for the job. After that, ‥‥‥‥‥‥‥‥‥‥‥‥‥ . The advertisement

contains information from the job description and the person description.

Next, ‥‥‥‥‥‥‥‥‥‥‥‥‥‥‥ because she wants a large number of people

to apply. Candidates contact the company. ‥‥‥‥‥‥‥‥‥‥‥‥‥‥‥ .

The candidates complete the form and return it to the company. Candidates must provide two

referees. After studying all the applications, ‥‥‥‥‥‥‥‥‥‥‥‥‥‥‥‥‥‥

‥‥‥‥‥‥‥‥‥‥‥‥‥‥‥‥‥‥‥‥‥‥‥‥‥‥‥‥‥‥‥‥‥‥ .

Then, ‥‥‥‥‥‥‥‥‥‥‥‥‥‥‥ . She writes to the referees and she telephones

them ‥‥‥‥‥‥‥‥‥‥‥‥‥‥‥‥‥‥‥‥‥‥‥‥‥‥‥‥‥‥‥‥‥ .

Finally, ‥‥‥‥‥‥‥‥‥‥‥‥‥‥‥‥‥‥‥‥‥‥‥‥‥‥‥‥‥‥‥‥‥ .

A Developing vocabulary

One or two letters are missing from each of these words from the course so far.

1. Complete each word with the missing letter(s).

   a. lan____ua____e
   b. mana____er
   c. en____oy
   d. ____ob
   e. su____est
   f. ____une

   g. en____ineer
   h. wa____e
   i. collea____ue
   j. a____ressive
   k. sub____ect
   l. assi____nment

2. Read the Pronunciation Check and check.

B Identifying a new skill (1)

1. Read Skills Check 1. How many stages are there in the process of making a cup of tea?

2. What stage is missing from the flow chart in Skills Check 1?

C Practising a new skill

Below are the stages of the writing process.

1. Number them in a logical order.

	Organize
	Rewrite
	Think
	Write

2. One stage is missing. Add the missing stage in the correct place.

3. Draw a flow chart of the process.

D Identifying a new skill (2)

Read Skills Check 2. Then write a chronological marker in each space in this short essay.

_Firstly_____, the writer thinks about the topic. The writer makes some notes or a spidergram.

_____, the writer organizes the information into paragraphs. Each paragraph contains information about one or two sub-topics.

_____, the writer produces the first draft of the essay.

_____, the writer edits the first draft. The writer corrects problems with grammar, spelling and punctuation.

_____, the writer rewrites the essay.

Pronunciation Check

Using the letters _g_ and _j_

We can write the sound /g/ as _g_ or _gg_.

Examples: _colleague, aggressive_

We can write the sound /dʒ/ as _g_, _gg_ or _j_.

Examples: _engineer, suggest, subject_

You must learn the correct form in each word.

Note:

Sometimes we must write the letter _g_ but it has no sound.

Examples: _assignment, weight, high_

Skills Check 1

Organizing information into a flow chart

You can organize information in a process into a flow chart.

Example:

Making a cup of tea

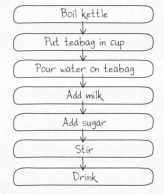

You must:

1. Find out the stages of the process.

2. Put them in order. Draw a box around each stage.

3. Draw an arrow to link each stage with the next one.

Skills Check 2

Chronological markers

We use words and phrases to show the stages of a process.

Firstly, Secondly, Thirdly, …

Next, / After that, / Then, …

Finally, …

We often use the passive in academic English. In passive sentences, we give important information in a ㉒ different order.

In the **present simple passive**, we use the verb *be* in the **present** and the **past participle** of the active verb. We often do not say who did the action.

1	2	3		3	2		1
subject	v. active	object		subject	v. passive		~~object~~
The manager	writes	a job description.	→	A job description	is	written	~~by the manager~~.
She	telephones	the referees.	→	The referees	are	telephoned	~~by her~~.

A Producing passive sentences

Rewrite each sentence in the space given.

1. The manager writes a person description. *A person description is written.*

2. The manager designs a job advertisement. ....

3. .... The advertisement is put in several newspapers.

4. .... Candidates are sent an application form.

5. The candidates complete the form. ....

We often give a **reason** for an **action** by using *because* or *so*. We can put the reason **after** or **before the action**. ㉓

action		reason
The advertisement is put in several newspapers	*because*	the company wants a large number of candidates.

reason		action
The company wants a large number of candidates,	*so*	the advertisement is put in several newspapers.

B Giving reasons

Complete each sentence with something logical.

1. Managers telephone referees because ....
2. Architects must be able to listen to clients because ....
3. You must go to work every day because ....
4. The news never stops, so ....
5. Journalists meet new people every day, so ....
6. Managers cannot interview all candidates, so ....

A Reviewing vocabulary

In a selection process, who or what can you …

1. write? *a job description / person description*
2. design? ....
3. send? ....
4. complete and return? ....
5. make? ....
6. take up? ....
7. telephone? ....
8. conduct? ....
9. interview? ....
10. select? ....

B Thinking and organizing

You are going to describe the interview process at a large company. There are three sections to the process:

- Before the interviews (B)
- During each interview (D)
- After the interviews (A)

1. Study the stages on the right. Mark each stage *B*, *D* or *A*.
2. Number the stages in each section in a logical order.
3. Add a reason for some of the stages.

C Making a flow chart

Make a flow chart for each section of the interview process.

D Describing a process

Write about the interview process.

Remember to:

- use the present simple passive where possible.
- give reasons for stages with *because* / *so*.

E Editing

Exchange descriptions with a partner. Read his/her description. Mark the description with *?*, *S*, *G* and *P*.

F Rewriting

Read your description again. Look at the *?*, *S*, *G* and *P* marks on your first draft. Rewrite the description.

An interview process

		Candidate can ask questions
		Check qualifications and experience
		Give candidates a personality test
		Give candidates tea / coffee / biscuits
		Interviewers discuss candidates
		Interviewers make a decision
		Introduce the interviewers
		Manager sends letter to successful candidate
		Manager sends letters to unsuccessful candidates
B	1	Organize interview room
		Question: Tell me about yourself.
		Question: Why do you want to work here?
		Question: Why should we hire you?
		Short conversation, e.g., weather, journey
		Take candidates on tour of company

Portfolio Jobs

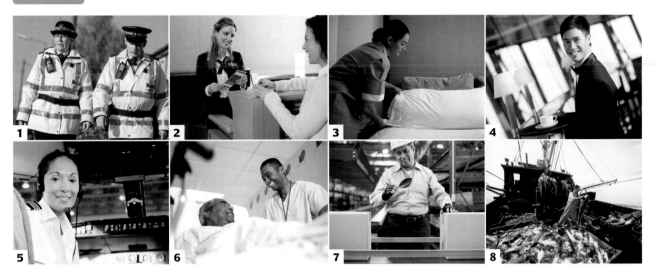

A Activating ideas

1. Look at the photographs of jobs above. What is the main task of each job?
2. Which of these jobs would you like to do? Which of these jobs would you hate?

B Gathering information (1)

1. Divide into two groups. Group A: ⓐ 3.26, Group B: ⓐ 3.27. Listen to the information about two jobs. Make notes to answer these questions.
   - What is the name of the job?
   - What does the job involve?
   - What sort of person is good at the job?
   - What are the working hours?
   - What are the benefits?
   - What qualifications do you need?
   - What experience do you need?
   - What is the starting salary?
2. Work in pairs, one student from Group A and the other from Group B. Exchange information about your job. Make notes.
3. Are you the right sort of person for one or both jobs? Explain your answer.

C Gathering information (2)

1. Work in pairs. Read one of the texts about jobs, *Advertising executive* or *Petroleum engineer,* on pages 102 and 103. Make notes.
2. Explain the information you read about to your partner. Your partner should make notes.

D Giving a talk

Choose one of the jobs from your portfolio notes, *Primary school teacher, Solicitor, Advertising executive* or *Petroleum engineer*. Write a short talk. Give your talk in a small group.

E Writing

ⓐ 3.28 Listen to a talk about the job of retail manager. Write a website page for **choose-a-career.com**.

choose-a-career.com

The website that helps you find the right career for you.

So you want to be an ...

advertising executive

The world of advertising looks very glamorous from the outside. Thinking up new ideas for advertisements, then making the advertisements with famous people in exotic locations. But in reality it is a very competitive field.

Personal qualities and abilities

Advertising executives must be knowledgeable about the world. They must be creative and passionate about their work. They also need determination to win, and they must not be afraid to compete with others. The business can be ruthless at times.

Working hours

Advertising executives do not have fixed hours. The office itself may be open from 9.00 a.m. to 5.00 p.m. to the general public, but the executives often start earlier and finish much, much later. There is a lot of weekend working, too.

Workplace

Advertising is largely office-based. Don't expect to be flying around the world all the time, although some very large agencies have offices overseas and you may be sent for a placement or a permanent job.

Qualifications

You need a degree, but it does not have to be in a particular subject. It can be an arts subject or a science subject. Most large advertising agencies will train you on the job, with lectures, presentations and placements in different departments.

Experience

It is good to show your creativity in some way. If you are studying art, you will have a portfolio of drawings and paintings, but if you are doing another subject, you need something else, for example, poetry you have written, or another type of creative writing.

Salary and benefits

Advertising executives start on about £18,000 per year but, if you are promoted regularly, you could earn around £40,000 after a few years.

File   Edit   View   Favorites   Tools   Help

http://www.choose-a-career.com/petroleumengineer

choose-a-career.com
The website that helps you find the right career for you.

So you want to be a …

petroleum engineer

The products of petroleum engineering are all around us, from car fuel to plastics, from perfume to fertilizer. Petroleum engineers make a vital contribution to the modern world. Perhaps they work with computers to design and build refineries. Or perhaps they work in a refinery with responsibility for maintenance, health and safety. Either way, it's an exciting world.

Personal qualities and abilities

Petroleum engineers must be interested in chemistry – and good at it! They must also be good at maths and be able to understand the principles of engineering. Because so much design and control is done by computers nowadays, they must have a high standard of computer literacy, especially using computer-aided design (CAD) programs.

Working hours

Petroleum engineers in a research and development team work about 37 to 40 hours per week. But engineers in a refinery often work much longer hours, 50 or 55, with a lot of evening and weekend work.

Workplace

Research and development teams work in offices. Maintenance and control engineers work in a refinery, both indoors and outdoors. Sometimes they need to work offshore or deep in the desert.

Qualifications

You need a degree in chemical engineering or a Higher National Diploma (in the UK).

Experience

Get as much experience as possible on computer programs, especially CAD.

Salary and benefits

Petroleum engineers earn around £19,000 during their training period. Experienced engineers can earn up to £35,000. If you get more qualifications on the job, you can expect to earn up to £50,000.

Theme 4

Science and nature

- The scientific method

- Diagrams and explanations

- Temperature and time

- A laboratory report

Listening: The scientific method

4.1 Vocabulary for listening Tables, graphs, experiments

Table 1: *Average temperature (in degrees C)*

	Jan	Feb	Mar	Apr	May	Jun	Jul	Aug	Sep	Oct	Nov	Dec
Abu Dhabi	19	20	23	27	31	33	35	34	32	29	25	20

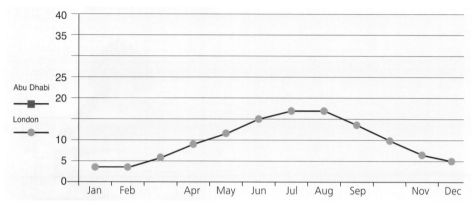

Figure 1: *Average temperature (in degrees C)*

A Developing vocabulary

Look at the table and the graph above. What do they show?

1. 🔊 4.1 Listen. Add the information to the table and the graph.
2. 🔊 4.2 Listen and answer the questions.

B Improving listening skills

🔊 4.3 Listen. Tick the correct column to show the stressed syllable.

		Oo	oO
1.	average	✓	
2.	axis		
3.	circle		
4.	column		
5.	compare		

		Oo	oO
6.	data		
7.	display		
8.	research		
9.	result		
10.	table		

C Understanding vocabulary in context

🔊 4.4 Listen. Complete the text with words from the list on the right.

Science is the study of how things work in the world. A .... usually works in a .... He/she works with many different kinds of ...., for example plastic or metal, and .... A scientist .... things to .... a hypothesis. A hypothesis is an idea that something is .... Scientists must .... all the facts first. Then he/she often puts the facts in a .... with columns of information, or in a ...., with blocks or lines that .... the information.

average *(adj)*
axis *(n)*
block *(n)*
collect *(v)*
column *(n)*
compare *(v)*
conclusion *(n)*
damage *(n and v)*
data *(n)*
display *(n and v)*
disprove *(v)*
draw *(v)*
experiment *(n and v)*
fact *(n)*
graph *(n)*
horizontal *(adj)*
hypothesis *(n)*
laboratory *(n)*
line *(n)*
liquid *(n)*
look up *(v)*
material *(n)*
method *(n)*
organize *(v)*
prove *(v)*
represent *(v)*
research *(n)*
result *(n)*
science *(n)*
scientific *(adj)*
scientist *(n)*
soft *(adj)*
sunlight *(n)*
table *(n)* [data]
test *(n and v)*
true *(adj)*
truth *(n)*
vertical *(adj)*

A Predicting content

1. Look at the information on the right. Think of answers to the three questions.

2. ⊙ 4.5 Listen to the introduction and answer the first two questions.

B Making notes of the main points

⊙ 4.6 Listen and complete the notes below about the scientific method.

> ## The scientific method
>
> 1. ___Make___ a hypothesis
> 2. _____ the hypothesis: _____ experiments
>   or _____ research
> 3. _____ data
> 4. _____ the results: table or graph
> 5. _____ conclusions = prove a hypothesis
>   or _____ it

9.15 | **So you want to be … a scientist**

In this week's programme, Arthur Burns looks at science as a career.
- What is science?
- What do scientists do?
- Is science the right career for you?

C Reconstructing information from notes

Explain the scientific method to your partner. Use the notes in Exercise B.

> Firstly, scientists make a hypothesis …

D Reviewing key skills

How does Arthur define these words?

1. proving   ☐ a test, usually in a laboratory
2. method   ☐ looking up information, e.g., in a library
3. hypothesis   ☐ an idea of the truth
4. experiment   ☐ information before it is organized
5. research   ☐ a way of doing something
6. data   ☐ what you learn from an experiment
7. conclusions   ☐1 showing that something is always true

E Reacting to information

Discuss the following questions.

1. What experiments can you remember doing at school?
2. What did you try to prove?
3. What was your method?
4. What conclusion did you draw?

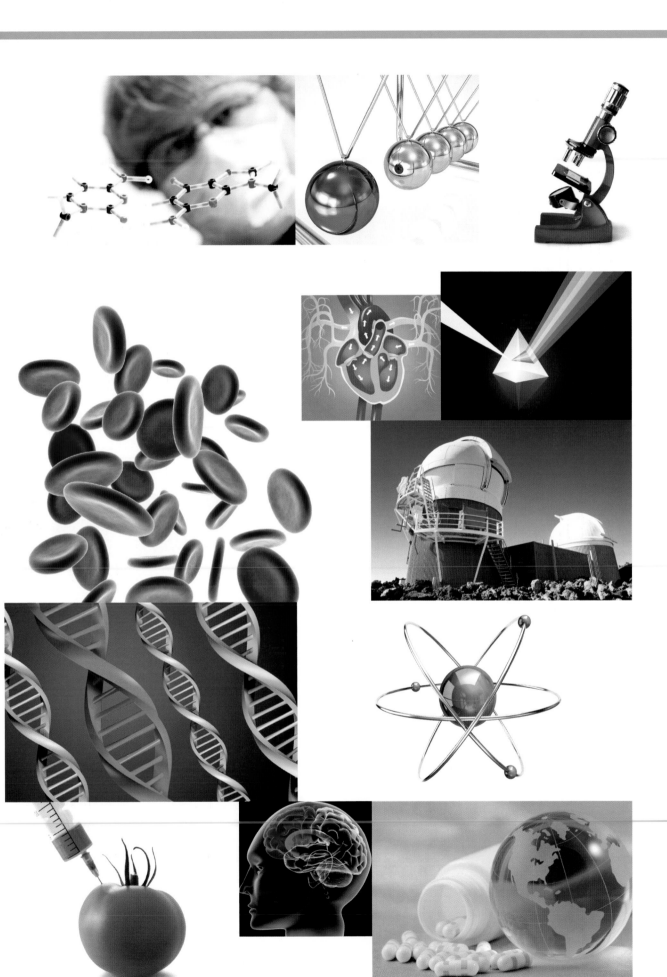

A Reviewing key words

Study each word in the table from the radio programme in Lesson 4.2.

1. What is the part of speech for each word in the table? (*n* = noun, *v* = verb, *adj* = adjective)

2. Think of another word with the same (underlined) vowel sound. Write it in the table.

d<u>a</u>ta	n	say
graph		
know		
m<u>e</u>thod		
true		
world	1	

B Learning to predict the next word

1. Read the Skills Check. Why should you predict the next word in a talk?

2. 🔊 4.7 Listen to some of Arthur's sentences from the radio programme. Number a word in the table in Exercise A each time Arthur pauses.

C Predicting the next word

You are going to hear about another experiment.

1. 🔊 4.8 Listen and predict the next word.

   1. hypothesis

2. 🔊 4.9 Listen to the complete talk. Check your ideas.

D Identifying consonants

Read Pronunciation Check 1. 🔊 4.10 Listen and copy each word from Arthur's talk into the correct column.

that the they both then there with
hypothesis thing truth think this

/θ/	/ð/

E Identifying vowel sounds

1. 🔊 4.11 Listen. Which is the odd one out?
   test when then pen she bed many any head again

2. What do all these words have in common?
   bird heard learn research surname turn work

3. Read Pronunciation Check 2 and check your ideas.

Skills Check

What comes next?

We can often predict the next word in a talk.

Examples:

Science is about knowing things, but even more it is about proving ... **things**.

I know that plants need sunlight and water to live. At least, I think that's ... **true**.

Pronunciation Check 1

Hearing consonants: *th*

The consonants *th* have two sounds:

1. the soft sound in *think, thing, hypothesis*.
   We can write the sound /θ/.
2. the harder sound in *this, that, the*.
   We can write the sound /ð/.

Pronunciation Check 2

Hearing vowels: *e* or *er*

The vowel sound in *then* /e/ is usually written with e. But there are some common words with *a* or *ea*.

Examples: *many, any, head*

The vowel sound in *her* /ɜː/ is written in many different ways.

Examples: *res<u>ea</u>rch, word, bird, turn*

There is often an article – *a*, *an*, *the*, *some* – in front of a noun. Here are some rules for using articles. ㉔

1. We use *a* or *an* to introduce a singular countable noun.
2. We use *the* to talk about specific singular countable nouns.
3. We use *the* to talk about specific plural countable nouns.
4. We use *some* to introduce a plural noun for a group of items.
5. We don't use an article with uncountable nouns to talk about things in general.
6. We don't use an article with plural nouns to talk about things in general.

A Understanding article usage

Which rule above does each sentence below follow? There is one sentence for each rule.

a. I made a hypothesis. ☐1   d. I tested the hypothesis. ☐

b. 'Plants need things to grow.' ☐   e. I bought some plants. ☐

c. 'They need sunlight and water.' ☐   f. The plants in Pot A died. ☐

B Recognizing words with and without articles

Look at part of the radio programme. Complete the spaces with –, *a*, *an* or *the*. ⓐ **4.12** Listen and check your answers.

Firstly, ____a____ scientist makes _____ hypothesis, which means _____ idea of the truth.

Then he/she tests _____ hypothesis. Scientists can test _____ hypotheses in two main ways.

They can do _____ experiment, which means a test in a laboratory. Scientists study what happens

during _____ experiment. Or they can do _____ research, which means looking up _____

information. They usually do research in _____ library or, nowadays, on _____ Internet.

Look at the simple SVO sentence pattern below, and the same sentence with an introductory phrase. ㉕

subject	verb	object		introductory phrase	subject	verb	object
Plants	need	water.	→	I know (that)	plants	need	water.
Water	damages	teeth.	→	I don't believe (that)	water	damages	teeth.

Here are some other introductory phrases.
I think (that) ... I believe (that) ... The results mean that ... The experiment proves that ...

C Recognizing introductory phrases

Put the words for each sentence in the correct order.

ⓐ **4.13** Listen and check your ideas.

1. know   I   that   need   plants   water

2. I   damages   think   teeth   that   sugar

3. don't   finished   I   believe   the   research   that   is

4. means   it   we   enough   don't   that   have   data

5. it   that   proves   the   correct   hypothesis   is

6. the   temperature   the   summer   shows   us   17°C   that   graph   average   in   is

7. have   proved   sea   scientists   getting   water   that   temperatures   are   warmer

> *1. I know that plants need water.*

A Collocating vocabulary

What do you expect to hear after each verb? Think of a suitable noun phrase.

1. do   *an experiment, an assignment*
2. make
3. collect
4. display
5. draw
6. prove

B Predicting content

1. A student is making a presentation about an experiment.

   🔊 4.14 Listen. Put these groups of words in the correct order.

   | cola | damage teeth | is | My hypothesis | that | and other sugary drinks |

2. What materials did she use for the experiment? Name the items in the diagram.

3. Can you work out the experiment?

C Practising a key skill

1. 🔊 4.15 Listen to the student describing the experiment. When she stops speaking, tick the correct word from each pair of words below.

   Remember, my hypothesis was that cola damages ...

a. ☐ tooth	✓ teeth	g. ☐ air	☐ liquid
b. ☐ water	☐ glasses	h. ☐ year	☐ week
c. ☐ teeth	☐ people	i. ☐ liquid	☐ eggshell
d. ☐ shell	☐ glass	j. ☐ soft	☐ hard
e. ☐ pen	☐ pin	k. ☐ damaged	☐ good
f. ☐ thread	☐ water	l. ☐ teeth	☐ mouth

2. Find the transcript on page 199. Take it in turns to read some of the sentences. Pause before the last word. Your partner must predict the last word.

D Transferring a new skill

Describe the complete experiment. Use the diagram above to help you. Don't look at the transcript this time.

Speaking: Diagrams and explanations

4.6 Vocabulary for speaking Diagrams and explanations

A Reviewing vocabulary

1. What is the connection between a scientist and each of these words?

> collect   conclusion   data   experiment   hypothesis
> method   prove   research   scientific   test

> *A scientist collects data. Collect is a verb. What's the noun? Collection.*

2. Ask your partner for another form of a word in the box.

B Understanding new vocabulary

1. 🎧 4.16 Listen and number the words below in the order that you hear them.

atmosphere		mix	
contains		natural	
explained	1	rainbow	
hits		splits	

2. Can you remember the sentences about sunlight?

C Practising new vocabulary

Study the conversations below.

1. Complete each conversation with words from the list on the right.
   🎧 4.17 Listen and check.
2. Practise the conversations in pairs.
3. Add more lines to each conversation.

1 A: What is the water _____?
   B: I'm not sure. Is it something to do with rain?

2 A: What's that _____?
   B: I think it's thunder.

3 A: What are _____ made of?
   B: Water vapour, I think.

4 A: Why do we have _____ at the coast?
   B: I don't know. Perhaps the wind causes them.

amount (n)
area (n)
atmosphere (n)
burst (v)
charge (n) [electrical]
cloud (n)
contain (v)
cool (adj and v)
cycle (n)
diagram (n)
directly (adv)
dust (n)
(the) Earth (n)
expand (v)
explain (v)
explanation (n)
fall (v)
full (adj)
gas (n)
gravity (n)
heat (n and v)
hit (v)
lake (n)
light (n)
lightning (n)
mix (v)
natural (adj)
negative (adj)
pass through (v)
positive (adj)
rainbow (n)
rise (v)
smoke (n)
sound (n)
split (v)
surface (n)
thunder (n)
tide (n)
together (adv)
vapour (n)

A Previewing vocabulary

Find connections between some of the words in the box.

fall – rise = They are opposites.
wind – cloud = The wind moves clouds.

cloud   cool   fall   gas   heat   lake
land   liquid   rain   rise   river   sea
surface   vapour   water   wind

B Activating ideas

You are going to watch two students working on a presentation. Cover the text below. Look at the diagrams. What is the presentation about?

C Studying a model

1. Uncover the text. ⏵ 4.18 DVD 4.A Watch and listen to the explanation. Complete the gaps, using the correct word from the box in Exercise A.

1. This is the sky. This is the _____. These are rivers and lakes.	
2. Rain is part of the _____ cycle. The Sun is here, and it heats up the _____ of the water, here.	
3. The water is a _____, of course, but it _____ up and it turns into a _____. The gas is called water vapour. The water vapour rises into the air, like this. It _____ because it's hot.	
4. But the atmosphere here, above the Earth, is cold. The vapour makes _____ because it _____. Here are the clouds.	
5. The clouds move with the _____. They collect more and more water, and get bigger and bigger, like this.	
6. Finally, they are full of water, and they burst. The water _____ from the clouds. In other words, it _____. This is the rain falling. Some rain falls directly into the rivers, lakes and _____.	
7. The rest falls onto the land, here, and from there it travels back to the seas, _____ and _____. And the cycle continues, round and round, like this.	

2. Cover the text again. Give an explanation of the water cycle, using the drawings.

D Developing critical thinking

Discuss these questions.

1. Why does water vapour rise?
2. What makes clouds grow?
3. Where does the water go after it falls from the clouds?
4. In general, what is a cycle?

A Understanding functions

Look at the photos above. Which conversations below do they show?

B Studying models

1. Study the conversations. Find examples of people:
   - offering.
   - accepting.
   - requesting.
   - refusing.
2. Decide where each conversation is taking place.

C Practising conversations

🔊 4.19 Listen to the conversations. Then practise them in pairs.

1
A: Are you OK there?
B: I don't understand this assignment.
A: Let me have a look.
B: Thank you.

2
A: Would you like some help with that?
B: No, thanks. I can manage.
A: Are you sure?
B: Yes, I'm fine. Thanks anyway.

3
A: Can I help you?
B: Yes, please. Black coffee please.
A: Medium or large?
B: Mm. Large.

4
A: Could you help me with this?
B: I'm afraid I can't. I haven't finished myself.
A: OK. Don't worry.
B: Give me a few minutes.

5
A: Could you help me with this?
B: Of course.
A: Sorry to trouble you.
B: It's no trouble.

6
A: Have you got a moment?
B: No, sorry. I'm in a hurry.
A: OK. That's fine.
B: Sorry.

D Real-time speaking

Choose three or four of the real-life situations below. Role-play a conversation in each case. Use expressions from the conversations above.

You have to:

- find your classroom.
- fill in a form for a student ID card.
- put in a code to open the door.
- carry something heavy.
- use a drinks machine.
- print your work in the computer room.
- write an essay.
- find a place to live.

A Saying vowels

1. Underline the words with the same vowel sound in each sentence on the right.

2. Read the Pronunciation Check to check your answers.

3. Practise saying the sentences aloud.

4. How do you pronounce the underlined sound in each word in the box on the right?

B Identifying a new skill

1. Read the Skills Check.

2. Look at the presentation in Lesson 4.7. Underline all the places where the student uses a diagram to help her explanation.

C Rehearsing a model

1. Look at each diagram below. Use it to help you give a scientific explanation.

2. 🔊 4.20 DVD 4.B Watch some students giving explanations.

1. Rainbows

> Look. The Sun is here, and this is water vapour. The white light from the Sun travels like this ...

2. Thunder

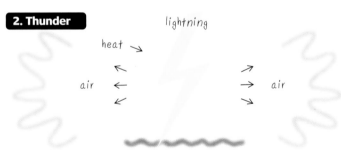

3. Tides

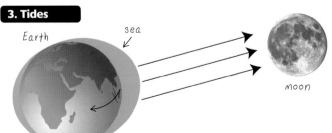

D Extended practice

Work in groups. Take it in turns to give one of the scientific explanations in Exercise C and draw a diagram.

> Then Ben's ten men went to bed.

> Were her first words 'bird' and 'learn'?

| get   water   surface   river   when |
| turns   Earth   bigger   burst   rest |

Pronunciation Check

Saying vowels: /e/, /ɜː/, /ə/

We pronounce most short words with e with the short sound /e/.

Examples: *test, then, method*

The letters *er* in the middle of a word are often pronounced /ɜː/.

Examples: *person, certainly, verb*

The letters *er* at the end of a word are often pronounced /ə/.

Examples: *river, water, bigger*

The sound /ɜː/ is in many words with these spellings: *first, earth, burst.*

Skills Check

Giving a scientific explanation

We give scientific explanations in the **present simple**.

Rain is part of the water cycle. The Sun heats up the liquid and it turns into a gas.

We often use a **diagram** to help us give a scientific explanation.

We can refer to **objects** in the diagram with *this, these, here.*

This is the Sun. These are lakes. Here is the sea. The clouds are here.

We can refer to **actions** in the diagram with a verb + *like this.*

The water vapour rises, like this ...

> We use *this* with singular nouns and uncountable nouns. We use *these* with plural nouns. ㉖
> *this + diagram, this + light, these + clouds*
> *This is the sky. This is the rain falling. These are rivers.*

A Referring to a diagram

Complete the text with *this* or *these*.

Look here. .... is a picture of Isaac Newton in his laboratory.
.... shows his experiment with light. .... is a ray
of light going into the prism here, and .... are the seven
colours coming out on .... side. Light has other colours too,
but .... colours are the only ones that humans can see.

> We can join two actions in several ways.
> Examples: ㉗
>
> | | | | | | | |
> |---|---|---|---|---|---|---|
> | *The liquid heats up **and** it turns into gas.* | = | action | + | *and* | + | next action |
> | *The water is a liquid, **but** it turns into a gas.* | = | action | + | *but* | + | surprising action |
> | *The vapour makes clouds **because** it cools.* | = | action | + | *because* | + | reason |
> | *The clouds have too much water, **so** they burst.* | = | action | + | *so* | + | result |

B Joining ideas

Make a sentence with each pair of words.
Then join the sentences in a logical way.

1. a. rain   land
    b. water   sea

> *The rain falls on the land.*
> *The water travels to the sea.*
> *The rain falls on the land, and the water travels to the sea.*

2. a. Sun   water
    b. liquid   gas

3. a. gas   warm
    b. gas   air

4. a. vapour   warm
    b. atmosphere   cold

5. a. atmosphere   cold
    b. clouds   sky

6. a. rain   clouds
    b. clouds   too big

7. a. rain   land
    b. cycle   again

A Reviewing sounds

Say these words aloud. Make sure you pronounce the vowel sounds correctly.

1. bed   bird
2. ten   turn
3. wed   word
4. head   heard
5. Ben   burn
6. went   weren't

B Preparing vocabulary

1. Read the Pronunciation Check.
2. Work in pairs. Use the questions in the Pronunciation Check to ask about the words in the box below.

> amount   atmosphere   cloud   contains
> straight   vapour

Pronunciation Check

Asking about pronunciation

Always ask for help in pronouncing a new word.

Point to the word and ask:
How do you say this word?

Spell the word. Ask:
How do you say S-C-A-T-T-E-R?

Say the word several times and check that your pronunciation is correct.

Mark the stress on multi-syllable words with a vertical line.

Examples: *'scatter, con'tains*

C Using a key skill

1. Which natural event does each diagram below show?
2. Form three groups. Group A: Look at page 173. Group B: Look at page 179. Group C: Look at page 177. Read your text. Ask for help with any new words.
3. Practise explaining your point to a partner in your own group. Write labels on the diagram as you speak to make your explanation clear.
4. Make new groups. There must be at least one A, one B and one C student in each group. Explain your point to the other students. Redraw the diagram as you speak.
5. DVD 4.A Watch some students doing the exercise.

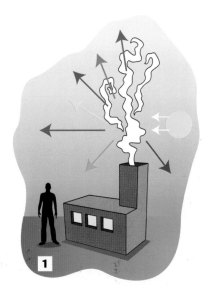

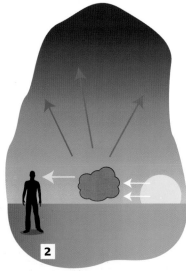

4.11 Vocabulary for reading   Location

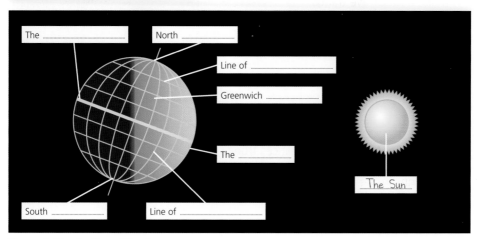

The ....
North ....
Line of ....
Greenwich ....
The ....
The Sun
South ....
Line of ....

Figure 1: *The Earth and the Sun*

A Understanding vocabulary in context

Read the text below and label Figure 1 with words from the text.

How can we locate a place on Earth? For example, where is Mexico City? We can use lines of latitude and longitude to give the position of any place on the Earth. Lines of latitude run around the Earth. The best-known line of latitude is the Equator (0°), which runs around the centre of the Earth. Lines of longitude run from the North Pole to the South Pole. The most important line of longitude is the Greenwich Meridian (0°), which runs through London. International time, or GMT, is taken from this line. So where is Mexico City? It is on latitude 19° north and longitude 99° west.

B Developing vocabulary

Look at Table 1 on the right. Answer these questions.

1. How many columns are there?
2. In which row are the column headings?
3. What does this table show?
4. What is the unit of measurement for this table?
5. Which city is nearest the Equator?
6. Where does this information come from?

Table 1: *Location of some capital cities*

city	lat (°)	long (°)
Mexico City, Mexico	19 N	99 W
Tokyo, Japan	35 N	139 E
Asunción, Paraguay	25 S	57 W
Beijing, China	40 N	116 E
Washington, D.C., USA	40 N	77 W
Helsinki, Finland	60 N	25 E
London, England	51 N	0 W
Wellington, New Zealand	41 S	174 E
Moscow, Russia	55 N	37 E
New Delhi, India	28 N	77 E

Source: www.infoplease.com

C Developing critical thinking

Discuss these questions.

1. Why is this table difficult to understand?
2. How could you improve it?

affect (*v*)
average (*adj*)
base (*n*)
centre (*n*)
coast (*n*)
degree (*n*)
distance (*n*)
(the) Equator (*n*)
extremely (*adv*)
factor (*n*)
furthest (*adj*)
ground (*n*)
hemisphere (*n*)
horizon (*n*)
influence (*n* and *v*)
inland (*adj* and *adv*)
latitude (*n*)
locate (*v*)
longitude (*n*)
measurement (*n*)
meridian (*n*)
minus (*prep*)
northern (*adj*)
peak (*n*)
pole (*n*)
rainfall (*n*)
row (*n*)
run (*v*) [= go]
single (*adj*)
slightly (*adv*)
source (*n*)
temperature (*n*)
thunderstorm (*n*)
tilt (*v*)
unit (*n*)

4.12 Real-time reading   Factors affecting temperature

A   Activating ideas

What should tables of information have? Look again at part of the table from Lesson 4.11. Make a list of five things.

1.   headings
2.   ....
3.   ....
4.   ....
5.   ....

Table 1: *Location of some capital cities*

city	lat (°)	long (°)
Mexico City, Mexico	19 N	99 W
Tokyo, Japan	35 N	139 E
Asunción, Paraguay	25 S	57 W
Beijing, China	40 N	116 E

Source: www.infoplease.com

B   Understanding a table

Look at the table on the opposite page. Mark these sentences true (*T*) or false (*F*).

1.   There are four columns in this table.   ☐ T
2.   The table has eight rows.   ☐
3.   In the first row, there are headings.   ☐
4.   The first column contains capital cities.   ☐
5.   In the second column, there is information about the average rainfall.   ☐
6.   All the information in this table comes from worldweather.wmo.int.   ☐
7.   Colombo has the highest average temperature of these capital cities.   ☐
8.   Petropavlovsk-Kamca has the lowest average temperature in the world.   ☐

C   Predicting the content of a text

1.   Keep the text on the opposite page covered. Look at the table again.
     Tick the sentences you expect to find in the text.

   a.   As you travel north or south from the Equator, the average temperature falls.   ☐
   b.   Cities are often much warmer in summer.   ☐
   c.   In Colombo on July 1ˢᵗ, sunrise is at 5.35 a.m.   ☐
   d.   Kampala is almost on the Equator.   ☐
   e.   Rangoon is 1,900 km north of the Equator.   ☐
   f.   The Sun rises in the east.   ☐
   g.   There are many factors that affect the average temperature.   ☐

2.   Uncover the text. Look quickly through the whole text to check your answers.

D   Dealing with new words

Look at the highlighted words in the text. Can you work out the meaning of each word?

E   Checking information

Read the text. Correct this summary.

                                            average
There are many factors that affect the ~~maximum~~ temperature of a city. One factor is the size of the city.

However, the main factor is how high the city is above sea level. Places near the Equator are colder

because the Sun is low in the sky during the day.

Why is it so hot ... or so cold?

Why are some places hotter than other places? Is there one single factor that affects the temperature at a location? The simple answer is: *no*.

Table 1: *Average temperature in selected cities: E. Asia*

city	average temp (°C)	latitude (°N)	distance from the Equator (km)
Colombo	27.4	7	770
Rangoon	27.2	17	1,870
Vientiane	25.9	18	2,000
Hanoi	23.0	21	2,330
Hong Kong	22.7	22	2,470
Taipei	22.0	25	2,780
Tokyo	16.7	36	3,960
Petropavlovsk-Kamca	3.9	55	5,890

Average temperature information from worldweather.wmo.int

There are many factors that affect the average temperature. These factors include:

- Where do the winds come from? Winds from the North Pole bring cold air to, say, Canada, while winds from the Equator keep places like South Africa warm.
- Is the city on the coast? Temperatures do not vary much in a city near the sea, such as Lisbon. At the centre of the USA, however, the temperature can be minus 10°C in winter and over 30°C in summer.
- How high is the city above sea level? The higher you go, the colder the air gets. For example, the peak of a mountain, like Kilimanjaro in Tanzania, may be covered in snow, while the base is warm and green.

However, there is one main factor that strongly influences the average temperature. That factor is the distance of the city from the Equator. Take Kampala, the capital city of Uganda, for instance. It is almost on the Equator, and the average temperature is extremely high, at 29°C.

As you travel north or south from the Equator, the average temperature falls. In Rangoon, the capital of Myanmar, for example, which is 1,900 kilometres north of the Equator, the average temperature is 27.2°C.

In Tokyo, which is another 2,100 kilometres north, the average is down to 16.7°C. So places close to the Equator are generally hotter than places close to the poles. But that still leaves one question.

Why is it so hot at the Equator? It is because the Sun is much higher in the sky during the day at the Equator. At the poles, the Sun is close to the horizon, so less heat reaches the ground.

Sources: http://www.videojug.com http://answers.yahoo.com

A   Identifying a new skill (1)

1. Read Skills Check 1.

2. Find and highlight the topic sentences in the article in Lesson 4.12.

3. Read the topic sentences A–D below. Which sentence or phrase (1 or 2) follows in each case?

A   There are many factors that affect the average temperature.

1. ☐   These factors include …

2. ☐   Is the city on the coast?

B   However, there is one main factor that strongly influences the average temperature.

1. ☐   Take Kampala, the capital city of Uganda, …

2. ☐   That factor is the distance …

C   As you travel north or south from the Equator, the average temperature falls.

1. ☐   In Rangoon, the capital of Myanmar, for example, …

2. ☐   In Tokyo, which is another 2,100 kilometres north, …

D   Why is it so hot at the Equator?

1. ☐   It is because the Sun is much higher …

2. ☐   At the poles, the Sun is close to the horizon …

B   Identifying a new skill (2)

1. Read Skills Check 2.

2. Read and match the statements below on the left with the examples on the right.

A   Try this experiment. Find five or six different kinds of food and leave them in a warm place,

B   There are a lot of hypotheses about the weather that scientists have not proved yet.

C   Scientists want to collect data in space to help answer some difficult questions.

D   We are beginning to understand large, violent weather events

E   Some scientists think that the Earth's weather is changing. They believe that average temperatures will be much higher in,

F   Everybody knows that water can fall from the sky in different forms.

Skills Check 1

Finding and using topic sentences

The first sentence of a paragraph is sometimes called the **topic sentence**. This sentence helps you to predict the **content of the paragraph**.

Find and highlight topic sentences while you are reading.
Think: *What information will come next?*

Skills Check 2

Looking for examples

Many paragraphs have this structure:

statement of fact then	As you travel north or south from the Equator, the average temperature falls.
example(s)	In Rangoon, **for example**, the average temperature is 27.2°C.

Look for examples to help you understand.

We introduce examples with:

For example, … For instance, …

Take …

include / including, such as, say, like

Find these words in the text on page 123.

☐   such as thunderstorms and hurricanes.

☐   For example, sometimes it falls as snow and sometimes as rain.

☐   say, 100 years from now.

☐   Take, for example, the idea that lightning is caused by ice in clouds.

☐   such as inside a sunny window.

☐   These include: What is the universe made of?

We can compare two things with two grammatical structures: ⁽²⁸⁾

1. with one-syllable adjectives, e.g., *hot, cold, big*   adjective + ~er (*than*)
2. with two-syllable adjectives ending in -y, e.g., *pretty, heavy*   adjective + ~ier (*than*)
3. with two-syllable adjectives ending in -ed, -ing, -ful, -less,   *more* + adjective (*than*)
   e.g., *worried, boring, careful, careless*

		first thing	comparative	**second thing**
Why	are	some places	hotter than	other places?

first thing		comparative	**second thing**
This factor	is	more important than	other factors.

Make sure you can identify the two things being compared when you read a comparative sentence.
We can add *much* to each structure: *much hotter than; much more important than.*

A   **Identifying comparatives**

1. Underline the comparative forms in the following text.
2. Circle the two things involved in each case.

Imagine two cities on the same continent. City A is closer to the Equator than City B. So is City B warmer

in winter than City A? No, it is colder, because it is inland, whereas City B is on the coast. Why are coastal

cities usually warmer in winter than places inland? It is because the sea in winter is warmer than the land.

In fact, the climate in coastal cities is more pleasant all year round. In summer, the sea is cooler than the

land, so coastal cities are cooler in summer than inland cities on the same latitude.

B   **Understanding long sentences**

subject		be	complement			
noun	**more information**		comparative	**noun**	**more information**	
A city	on the coast	is	cooler than	a city	inland.	
Places	near the Equator	are	much hotter than	places	close to the poles.	

What do you expect to come next?

1. A city on the coast is cooler in summer than ..a city inland...
2. Places near the poles are much colder than ....
3. A country on the Equator is much hotter than ....
4. Cities at sea level are usually hotter than ....
5. The sea on the side near the moon is higher because ....
6. The sky in the evening is redder because ....

A Reviewing vocabulary

1. Find pairs of words in the box below. Explain the connection.

> east   high   low   horizontal   north   far   near   vertical   south   west

2. Read the text in the box below aloud. Don't write anything.

> The dist_____ of a place from the Equ_____ is the ma_____ fac_____ that inf_____ the ave_____
>
> temp_____ of that place. The lat_____ of the loca_____ indicates its dist_____ from the Equ_____.
>
> Other fact_____ include wind dir_____ and hei_____ above sea lev_____.

B Using a key skill (1)

You are going to read the article on the opposite page. After each of the steps listed below, stop and discuss with your partner the question: *What will the article be about?*

1. Look at the title of the text.
2. Look at the illustration.
3. Look at the table.
4. Read the first paragraph only.
5. Read the topic sentences of paragraphs 2, 3 and 4.

C Using a key skill (2)

Read the article. Match the left and right columns to make true sentences.

	example		... *is (are) an example(s) of* ...
1.	The Arabian Gulf		the location of an old meridian.
2.	Paris		places on the same line of longitude but with different sunrise times.
3.	Muscat and Damascus		a place where the Sun rises early in winter.
4.	Tehran and Abu Dhabi		places on different lines of longitude with different sunrise times.

D Showing comprehension

Cover the text. Decide if each sentence is true or false.

1. The table shows information about selected capital cities in the Arabian Gulf. ......
2. The text explains why it is darker in winter in London. ......
3. Summer and winter are the two factors which affect sunrise times. ......
4. Sunrise is later in Damascus than in Muscat because it is closer to Greenwich. ......
5. Sunrise is earlier in Tehran than in Abu Dhabi because it is on the same line of longitude. ......

E Developing critical thinking

How does the location of your city influence its daylight hours?

Why is it still dark?

Table 1: *Sunrise on July 1ˢᵗ in selected capital cities: Arabian Gulf*

capital city	sunrise (July 1ˢᵗ)	longitude (°N)	distance from Greenwich Meridian (km)
Muscat	5.22	59	6,490
Abu Dhabi	5.38	54	5,940
Doha	5.47	52	5,610
Manama	5.49	51	5,720
Kuwait City	5.52	48	5,280
Baghdad	5.57	45	4,950
Damascus	6.28	36	3,960

Sunrise times from timeanddate.com

People who travel in winter to London sometimes find that the climate is very different from the climate at home. Visitors from, say, the Arabian Gulf, are often surprised that the Sun does not rise in London until 7.30 or 8.00 a.m. Why does the Sun rise at different times in different places?

There are two factors that affect the time of sunrise. The first factor is related to the distance of the place from the Greenwich meridian. A meridian is a line of longitude. The second factor is related to the distance of the place from the Equator.

The Greenwich meridian, which runs through London, is the 0° line of longitude. The modern measurement of longitude begins here although, in the past, other meridians have been used. These include the old meridians in Paris, Antwerp and the Canary Islands in the Atlantic.

Let's consider the first factor. The Sun rises in the east. This means that, as we travel to the west, we leave the Sun behind, so sunrise is later. For instance, in Muscat in Oman on July 1ˢᵗ, sunrise is at 5.22 a.m., whereas in Damascus (Syria), sunrise on the same day of the year is over an hour later, at 6.28 a.m. This is because Damascus is around 2,500 kilometres west, closer to Greenwich than Muscat.

What about the second factor? In summer, the northern hemisphere of the Earth is tilted slightly towards the Sun. So if you travel north from the Equator, you are actually moving closer to the Sun. Take Tehran, for example. The capital of Iran is on almost the same line of longitude as Abu Dhabi, but it is 1,400 kilometres north. Sunrise in Tehran on July 1ˢᵗ is 5.25 a.m. – nearly a quarter of an hour earlier than in Abu Dhabi.

Sources: http://www.videojug.com http://answers.yahoo.com

How much have you learnt about science and nature in Theme 4 so far?

Test your knowledge, and your partner's knowledge.

1 How do you do this experiment?

2 What does this show?

3 What does this table show?

Table 1: *Location of some capital cities*

city	lat (°)	long (°)
Mexico City, Mexico	19 N	99 W
Tokyo, Japan	35 N	139 E
Asunción, Paraguay	25 S	57 W
Beijing, China	40 N	116 E

Source: www.infoplease.com

4 What do scientists do?

5 What does this diagram describe?

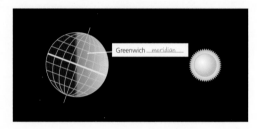

6 Why is Greenwich important?

Greenwich ___meridian___

7 How does a rainbow form?

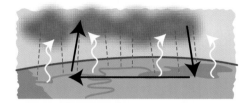

8 Why is the sky blue during the day, but red at sunset?

Writing: A laboratory report

4.16 Vocabulary for writing   Materials and experiments

A   Understanding new vocabulary

1. Look at Figure 1. Complete **The method** and **The result** below with the verbs from the box. Put the verbs into the past simple. You can use the same verb more than once.

> do   fill   lift   put   stay   take   turn

The method:

We ____did____ an experiment. We _____ a glass and a bowl. We _____ them with water. We _____ two coins in the bottom of the bowl. We _____ a piece of cardboard on top of the glass. We _____ the glass upside down. We _____ it into the bowl on the coins. We _____ the glass a little and _____ away the cardboard.

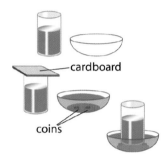

Figure 1: *Method*

The result: Some of the water _____ in the glass.

2. Look at Figure 2. Complete **The conclusion** below with words from the list on the right.

The conclusion:

This experiment proves that air has _____. Some of the water stays in the glass because air is pressing down on the _____ of the water in the bowl. Air _____ stops some of the water coming out of the glass. The _____ of the water in the glass shows the _____ of air pressure. We could put a _____ in centimetres on the side of the glass. This is a simple measuring _____. It is called a barometer.

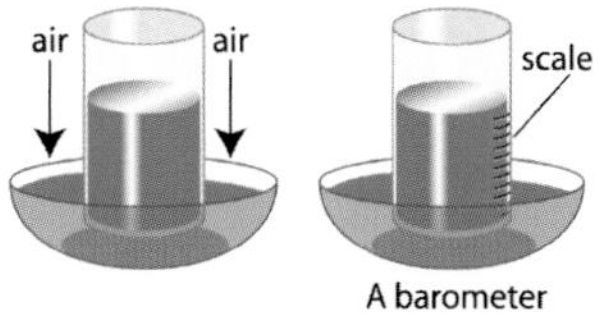

Figure 2: *A measuring device*

B   Developing critical thinking

Answer these questions.

1. How many containers did you need for the experiment?
2. Why didn't the water flow out of the glass when you turned it upside down?
3. What can you conclude from this experiment?

base (*n*)
conclude (*v*)
conclusion (*n*)
constant (*adj*)
container (*n*)
deep (*adj*)
depth (*n*)
device (*n*)
distance (*n*)
do (*v*) [= conduct]
figure (*n*)
fill (*v*)
flow (*v*)
force (*n*)
height (*n*)
high (*adj*)
hole (*n*)
implication (*n*)
indicate (*v*)
introduction (*n*)
investigate (*v*)
lift (*v*)
mark (*v*)
measure (*v*)
plot (*v*) [on a graph]
point (*n*)
pressure (*n*)
put (*v*)
result (*n*)
scale (*n*)
shape (*n*)
show (*v*)
surface (*n*)
take (*v*)
turn (*v*)
volume (*n*)
weigh (*v*)
weight (*n*)

You are going to write part of a laboratory report.

A Understanding a discourse structure

What information is in each section of a laboratory report? Match each section to the question it answers.

1.	Introduction	☐ What did you do?
2.	The materials	☐ What did you find out?
3.	The method	☐ What did you use?
4.	The results	☐ What do the results mean?
5.	The conclusions	☐ What else could you do in this area?
6.	Ideas for further research	1 What is the hypothesis for this experiment?

B Gathering information

Imagine you did an experiment into water pressure.
Study the figures below. Discuss the method.

Hypothesis:
Water pressure increases with depth.

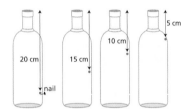

Figure 1: *Method (1)*

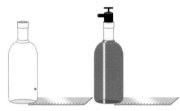

Figure 2: *Method (2)*

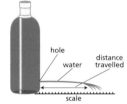

Figure 3: *Method (3)*

C Writing about the method

Write one sentence for each set of words below. Use the past simple.

make / hole / nail — We made a hole in each bottle with a nail.

1. 1ˢᵗ bottle / hole / 5 cm — In the first bottle,
2. 2ⁿᵈ bottle / 10 cm
3. 3ʳᵈ / 15 cm
4. 4ᵗʰ / 20 cm
5. put / bottle / ruler
6. fill / water
7. water / flow / hole
8. measure / distance
9. water / 1ˢᵗ / 30 cm
10. water / 2ⁿᵈ / 25 cm
11. water / 3ʳᵈ / 20 cm
12. water / 4ᵗʰ / 15 cm

Copy your sentences into **The method** section of the report opposite.

D Writing about the results

Complete Table 1 and Figure 1 in the report opposite. Use information from **The method** section.

E Developing critical thinking

Discuss these questions.

1. How far does the water travel if the bottle is twice as tall and the water is 40 cm deep?
2. What are the practical implications of the results of this experiment?

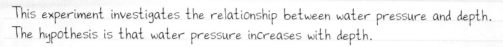

Laboratory report

This experiment investigates the relationship between water pressure and depth. The hypothesis is that water pressure increases with depth.

The materials

We needed four containers of the same size and shape. We chose mineral-water bottles of the same type. We also needed four measuring devices. We chose 30-centimetre rulers.

The method

We made a hole of the same size in each bottle with a nail. In the first bottle,

The results

We recorded the results. We put them into a table (see Table 1). As we can see from the table, water from the first bottle travelled the largest distance. Water from the fourth bottle travelled the smallest distance. We then plotted the results on a graph (Figure 1). The graph shows that distance travelled increases with depth.

Table 1: Depth and distance travelled (cm)

Bottle	1	2	3	4
Depth of water	20			
Distance travelled	30			

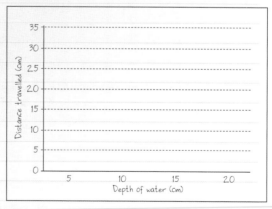

Figure 1: Depth and distance travelled (cm)

The conclusions

The experiment proves that water pressure increases with depth. The water from the lowest hole travels the furthest because this is the deepest part of the container. The experiment proves the hypothesis.

Ideas for further research

In this study, the bottles were the same size and shape and they were all filled to the top. Therefore, there was an equal volume of water in each bottle. We should do another experiment with different volumes of water. We should test the hypothesis that pressure increases with volume.

A Developing vocabulary

All the words below have the same vowel sound as the word *her*. What is each word? How do you spell it?

1. b_i_r_d
2. b_____st
3. _____th
4. f_____st
5. f_____ther
6. h_____d
7. res_____ch
8. s_____face
9. v_____tical
10. w_____ld

Read Skills Check 1 and check your answers.

B Choosing the correct tense

Which tense do you use in each section? Tick under *present* or *past* or both.

sections	present	past
Introduction	✓	
The materials		
The method		
The results		
The conclusions		

Look back at the report on page 129 and check your answers.

C Identifying a new skill

Find the mistakes below. Rewrite each section.

1 We <u>measure</u> the distance from the bottle (see Figure <u>Four</u>).

We measured the distance from the bottle (see Figure 4).

2 We were putting the results into a table (look Table 1).

3 As we could see from table, the water travels different distances from each bottle.

4 We then plot the results on a Figure 1.

5 This graph is indicating that distance increased at a constant rate with depth.

Read Skills Check 2 and Skills Check 3 and check your work.

D Transferring a new skill

Look at the table on page 121. Write a paragraph about the information. Use the patterns in Skills Check 3.

Skills Check 1

Spelling the /ɜː/ sound

Many words have the vowel sound in *her* – /ɜː/, but the sound can be spelt in different ways.

with *er*	vertical, were, person
with *ear*	research, learn, heard
with *ir*	first, third, bird
with *ur*	further, surface, burst
with *or*	world, work, worse

When you hear the sound /ɜː/, always ask:
How do you spell that word?

Skills Check 2

Present or past?

Always think: *What **tense** do I need for this paragraph?* It helps to think: *What question does this paragraph answer?*

Introduction: What **is** the hypothesis?

The materials: What **did** you use?

The method: What **did** you do?

The results: What **did** you find?

The conclusions: What **do** the results mean?

Skills Check 3

Referring to tables and figures

We want readers to notice important data. Learn these ways of referring to tables and figures.

We put the results in a table (see Table 1). As we can see from the table, ...
Table 1 shows that ...

We then plotted the results on a graph (Figure 1).
This graph indicates that ...

As we saw in Lesson 3.19, we often use the passive in academic English. In passive sentences, we give important information in a different order.

In the **past simple passive**, we use the verb *be* in the **past** and the **past participle** of the active verb. We often do not say who did the action.

1	2	3
subject	v. active	object
We	needed	four containers.
We	chose	a mineral bottle.

3	2		1
subject	v. passive		object
Four containers	were	needed.	~~by us.~~
A mineral bottle	was	chosen.	~~by us.~~

A Producing passive sentences

Rewrite each sentence in the space.

1. We did a simple experiment.   *A simple experiment was done.*

2. We needed containers.   _____

3. _____   Glasses were chosen.

4. _____   Rainfall was measured.

5. We required a measuring device.   _____

We sometimes want to give more information about the object or the verb in passive sentences.

subject	extra information about S	verb		extra information about V
Four containers	of the same size	were	needed	for the experiment.

B Producing passives in longer sentences

Rewrite each sentence in the space.

1. We needed four containers of the same size and shape.

   Four measuring devices were required.

2. We chose mineral-water bottles of the same type.

   _____

3. We also required four measuring devices.

   _____

4. We chose rulers with a scale in centimetres.

   _____

5. We made a small hole in each bottle with a nail.

   _____

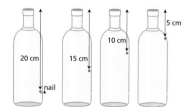

A Developing vocabulary

Match each verb with a noun phrase.

1. investigate ☐ the containers
2. do ☐1☐ the relationship
3. make ☐ the hypothesis
4. fill ☐ an experiment
5. mark ☐ the point
6. prove ☐ a hole

B Developing critical thinking

What does the experiment in Real-time writing (4.17) prove?

....

....

C Thinking

Study all the notes and drawings on the right.
Answer the questions below.

1. What is the hypothesis?

....

2. What materials did the researcher use?

....

3. What did the researcher do?

....

4. What did the researcher discover?

....

5. What do the results mean?

....

D Organizing a laboratory report

1. Write the six headings for a laboratory report.
   Leave space to write in each section.
2. Study the information on the right. Make notes under
   the best heading.

E Writing a laboratory report

Write the report. Remember:

- to use the correct tense, present simple or past simple.
- to use passives where necessary.
- to give a caption to each table and figure.
- to refer to the table(s) and the figure(s) in the report.

F Editing and rewriting

1. Exchange drafts with a partner. Check your partner's work.
2. Write a final version of your report.

Hypothesis:
Water pressure increases with volume

bottle x1   bucket x1   pipette x1   rainwater butt x1

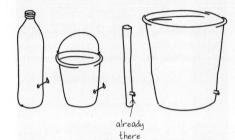

already there

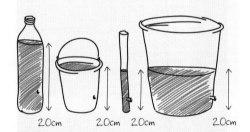

2.0cm   2.0cm 2.0cm   2.0cm

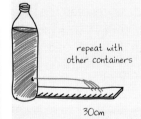

repeat with other containers

30cm

Container	bottle	bucket	pipette	butt
Distance travelled	30	30	30	30

Distance travelled (cm)

40
30
20
10

bottle   bucket pipette   butt

Container

A Activating schemata

1. Look at the pictures of natural events. What is the correct word for each natural event?
2. Can you explain why each natural event happens?

B Gathering information (1)

1. Divide into two groups. Group 1: ⊚ 4.21, Group 2: ⊚ 4.22. Listen to the information about tides or wind. Make notes about:
   - the topic.
   - new words.
   - what happens.
2. Work in pairs, one student from Group 1 and the other from Group 2. Exchange information about your natural events. Make notes and draw a diagram.
3. Are there any similarities between the two natural events?

C Gathering information (2)

1. Read one of the texts about rain, rainbows, thunder and lightning or snow and hail on pages 134–135. Make notes. Draw a diagram.
2. Explain the information you read about to a partner. Your partner should make notes.

D Using a diagram

1. Choose one of the natural events from your project notes. Write a short talk about the events.
2. Give your talk in a small group. Use a diagram to help you to explain what happens.

E Writing

1. Choose a different natural event from your project notes. Draw a diagram of the event.
2. Write a description of the diagram and explain what it shows.

F Extended writing

1. Research some information about waves on the seashore.
2. Write a short description of this natural event. Use a diagram to explain what happens.

Why does it rain?

Why does rain fall from the sky? And where does the rain come from? Why don't we use up all the rain in the clouds?

Rain is part of the water cycle. A cycle is something which goes round and round with no end. The water cycle is powered by the sun. It heats up the surface of areas of water, for example, rivers, lakes and seas. The water is a liquid, but as it heats, it turns into a gas. This gas is called water vapour. The hot gas rises into the air.

The air high above the Earth is cold, so the water vapour cools. This cool water vapour is called clouds.

The clouds move from areas of high pressure to areas of low pressure. As they move, they collect more water vapour and they get bigger and bigger. Finally, the clouds are so full of water that they burst. It rains.

Why don't we use up all the rain? Because some of the rain falls directly onto seas, rivers and lakes. The rest falls onto land and, from there, it travels back into seas, rivers and lakes. The cycle continues.

What are rainbows?

Why do we sometimes see a rainbow after it rains? Why don't we see them all the time? And where do rainbows end?

White light is made of all the colours of the rainbow, for example, red, orange and green. The sun sends white light to the Earth. We usually see only this white light.

However, when white light from the sun hits a raindrop, or tiny piece of rain, it is scattered. *Scattered* means 'sent in different directions'. When white light scatters, it becomes all the colours of the rainbow again.

So why don't we see rainbows all the time? Because the sun is usually behind clouds during a rainstorm. We only see rainbows if the sun comes out while there are still raindrops in the air. And you only see a rainbow if your back is to the sun.

Where do rainbows end? That is a difficult question to answer. They end when you move, because they don't really exist. You see a rainbow because you are standing in a particular place. If you try to go to the end of the rainbow, it disappears.

What are thunder and lightning?

Why do some storms produce thunder and lightning? And what is thunder? What is lightning?

Thunder and lightning are caused by electricity. The earth normally has no charge, but during a thunderstorm, the ground under the clouds gets a positive charge, just like the positive (+) end of a battery. At the same time, the clouds become negatively charged, like the negative (-) end of a battery. Scientists do not know for certain the cause of this charging.

Electricity flows between positive and negative areas. When the negative clouds come close to the positive earth, electricity flows. We see this as a flash of lightning. Most people think that lightning comes from the sky down to the earth but, in fact, lightning moves from the earth up to the clouds.

What about thunder? Lightning is hotter than the surface of the sun. The lightning heats the air very quickly and it expands, or gets bigger. We hear the sudden expansion as a loud noise. If we are near the lightning, we hear one sound. If we are far away, we hear a number of sounds.

What is snow and hail?

Why does water sometimes fall from the clouds as rain, sometimes as snow and sometimes as hail or hailstones?

Rain is water in liquid form. Snow is water in the form of ice crystals. Hail is a ball of frozen water.

Rain falls when the clouds become too full of water. In very cold weather, tiny drops of water in the clouds freeze and form ice crystals. The ice crystals are heavy so they fall from the clouds. If the air temperature below the clouds is less than 0°C, they will fall as snow. If it is more than zero, they will melt, or change back to water, and become rain.

During a thunderstorm, there are winds inside the clouds. As the raindrops fall through the clouds, these winds carry them up again. In very cold weather, the raindrops freeze as they rise to the top of the cloud. Now they are heavy and begin to fall again, but sometimes another wind carries them up. This can happen many times, and every time, the frozen drop becomes bigger.

Finally, the frozen raindrops, or hail, fall to the ground. Hailstones can be as big as footballs.

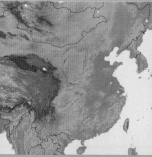

Theme 5

The physical world

- Geographical location

- Location and physical features

- Encyclopedia research

- Advantages and disadvantages

Listening: Geographical location

5.1 Vocabulary for listening Location in the world, physical features

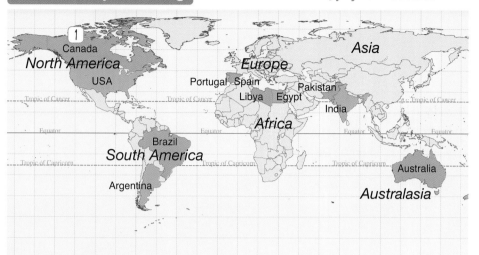

A Activating ideas

Look at the map of the world above. Which countries are:

1. north of the Equator?
2. south of the Equator?
3. on the Tropic of Cancer?
4. on the Tropic of Capricorn?

B Developing vocabulary (1)

1. 🔊 5.1 Listen to descriptions of six countries and look at the map. Number each country in the correct order on the map.

2. How did the speaker describe each country? Use some words from the list on the right.

   > It is in North America. It is north of the USA.

3. 🔊 5.2 Listen. Is each sentence true or false?

   > The Equator runs through Central America. True.

C Developing vocabulary (2)

1. 🔊 5.3 Listen to the pronunciation of ten words for physical features. Find and number them in the list on the right.

2. 🔊 5.4 Listen to a sentence about each physical feature. Find an example of each feature on the map.

   > A peninsula is a piece of land with water on three sides.

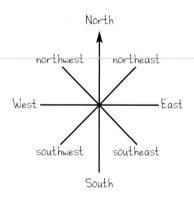

area (n)
border (n and v)
central (adj)
coast (n)
coastline (n)
consist of (v)
contain (v)
continent (n)
(the) Equator (n)
feature (n)
fifth (n)
flat (adj)
freshwater (adj)
geographical (adj)
gulf (n)
hometown (n)
island (n)
locate (v)
location (n)
low (adj)
main (adj)
mountainous (adj)
ocean (n)
peak (n)
peninsula (n)
physical (adj)
plateau (n)
rainforest (n)
range (n)
square (adj)
(the) Tropic of Cancer (n)
(the) Tropic of Capricorn (n)
volcano (n)
whole (adj)

A Activating ideas

Look at the map opposite.

1. Where are the countries?
2. Find some physical features.

> Panama is east of Costa Rica.

> Yucatán is a peninsula.

Greenhill University
Geography Faculty
Focus on Central America
———————————————
Lecture 1: Nicaragua –
Location and Physical Features

B Predicting content

1. Cover the map opposite. Look at the title of this lecture on the right. What information do you expect to hear in the lecture? Write five ideas.

   1. names of rivers and lakes

2. 🔊 5.5 [DVD] 5.A Watch the lecture. What are the things listed below? Mark them L = lake, M = mountain, R = river, V = volcano, S = sea, N = neighbour, C = city.

   a. Managua .... C ....
   b. Nicaragua ....
   c. San Cristóbal ....
   d. Honduras ....
   e. Costa Rica ....
   f. Central Highlands ....
   g. Caribbean ....
   h. Coco ....

C Transferring information

[DVD] 5.A Watch the lecture again. Complete the summary below.

The country is in .... America. It is situated .... of the Equator and south of the .... of Cancer. It is .... of Honduras and .... of Costa Rica. The .... is Managua in the southwest. The country has a .... on two seas, and there is a very large lake in the .... and a large river in the ....

D Practising vocabulary

1. Study the map opposite. Answer these questions.

   a. How far is it from Managua to Panama City? ....
   b. How long is the River Coco? ....
   c. How big is Jamaica? ....
   d. What is the exact location of Managua? ....

2. 🔊 5.6 Listen to the words and tick the pronunciation that you hear.

/rɪve/		/rɪvə/	✓	/kæns ɜː/		/kænsə/	
/saʊθ/		/saʊð/		/kɪlɒmɪte/		/kɪlɒmɪtə/	
/wɜːst/		/west/		/nɔːθ/		/nɔːð/	
/bɔːdəd/		/bɔːded/		/freʃwɔːtə/		/freʃwɔːtɜː/	

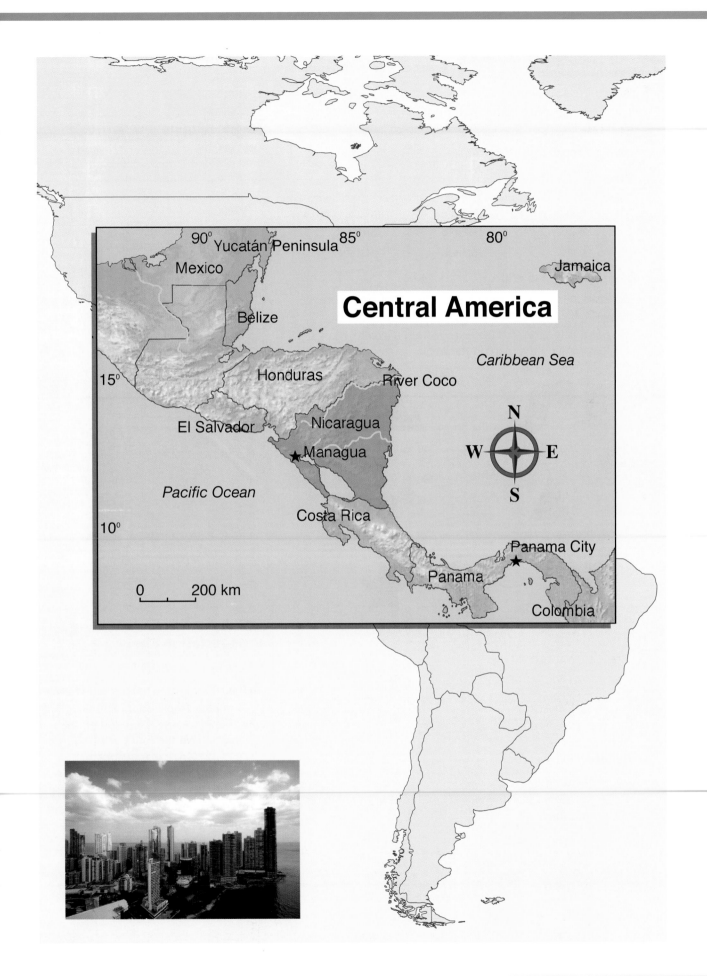

90° Yucatán Peninsula 85° 80°

Mexico

Jamaica

Central America

Belize

Caribbean Sea

15° Honduras River Coco

El Salvador Nicaragua

★ Managua

Pacific Ocean

N

W E

S

10° Costa Rica

Panama City ★

0 200 km

Panama

Colombia

A Reviewing key words

🎧 **5.7** Listen and tick the form of the word that you hear in each case.

a. ☐ Tropic   ✓ tropical   ☐ Tropics
b. ☐ centrally   ☐ centre   ☐ central
c. ☐ location   ☐ located   ☐ locates
d. ☐ raining   ☐ rainforest   ☐ forests
e. ☐ bordering   ☐ borders   ☐ border
f. ☐ coast   ☐ coastal   ☐ coastline

B Identifying a new skill

1. Read the Skills Check. Look at the transcript for 5.5 on page 202. Underline all the expressions of location.

2. 🎧 **5.8** [DVD] **5.B** Watch the extracts from a lecture. Mark the following on the map on the right.

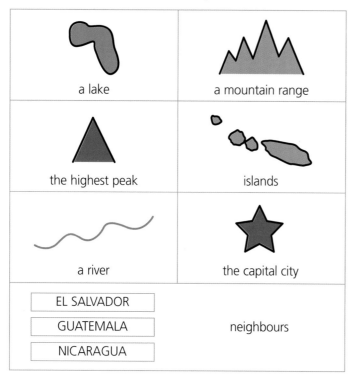

a lake	a mountain range
the highest peak	islands
a river	the capital city

EL SALVADOR
GUATEMALA   neighbours
NICARAGUA

C Identifying vowel sounds

1. Read the Pronunciation Check.

2. 🎧 **5.9** Listen. Circle the word in each row with a different vowel sound.

a. what   (four)   not   on
b. sorry   wash   come   from
c. more   coast   fall   for
d. long   not   was   north
e. locate   border   draw   for
f. before   small   home   warm

3. 🎧 **5.10** Listen and write the words you hear.

Skills Check

Understanding location

We sometimes need to be able **to follow a description** using a map and **find the places** described.

There are many expressions to describe locations.

Examples:

It is located at 35 degrees north, 28 degrees west.

It's in the centre of the country.

It is situated to the east of ...

It is bordered by ...

Pronunciation Check

Hearing vowels: /ɒ/ and /ɔː/

1. The letter *o* often has the sound /ɒ/.
   Examples: *Tropic, continent, on*
   But some common words with the letter *a* have the sound /ɒ/.
   Example: *what, was, want*

2. The letter *o* also often has the sound /ɔː/.
   Example: *border, Capricorn, north*
   But some common words with the letter *a* have the sound /ɔː/.
   Example: *warm, water, small*

There as replacement subject

We normally introduce new information with *There is / There are* … ㉛

| *There* | verb | complement | | extra information |
		(adjective) noun		
There	is	a peninsula	in the southeast.
	isn't	any fresh water	in the country.
	are	high mountains	near the coast.
	aren't	any permanent rivers	in the south.

We do not normally begin with a noun when we introduce new information: ~~A lake is in the south.~~

A Using *There is / There are*

These sentences are not very English.

1. Say each sentence in an English way.
   1. A lake is in the south.
   2. Many natural features are in the country.
   3. Several islands are in the gulf.
   4. A long, thin peninsula is south of the capital.
   5. No mountain range is in the east.
2. 🔊 5.11 Listen and check.

> There's a lake in the south.

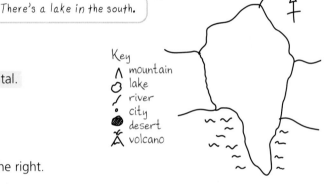

Key
∧ mountain
◯ lake
⁄ river
• city
🌑 desert
⩕ volcano

B Hearing *There is / There are*

🔊 5.12 Listen. Mark the features on the map on the right.

There are mountains in the north.

We often give information about a new item in the next sentence. ㉜

| introducing a new item | | | | giving information about the item | | |
There	verb	complement	extra information	*It / They*	verb	complement
There	is	a lake	in the south.	It	is	very large.
	are	mountains	along the coast.	They	are	the Andes.

C Using *It is / They are*

Give more information about each item. Use the words in the brackets.

1. There is a mountain in the east. (highest / country)
2. There is a river in the north. (longest / C. Am.)
3. There are some islands off the coast. (Bay Is.)
4. There are two volcanoes in the west. (middle / lake)

> It is the highest in the country.

D Using *There is / There are* to predict content

🔊 5.13 Listen. Which piece of information will come next?

1. There are some containers in the lab.

_____ It is dead.   _____ It's for Education Faculty students.

_____ It's all gone.   __1__ They are full of water.

_____ It's empty.   _____ They are talking.

A   Predicting content

Look at the presentation title on the right. Study the research questions below. Tick the questions the presentation will answer.

1. ☐   Where is Mexico?
2. ☐   What are the major cities?
3. ☐   How many people live there?
4. ☐   What does the country look like?
5. ☐   Does the country have any important rivers?
6. ☐   How can you get to the country?

Presentation:

Mexico
• Location
• Physical features

B   Practising a key skill

🔊 5.14 DVD 5.C Watch the presentation. Label the map of Mexico below.

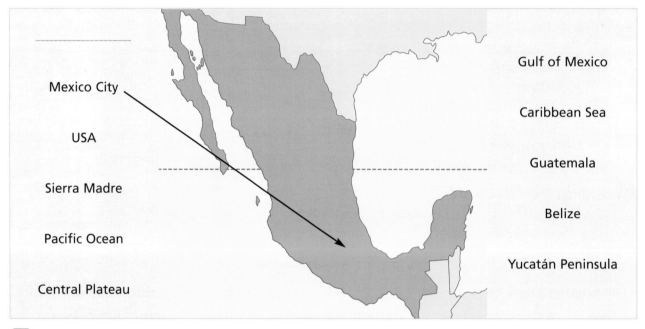

Gulf of Mexico

Mexico City

Caribbean Sea

USA

Guatemala

Sierra Madre

Belize

Pacific Ocean

Yucatán Peninsula

Central Plateau

C   Showing understanding

1. Which questions from Exercise A can you answer?
2. Discuss the answers in pairs. Use the map to help you.

D   Transferring a new skill

Student A

Look at page 174.

Read your description to your partner. Then listen to your partner and complete the map.

Student B

Look at page 176.

Read your description to your partner. Then listen to your partner and complete the map.

Speaking: Location and physical features

5

5.6 Vocabulary for speaking Continents

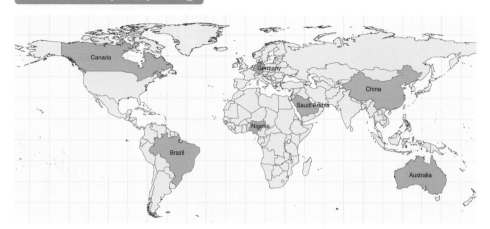

A Reviewing vocabulary

1. Which countries border the country you are in now? On which sides?

> It has a border with two countries. We have Norway to the northeast and Finland to the west.

2. What is in the north / south / east / west of the country?

B Understanding new vocabulary

Cover the map above.
Match the countries and continents.
Which area of each continent are they in?

1. Australia ☐ Africa
2. Brazil ☐ Europe
3. Canada ☐ Asia
4. China ☐ North America
5. Nigeria ☐ South America
6. Germany ☐ the Middle East
7. Saudi Arabia ☐ Oceania

> Is Brazil in Africa?

> No, I don't think so. I think it's in South America.

> Where exactly?

> I think it's in the east, on the coast.

C Practising new vocabulary

1. Complete each conversation with words from the list on the right.
   🔊 5.15 Listen and check.

2. Practise the conversations in pairs.

3. Add more lines to each conversation.

1 A: We have a big mountain _____ in my country.

B: What is a range?

2 A: Is your country _____?

B: No, it has a coastline on the Mediterranean.

3 A: What's a _____?

B: It's a big flat area of land.

Africa (*n*)
America (*n*)
Asia (*n*)
behind (*prep*)
between (*prep*)
border (*n* and *v*)
coastline (*n*)
continent (*n*)
corner (*n*)
double (*adj*)
Europe (*n*)
European (*adj*)
exactly (*adv*)
feature (*n*)
flat (*adj*)
geographical (*adj*)
in the centre of (*prep*)
landlocked (*adj*)
left (*n*)
(the) Middle East (*n*)
mountainous (*adj*)
next to (*prep*)
Oceania (*n*)
opposite (*prep*)
physical (*adj*)
plain (*n*)
range (*n*)
right (*n*)
river (*n*)
rocky (*adj*)
through (*adv*)
valley (*n*)
waterfall (*n*)
western (*adj*)

A **Previewing vocabulary**

1. 🔊 5.16 Listen to the words. Tick the correct column to show the number of syllables.

2. Mark the stressed syllable on each two- and three-syllable word.

3. 🔊 5.17 Listen again and repeat the words.

B **Activating ideas**

You are going to listen to a student giving a short talk about her country.

Look at the map on the right and answer these questions.

1. Where is the student from?

2. What is the geographical location of her country?

3. What are the main physical features of her country?

C **Studying a model**

1. 🔊 5.18 Listen. Make notes beside each heading in the table at the bottom of the page.

2. Complete the sentences from the introduction below.

	1	2	3
'Europe		✓	
capital			
coastline			
feature			
low			
mountainous			
north			
plain			
range			
rocky			

Introduction

I'm going .... about my country ...

First of all, I will .... the size and location ...

Then, I'll .... you about the capital city ...

Finally, I'll .... some of the physical features.

D **Practising a model**

Talk about your own country. Complete the sentences below in as many ways as you can.

- The country is ...   • It has ...   • There is ...   • There are ...

country	Croatia
continent	
size	
location	
capital	
physical features	

A   Activating ideas

Where are the people in each photo? What are they saying?

B   Studying models

Match each conversation (1–6) below to a photo. 🔊 5.19 Listen and check your ideas.

C   Practising conversations

Work in pairs to practise the conversations.

1
A: Excuse me.
B: Yes, sir. Can I help you?
A: Yes, please. Where's the nearest *tube station*?
B: *Go straight down this road. It's on the next corner.*

2
A: Where are we on this map?
B: Let's see. We're *here*.
A: And where's the *hotel*?
B: Mm. About a *ten-minute walk*, I think.

3
A: Which room are we in?
B: *J32*. But I'm not sure where it is.
A: Here we are. It's on the *fourth floor*.
B: OK. We'd better take the lift.

4
A: Are you going to *the meeting about fees*?
B: Yes, I am. I think it's in *the main hall*.
A: Where's that?
B: *Not far*. I'll show you.

5
A: How far are we from *the bus station*?
B: I think it's *in the next road on the left*.
A: No it isn't! It's *the second on the right*.
B: Oh, yes. I've got the map the wrong way round!

6
A: Hi you two! Where are you going?
B: We're on our way to *the café*.
A: Can I join you?
B: Yeah, sure. But hurry up, we're starving.

D   Real-time speaking

Practise the conversations again. Use different ideas for the words and phrases in italics. Make sure the conversation still makes sense!

A Saying consonants

1. 🔊 5.20 Listen to these sentences. What is the sound of the letter *s* in each case?

a. Where's that? ....

b. Yes, that's right. ....

c. How do you spell that? ....

d. Sorry. What did you say? ....

e. It goes through the capital. ....

2. Read Pronunciation Check 1 to check your answers.

B Saying vowels

Read Pronunciation Check 2. Then try these tongue twisters.

- What I wanted was a wash.
- A warm August morning before dawn.
- What was your fourth drawing?

C Identifying a new skill

1. Read the Skills Check.

2. Correct the introduction below.

> I going to tell about my country …
> First all, I describe the size …
> Then, I'll talk you about the capital city …
> Final, I'll mentioning some of the physical features.

D Rehearsing a model

Introduce the talks below.

1.
> Topic: The science of light
> Contents:
> 1. Isaac Newton
> 2. Newton's experiment with light
> 3. Results of the experiment

2.
> Topic: My education
> Contents:
> 1. primary school
> 2. secondary school
> 3. sixth form
> 4. university course

E Extended practice

You have to give a talk to your study group. Think of an interesting topic, make a list of contents, then practise giving the introduction.

Pronunciation Check 1

Saying consonants: /s/ and /z/

We say the letter *s* in two ways: /s/ and /z/.

The letter *s* has the sound /s/ at the beginning of a word.

Examples: *south, say, sea*

It also has the sound /s/ before another consonant.

Examples: *spell, small, Australia*

When we say /s/, the air passes out between our tongue and teeth.

The letter *z* has the sound /z/.

Examples: *zero, Zagreb*

We make /z/ like /s/, but we use our voice at the same time. The letter *s* sometimes has the sound /z/, too.

Examples: *was, does, goes, where's*

Pronunciation Check 2

Saying vowels: /ɒ/ and /ɔː/

You need to make your lips round for both of these sounds.

The sound /ɒ/ is short.

Examples: *top, was, not, often*

The sound /ɔː/ is longer.

Examples: *north, more, warm, fall, tall*

Skills Check

Introducing a talk

We must introduce a talk.

Tell people:

- the **topic** of the talk.
- the **contents** of the talk.
- the **order** of the talk.

Use **sequencers** – *First of all, then …*

Use a **range of verbs** – *talk about, tell …*

Use *going to* and *will*.

Examples:

I'm going to talk about my country …

First of all, I will describe the size …

Then, I'll tell you about the capital city …

Finally, I'll mention some of the physical features.

We often use prepositions to talk about location. ㉝

S	V	prepositional phrase	
Zagreb	is	in	the north.
Ludbreg	is	near	Zagreb.
Ludbreg	is	between	the capital **and** the border.

A   Talking about location

1. Study the sketch map on the right.
2. 🔊 **5.21** Listen. Which place are they talking about in each case?

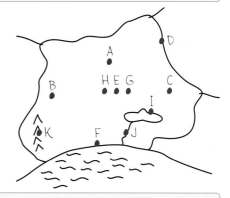

> 1. It's on a river near the coast.   It's J.

3. Where is each place, A to K? Describe the location.

> A is in the north near the border.

We can use *which* to give extra information about the **object** of a sentence. ㉞

	object	subject	extra information
I am going to talk about	Croatia.	Croatia	is my country.
	Croatia,	which	is my country.

B   Joining sentences with *which*

Join these sentences, using *which*.

1. The capital is Zagreb. Zagreb is in the north.

> The capital is Zagreb, which is in the north.

2. There are many rivers. The rivers cross the plain.
3. There are many lakes. The lakes are part of a national park.
4. The country has many mountains. They are very beautiful.
5. There is a tiny border with Montenegro. Montenegro is in the southeast.
6. The eastern border of Croatia is the River Danube. It is the second longest river in Europe.

A Reviewing sounds

1. Say the words on the right aloud. Make sure you pronounce the vowel sounds correctly.

2. Work in pairs. Say one of the words in each pair. Your partner ticks the word.

1.	☐	not	☐	north
2.	☐	got	☐	caught
3.	☐	what	☐	water
4.	☐	top	☐	talk
5.	☐	was	☐	wars
6.	☐	want	☐	warn
7.	☐	shot	☐	short
8.	☐	pot	☐	port
9.	☐	lot	☐	law
10.	☐	shock	☐	chalk

B Practising vocabulary

> south   east   west   north   town   village
> Europe   which   called   Asia

1. You will need to say the words above in the final exercise in this lesson. What is the pronunciation of each word?

2. Read the Pronunciation Check.

3. Ask your partner or your teacher about the words you are not sure of.

C Using a key skill

1. Form three groups.

   Group A: Look at page 175.

   Group B: Look at page 178.

   Group C: Look at page 172.

2. Read the notes about the country. Prepare a short talk with the other people in your group.

3. Make new groups. There must be at least one A, one B and one C in each group. Give your talk.

4. Listen to the other two talks. Make notes about them in the table below.

Pronunciation Check

Asking about pronunciation

Remember: Always ask for help with pronouncing a new word.

Spell the word so that the person can recognize it.

Example:

How do you say this word:

E-U-R-O-P-E?

Check the stress.

Example:

Is the stress on the first syllable?

---

country	
continent	
size	
location	
capital	
physical features	

Reading: Encyclopedia research

5.11 Vocabulary for reading The countries of East Asia

A Reviewing vocabulary

Write four words in each of these groups. Look back at the lessons in this theme.

physical features	location
desert	longitude

B Developing vocabulary

Label the picture. Use the list on the right. You already know some of the words.

lake

C Understanding vocabulary

Read the text and complete the gaps with words from the list on the right.

We call the geographical features of a country its ……landscape……. These
features have an important influence on human activity. In East Asia, like the rest
of the ………………………, the majority of farming happens in ………………………
areas, where the land is flat and easy to work. Large cities are also often situated
near ………………………. In countries which occupy islands or a
………………………, the main activity is often ………………………. In these areas,
most people live ……………………… the coast. Very hot or cold areas
………………………, such as ……………………… and high mountain ranges, are
often ……………………… or have few people.

D Developing critical thinking

Discuss these questions.

1. Why are large cities usually in lowland areas?
2. What kind of farming can be done in mountainous areas? What about in lowland areas?
3. Why do deserts form inland?

agriculture (n)
almost (adv)
along (prep)
between (prep)
chain (n)
compass (n)
corner (n)
cover (v)
desert (n)
exactly (adv)
extinct (adj)
fairly (adv)
farmland (n)
feature (n)
height (n)
inland (adv)
landscape (n)
lie (v)
lowland (n)
major (adj)
majority (n)
mostly (adv)
neighbour (n)
notes (n pl)
occupy (v)
officially (adv)
peninsula (n)
permanent (adj)
port (n)
reach (v)
record (v)
region (n)
sea level (n)
situated (adj)
slope (n and v)
table (n)
uninhabited (adj)
valley (n)
world (n)

A Activating ideas

1. Look at the map on the right. Match a flag to each country.

2. What do you know about these countries?

B Using topic sentences

1. Read the title of the text opposite, then the first paragraph, and then the topic sentences. What information will you read in this text?

2. Which paragraph do you think these sentences come from?

.... The highest point in South Korea is Halla-san.

.... It occupies the majority of the Korean Peninsula.

.... To the north, it is bordered by North Korea.

.... There is another big city on the southeast coast, opposite Japan.

.... There are about 3,000 islands.

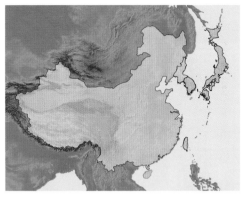

a   b   c

d   e   f

C Showing comprehension

The numbers below are from the text. Read the text and correct the explanations in the right-hand column.

125°–130° east is the longitude of South Korea.

                                                  longitudes

1. 125°–130°   South Korea lies between these ~~latitudes.~~

2. 30%   The amount of land around Kwangju used for farmland.

3. 100,000 km²   The exact area of the country.

4. 125 km   The distance from Pusan to Japan.

5. 3,000   The number of uninhabited islands which form part of South Korea.

6. 1,950 m   The distance from Cheju to the south coast of the peninsula.

7. 33°–39°   Average temperature of South Korea in summer.

8. three   The number of rivers in South Korea.

D Dealing with word combinations

Cover the text. Match the verbs on the left below with words on the right to make phrases from the text.

1. occupies   [ ] a height of 1,950 metres

2. is located   [ ] down to the Yellow Sea

3. covers   [1] the majority of the Korean Peninsula

4. is bordered by   [ ] an area of almost exactly 100,000 square kilometres

5. reaches   [ ] in the northwest of the country

6. slope   [ ] North Korea

E Developing critical thinking

Which other countries are sometimes included in East Asia?

South Korea

Location

South Korea (officially the Republic of Korea) is a fairly small country. It is situated in the region of East Asia. It occupies the majority of the Korean Peninsula. It lies between latitude 33° and 39° north and longitude 125° and 130° east.

Capital and other main cities

The capital is Seoul. It is the largest city in the country. In fact, it is one of the largest cities in the world. It is located in the northwest of the country. It is 125 kilometres inland from the Yellow Sea. There is another big city on the southeast coast, opposite Japan. It is called Pusan. It is the most important seaport in the country. There is also a seaport and an international airport at Inch'on, on the west coast.

Area and borders

The country covers an area of almost exactly 100,000 square kilometres. To the north, it is bordered by North Korea, or the Democratic People's Republic of Korea. Its nearest neighbours are China to the west and Japan to the east. There are about 3,000 islands. They are near the western and southern coasts of the peninsula. They are mostly small and uninhabited. The peninsula has coastlines on three seas. The Sea of Japan is between Korea, Russia and Japan, while the Yellow Sea lies between Korea and China. To the south, there is the East China Sea.

Landscape

South Korea is a mountainous country. There are mountains and valleys along the coast in the east and in the southwest corner of the country. The lowlands, which are in the western region, slope down to the Yellow Sea. Only about 30 per cent of the land is farmland, but the best area is around Kwangju, near the southwest coast. The country has many permanent rivers, so there is a lot of fresh water. The River Nakdong runs into the sea at Pusan. There are no deserts. The highest point in South Korea is Halla-san, on the island of Cheju, which is south of the peninsula. It is an extinct volcano which reaches a height of 1,950 metres.

A Reviewing phrases

1. Make phrases with one word from each column below.
2. Does each phrase normally have *the*?

East Asia; the Korean Peninsula

a. East	☐	Peninsula
b. Korean	☐	Nakdong
c. capital	☐	rivers
d. Yellow	a	Asia
e. square	☐	Sea
f. highest	☐	waters
g. River	☐	east
h. fresh	☐	point
i. south	☐	kilometres
j. permanent	☐	city

B Identifying a new skill

1. Read the Skills Check.
2. Look at the texts below. Underline words that you can use as section headings. Circle the important information.

a. In total, it covers an area of nearly 400,000 square kilometres.

b. Most towns and cities are situated on the coast.

c. The landscape is mountainous, with high valleys and thick forest.

d. It is bordered by Russia to the east and Latvia to the southwest.

e. The islands are all located on or near the Tropic of Capricorn.

f. This is a country in the Middle East region, also called the Near East.

C Using a new skill

Study the student's notes on Japan on the right. Some of the notes are too long. Correct them.

Skills Check

Transferring information

We often want to make notes of the important information in a factual text.

We can often record this information in a table.

The headings in tables are usually one or two nouns. These nouns often appear in the original text.

Example:

South Korea is a fairly small country situated in the <u>region</u> of East Asia.

Sometimes, you must change **a verb** in the text to **a noun** for the section heading.

Example:

It **is located** between latitudes …

located → location

country	South Korea
region	East Asia
location	between latitude …

Notes should be **short**. Only include the important information. **Do not copy out the text!**

---

country	Japan
location	~~Japan is in the geographical region of~~ East Asia, ~~sometimes called the~~ Far East.
	Between 26° and 46° north and 128° to 146° east.
cities	The biggest cities are Nagoya and Osaka, which are very modern places.
	Main cities are in coastal areas.
	The capital is Tokyo.
area & borders	Japan does not have land borders, because it is formed by a chain of four main islands. They are called Hokkaido, Honshu, Kyushu and Shikoku.
	Sea of Japan, Pacific Ocean.
	The country covers a total area of about 378,000 square kilometres, including all its small islands.
landscape	There are large forests in all areas of Japan, which are very beautiful.
	Highest point Mount Fuji.
	Most of the country is very mountainous (about 75%), so there is not much space for cities or agriculture.

We can talk about *the largest*, *the most interesting*, etc., item in a particular group, e.g., the cities in a country. ㉟

item	verb	superlative adjective	noun	prepositional phrase
Seoul	is	the largest	city	in South Korea.
Pusan		the most important	port	

We can give the same information in a different order.

superlative adjective	noun	prepositional phrase	verb	item
The largest	city	in South Korea	is	Seoul.
The most important	port			Pusan.

When you read a superlative sentence, think:

- What is the **superlative adjective**? e.g., *the most important*
- What **noun** is the superlative adjective describing? e.g., *Pusan*
- What is the **group** (noun + prepositional phrase)? e.g., *port in South Korea*

A   **Predicting content**

Read the sentences below. How do you expect each sentence to end?

1. The longest river in the world is ... *the Nile.*
2. The highest mountain in the world is ...
3. The largest island in the world is ...
4. The Caspian Sea is the ...
5. The Pacific Ocean is the ...
6. The largest organ in the body is the ...
7. The most famous footballer in the world is ...
8. The most popular tourist attraction in the world is ...
9. The best writer in my country is ...
10. The most interesting place in my country is ...

A prepositional phrase has a preposition and a noun. The subject of the sentence comes **after the noun** ㊱ in the prepositional phrase. Always find the subject of the sentence. Look for **nouns / pronouns**. Sometimes, the subject is *there*. In this case, the **object or complement** is the important item.

prepositional phrase		subject	verb	object / complement	
preposition	noun			noun	extra information
In	the west,	the country	has	a border	with China.
To	the north,	it	is bordered by	North Korea.	
On	the coast,	there	are	mountains.	

B   **Finding the subject**

Find and circle the important item (subject) in each sentence.

1. In the north, (the country) is very mountainous.
2. In the west, the land slopes to the Yellow Sea.
3. Near the western and southern coasts of the peninsula, there are about 3,000 islands.
4. Between the two mountain ranges, the country is very flat.
5. On the southeast coast, there is another big city.
6. Around the peninsula, there are three seas.

A Reviewing vocabulary

Complete these words from the theme.

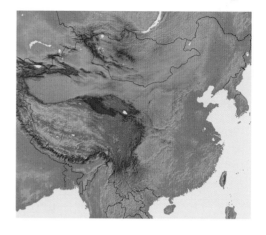

1. peni nsula
2. lati
3. longi
4. bord
5. situa
6. loca
7. reg
8. coa
9. lan
10. des

B Using a key skill (1)

1. Scan the topic sentences in the text opposite.
   Find a heading on the right for each section.

2. Cover the text. What specific information will
   be in each section? Write one thing.

3. Which sections do you think these phrases are from?

   .... 18,000-kilometre-long coastline

   .... contains the highest point on Earth

   .... longitude 73° east

   .... not the largest city

   .... a total area

Borders Location Landscape
Area   Main cities

C Using a key skill (2)

Read the text. Complete the table with information from the text. Use notes.

country		
region		Southeast Asia
location	latitude	
	longitude	
		• 15 countries, inc. Kazakhstan, India, Vietnam and Russia • 18,000-km coastline on Yellow Sea and China Sea
landscape		

China
(People's Republic of China, PRC)

1. The People's Republic of China (PRC) is in East Asia. It is usually called simply China. It lies in the northern hemisphere between latitude 18° and 53° north and longitude 73° and 135° east.

2. China's largest cities are located in the east of the country. The capital is Beijing. It is located in the north, near the Yellow Sea coast. However, the capital is not the largest city in the country. The largest city is Shanghai, which is situated 1,000 kilometres to the south of the capital, on the East China Sea coast. The third city is Tianjin.

3. China is one of the largest countries in the world. It covers a total area of around 9,600,000 square kilometres.

4. China is bordered by 15 countries, from Kazakhstan in the east and India and Vietnam in the south, to Russia in the north. In the west, China has an 18,000-kilometre-long coastline on the Yellow Sea and the China Sea.

5. China has many types of landscape, from high plateaus and mountains to the eastern lowlands. Off the Pacific coast, there are hundreds of islands. In the west, the Himalaya mountain range contains the ten highest peaks on the globe, including Mount Everest. This mountain reaches 8,848 metres and is the highest point on Earth. But Everest is not actually in China. In the north, the Gobi and Taklamakan deserts cover many thousands of square kilometres. Fresh water comes from China's many large rivers. These include the Yangtze, the Huang He (Yellow), the Pearl and the Mekong. Most rivers in China run from west to east and flow into the Pacific Ocean.

1. What have you learnt about the physical world so far in Theme 5? Try this quiz.

A The Americas

1. Name two countries that have a border with Mexico.
2. Where is the biggest lake in Central America?
3. Which name is wrong: Pacific Ocean, Atlantic Sea, Caribbean Sea?
4. What is the capital of Panama?

B Europe

1. Is Germany landlocked?
2. There are 203 countries. In size, is Croatia number 12, number 27 or number 127?
3. What country is opposite Croatia, on the other side of the Adriatic Sea?
4. What is the capital of Latvia?

C Chile

1. True or false? Chile has a very long coastline to the east.
2. What is the Atacama?
3. Which continent is Chile in?
4. Name the main mountain range in Chile.

D Sudan

1. Which famous river flows through Sudan?
2. True or false? Sudan is bordered by nine countries.
3. Name the desert in Sudan.
4. On which sea does Sudan have a coastline?

E East Asia

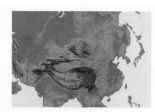

1. Is the centre of China 105° E, 15° E or 55° W?
2. How many main islands form Japan?
3. Which country is Mount Fuji in?
4. Is Halla-san a river, a volcano or a seaport?

F General knowledge

1. Which is north of the Equator, the Tropic of Cancer or the Tropic of Capricorn?
2. What is a peninsula?
3. True or false? New Zealand is in Oceania.
4. Name four of the continents.

2. Look through Theme 5. Write some more questions to continue the quiz.

Writing: Advantages and disadvantages

5

5.16 Vocabulary for writing   Location

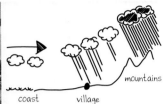

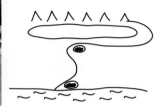

coast   village   mountains

A Reviewing vocabulary

Write the missing letters in these words and phrases.

1. v i ll a g e   3. r____ng____   5. f___r___st   7. d___s___rt
2. m_____nt_____n 4. tr_____s   6. pl____n   8. ____gr___c___lt___r____

B Understanding new vocabulary

Look at the photograph and the diagrams above. This is an African village. Complete the advantages and disadvantages about its location. Use a word from the list on the right in each case. Make any necessary changes.

1. The low flat land is good for growing _____.

2. The village is near a river which _____ *crops* _____ fresh water.

3. The river is also a good _____ of food.

4. The river provides good _____ links to the nearest town.

5. The _____ wind from the sea helps the annual rainfall.

6. In winter, a lot of rain falls, so the river bursts its _____.

7. Sometimes, the water from the river _____ the plain.

8. _____ to the village is difficult by road.

9. The village is surrounded by _____ land.

10. There is little _____, and the main employment is farming or fishing.

11. There is not much _____ activity in the village.

C Using new vocabulary

Complete these sentences about your hometown.

1. My hometown is near _____.

2. The main employment is _____.

3. The town has _____.

4. There aren't any _____.

5. There isn't much _____.

---

access (*n*)
active (*adj*)
 [of a volcano]
advantage (*n*)
agricultural (*adj*)
annual (*adj*)
area (*n*)
 [= location]
background (*n*)
bank (*n*)
 [of a river]
bay (*n*)
coast (*n*)
crop (*n*)
delta (*n*)
disadvantage (*n*)
disease (*n*)
economic (*adj*)
environmental (*adj*)
fertile (*adj*)
flat (*adj*)
flood (*n* and *v*)
foreground (*n*)
impact (*n*)
industry (*n*)
insect (*n*)
link (*n* and *v*)
marsh (*n*)
middle (*n*)
plain (*n*)
prevailing (*adj*)
provide (*v*)
rainfall (*n*)
shelter (*n*)
source (*n*)
storm (*n*)
surround (*v*)
transport (*n*)

You are going to write about the advantages and disadvantages of a location.

A   Understanding a discourse structure

Study the Writing Plan at the bottom of the page.

1. How many paragraphs do you need?
2. How should you start each paragraph? Read the Skills Check on the right and check.

B   Gathering information

Study the photograph opposite.

1. What can you see? Add to the list of Vocabulary on the plan.
2. What are the advantages and disadvantages of this location? Write notes in the Advantages and Disadvantages table.
3. Look at the Sketch Map of the location and the Notes below it. Add the extra information to your notes under Advantages and Disadvantages.

C   Writing (1)

1. Use your Advantages notes to write more sentences in the second paragraph on the page opposite.
2. Use your Disadvantages notes to complete the third paragraph.

D   Writing (2)

Think about a town or village in your country.

1. What are the advantages and disadvantages of the location? Make a table with notes.
2. Write three sentences about the advantages.
3. Write two sentences about the disadvantages.

Skills Check

Introducing paragraphs

In English, we normally put all the information about one point in the same paragraph.

Example:

Para 1:   **Introduction**

Para 2:   **Advantages**

Para 3:   **Disadvantages**

We must introduce each paragraph with a topic sentence.

Example:

Para 1:   *This is a photograph of a town in Africa.*

Para 2:   *There are several advantages to this location.*

Para 3:   *There are two main disadvantages.*

Writing Plan

- Description of the picture
- Advantages
- Disadvantages

Vocabulary

sea

fishing boats

Advantages	Disadvantages
on coast = gd. for fish	

Sketch Map

N

river delta

agricultural land

marsh (insects)

bay = shelter from storms

Notes:

1. Prevailing wind from the sea = cool summers, warm winters
2. Insects carry disease to the town in summer

This photograph shows a town in Africa. The town is on the coast.
In the foreground, there are some fishing boats.
In the middle of the photograph, we can see shops and houses on the seafront.
On the right, there is a small hill with trees.
In the background, we can see a range of low mountains.

There are several advantages to this location. Firstly, this area of the sea has many fish. Secondly,

There are two main disadvantages to this location. Firstly, ...

A Developing vocabulary

Read each sentence. All the incomplete words include the sound /ɔː/, but what is the correct spelling?

1. There is a sm..a..ll lake in the south.

2. In the f............ground of the picture, there are some fishing boats.

3. The country does not have any fresh w............ter.

4. It is m............ pleasant to live on the coast than in the interior.

5. There are good transp............t links to the interior.

6. ....lmost two-thirds of the country is desert.

7. The bay provides shelter from st............ms in winter.

8. The wind from the sea is w............m in winter.

9. The town is ....lso on a river.

10. There are high tides in spring and ....tumn.

Read Skills Check 1 and check your answers.

B Identifying a new skill

Study the photograph. Read the sentences below.
There are two mistakes in each sentence. Correct them.

1. This is ₍ₐ₎ photograph of a town in ~~the~~ Africa.

2. Town is in a lake.

3. In foreground, we are seeing the lake.

4. In the left, there is some trees.

5. On right, we see a castle.

6. In the back, there is a hill low.

Read Skills Check 2 and check your sentences.

C Transferring a new skill

Study the photograph on the right. Write six sentences about the photograph.

Skills Check 1

Spelling the /ɔː/ sound

The vowel sound in *north* is usually written with *or(e)*.

Examples: *border, more, corner*

But there are some common words with *a(l), ar, au, aw* and *our*.

Examples: *almost, small, warm, autumn, four*

Skills Check 2

Writing about a photograph

Sometimes, we want to describe a photograph.

First, we **introduce the subject** of the photograph and give some **information.**

Example:

This is a photograph of a village in Africa. The village is on a river.

Then we talk about items in **different areas** of the photograph.

There are five main areas:

We use *in* with *foreground, middle* and *background.*

	the background	
the left	the middle	the right
	the foreground	

We use *on* with *left* and *right.*

Examples:

In *the foreground, we can see some fishing boats.*

On *the right, there is a low hill.*

Some sentences have **a single noun** as the subject or the object / complement.
But we often want to give **extra information** about the noun. This is called *modifying* the noun.
We can modify a noun in several ways.

The	wide	river	provides		fresh	water.	*with an* adjective
There			is	a	low	hill.	
There			are		several	advantages.	
The river			provides	water		for the crops.	*with a* prepositional phrase
There			is	a hill		with trees.	
There			are	advantages		to this location.	

In many cases, we use several of these methods in the same sentence.
*There are **several advantages to this location**. **The warm wind in winter** blows from the sea.*
***The wide river** provides **fresh water for the crops**.*

A Building a noun phrase (1)

Study each set of sentences. Then add extra information from the box in the correct place.

1. There is land. There is agricultural land near the town.
2. The town has transport links. ....
3. The bay provides shelter. ....
4. This area has fish. ....
5. There are tides. ....

> ~~agricultural~~   from storms   good   high   in spring
> many   ~~near the town~~   of the sea   to the interior

B Building a noun phrase (2)

These sentences are a little harder.

1. There are disadvantages. ....
2. There are insects. ....
3. Insects carry diseases. ....
4. There is activity. ....
5. The village has impact. ....

> dangerous   economic   in the marsh   in the village   little   main   many
> some   not much   on the environment   to this location   two

A Reviewing vocabulary

Add a word to make a phrase.

1. fishing   _boat_
2. fresh
3. high
4. prevailing
5. river
6. transport
7. tourist
8. fertile

B Thinking

1. Match some of the phrases in Exercise A to photograph 1 or photograph 2, or both.
2. Study the sketch map below the photographs. What is the location of each photograph? Choose one of the locations, A to I.

C Organizing

Choose one of the photographs and locations.

1. Study the photograph. Make some notes for the first paragraph.
2. Think about the advantages and disadvantages of the location. Make a table for paragraphs 2 and 3.

D Writing

Write your description. Remember:

- Use *in the foreground*, *in the middle*, etc.
- Modify nouns with adjectives.
- Modify nouns with quantifiers.
- Modify nouns with prepositional phrases.

E Editing and rewriting

1. Exchange drafts with a partner. Check your partner's work.
2. Write a final version of your description.

Notes:
1. High tides in spring and autumn
2. Prevailing wind from the south
3. Volcano on island is active

1   2   3   4

A Activating ideas

1. Look at the photographs of villages and towns in the Arabian Gulf. Describe each photograph.

2. Can you explain why each village or town is located in each place?

B Gathering information (1)

1. Divide into two groups. Group A: 🔊 5.22, Group B: 🔊 5.23. Listen to the information about two countries in the Gulf: Kuwait and Yemen. Make notes about:

  • the location

  • the capital

  • other main cities

  • the area

  • the borders

  • the landscape

2. Work in pairs, one student from Group A and the other from Group B. Exchange information about your countries. Make notes.

3. Are there any similarities between the two countries?

C Gathering information (2)

1. Read one of the texts about the countries, Iraq or Iran, on pages 166/167. Make notes.

2. Explain the information you read about to a partner. Your partner should make notes.

D Giving a talk

Choose one of the countries from your portfolio notes: Kuwait, Yemen, Iran or Iraq. Write a short talk about the location. Find some photographs and maps on the Internet to illustrate your talk.
Give your talk in a small group. Use photographs or maps to help with your description.

E Writing a description

1. Select a suitable photograph of a village or a town in Qatar, Saudi Arabia or Bahrain.

2. Write a description of the photograph and explain some of the advantages and disadvantages of the location.

F Extended writing

Research some information about Qatar, Saudi Arabia or Bahrain. Write a short description of the location. Use a photo and maps to help you. You can make your description a poster, webpage or encyclopedia entry.

Iraq A brief introduction

Location Iraq is a large country situated in a region called the Middle East. It is located between latitudes 29° and 36° north and longitudes 38° and 48° east.

Capital and other main cities The capital is Baghdad. It is in the centre of the country, on the Tigris River. Other main cities are Mosul in the north and Basra in the south.

Area The country covers an area of 437,072 square kilometres.

Borders Iraq is bordered by several countries. In the north, it is bordered by Turkey. In the west lie Syria and Jordan. In the southwest is Saudi Arabia, while in the south is Kuwait. In the east, Iraq has a long border with Iran. The country is almost completely surrounded by land, with only a tiny coastal area on the Gulf.

Physical features Iraq's terrain is mostly wide plains. There are marshes in the south along the Iranian border and mountains along the borders with Turkey and Iran. There are two main rivers, called the Euphrates and the Tigris.

Iran A brief introduction

Location	Iran is in a region called the Middle East. It is located between latitudes 25° and 40° north and longitudes 45° and 62° east.
Capital and other main cities	The capital is Tehran. It is in the north of the country, near the Caspian Sea. Other main cities are Isfahan in the centre and Shiraz near the Gulf coast.
Area	The country covers an area of 1.648 million square kilometres.
Borders	Iran is bordered by many countries. In the north, there are borders with several countries, including Armenia, Azerbaijan and Turkmenistan. In the east, it is bordered by Afghanistan and Pakistan, while in the west there is a long border with Iraq. There is a short border in the north with Turkey. Iran also has a very long coastline on the Arabian Gulf and the Gulf of Oman.
Landscape	Iran's terrain is varied. There are mountainous areas and deserts. There are also plains along the coast.

Resources

Personality quiz scoring guide

1 I feel best ...

  a. in the morning.
  b. at lunchtime.
  c. during the afternoon.
  d. in the early evening.
  e. late at night.

	2
	3
	4
	5
	6

2 I usually walk ...

  a. fast, with long steps.
  b. fast, with short steps.
  c. quite fast, with my head up.
  d. quite fast, with my head down.
  e. slowly.

	6
	4
	7
	2
	1

3 When I talk to someone, I ...

  a. stand with my arms folded.
  b. clasp my hands behind my back.
  c. have one or both of my hands on my hips.
  d. touch the arm of the other person.
  e. play with my hair or touch my face.

	4
	2
	5
	7
	6

4 When I relax, I sit ...

  a. with my legs side by side.
  b. with my legs crossed.
  c. with my legs out straight.
  d. with one leg under the other leg.
  e. on the floor.

	4
	6
	3
	2
	1

5 When I find something funny, I ...

  a. laugh loudly.
  b. laugh quietly.
  c. smile broadly.
  d. smile slightly.
  e. smile to myself.

	6
	4
	3
	2
	1

6 When I go to a party, I ...

  a. make sure everyone notices me.
  b. look for a new person to speak to.
  c. look for a friend to speak to.
  d. enter quietly and speak to the host.
  e. enter quietly and do not speak to anyone.

	6
	5
	4
	2
	1

7 When I am working and someone interrupts me, I ...

a. am always happy to stop.
b. always get angry, but do not show my feelings.
c. always get angry and show my feelings.
d. sometimes get angry, sometimes not.
e. carry on working.

	6
	2
	1
	4
	3

8 My favourite colour is ...

a. red or orange.
b. black.
c. yellow, light blue or green.
d. dark blue or purple.
e. white, brown or grey.

	6
	7
	5
	4
	1

9 When I am going to sleep, I lie ...

a. on my back.
b. on my front.
c. on my side.
d. with my head on one arm.
e. with my head under the sheet

	7
	6
	4
	2
	1

10 I often dream about ...

a. falling.
b. fighting.
c. searching for something or somebody.
d. flying.
e. running away from something or somebody.

	4
	2
	3
	5
	6

Interpretation

This interpretation of your score answers the question: *How do people see you?*
Do you agree with this interpretation?

Over 60 points:
You are very dominant. You are self-centred. Some people admire you. Some people are afraid of you.

51–60 points:
You are an exciting person. You are impulsive. You take chances. You are a natural leader.

41–50 points:
You are lively. You are funny. You always have something interesting to say. You are kind and considerate.

31–40 points:
You are a sensible person. You are cautious. You are practical. You are clever but modest. You are loyal to your friends.

21–30 points:
You are very cautious. You take a long time to make decisions. You do not like doing new things.

Under 21 points:
You are very introvert. You are shy. You find it very difficult to make decisions. You worry a lot. You prefer being on your own.

Group C		Capital	Khartoum
Country	Sudan	Physical features	flat plains, Nile flows south–north through country, mountains – Jebel Marra, Nubian Desert, highest mountain = Kinyeti + swamps and rainforests
Continent	N.E. Africa		
Size	10 / 203		

Location

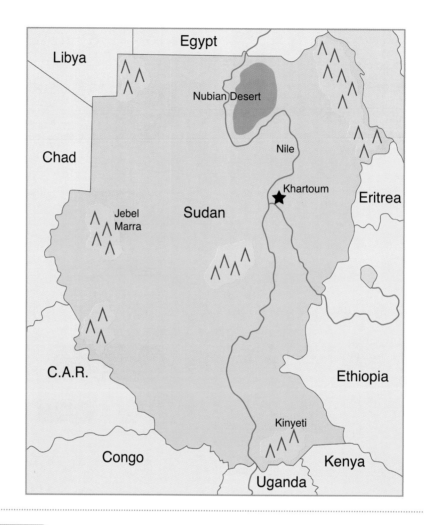

Group C

Do psychologists and sociologists help us?

Sociology is more important than psychology. Humans do not usually live alone. This means *individual* behaviour is not important. We must understand *group* behaviour. Sociologists can predict group behaviour in all situations. They can predict it in the home, in business, between countries. We need sociologists, **not** psychologists.

Debate Club Journal, Broadmead College

Student A

tertiary (adj)	Tertiary means 'after secondary school'. So universities are part of tertiary education.
form (n)	
set (v)	To set means 'to give'. We use it about exams, e.g., teachers set exams at the end of each term.
graduate (n and v)	
cram (v)	To cram means 'to study very hard for a short period of time'. It is not a good idea. You forget things very quickly if you cram.
residential (adj)	
kindergarten (n)	A kindergarten is a nursery school.
dormitory (n)	

Theme 4: Speaking 4.10

Group A

Why is the sky blue?

Light from the sun is white.
White light contains all the colours – red, orange, yellow, green and blue. The white light hits dust and smoke in the air. The blue light scatters more than all the other colours. The blue light makes the sky blue.

Theme 1: Speaking 1.10

Group B

What is a bad teacher?

Research shows that children have very clear ideas about teachers. Bad teachers are not interested in their subject. They are sarcastic. In other words, they make fun of the children, their work or their ideas. Bad teachers belittle children. To belittle means to make them feel small. Finally, bad teachers are unfair. They give rewards, or good things, to the wrong children. They give punishments, or bad things, to the wrong children, too.

Adapted from an article in The Guardian Unlimited (October 31, 2000)

Student A

Read this description for your partner. Spell names aloud if you need to.

Panama has borders to the west with Costa Rica and to the east with Colombia.
It has coastlines on the Caribbean Sea to the north and the Pacific Ocean to the south.
The capital of the country is Panama City.
There is a mountain range in the centre called the Cordillera Central.
In the east, near the border with Colombia, there is an area of rainforest called Darien.

Listen to your partner. Complete this map.

Group A

Country	Latvia
Continent	N.E. Europe
Size	124 / 203

Capital	Riga
Physical features	plains
	forests
	highest pt = only 311 m
	many rivers

Location

Group A

Do psychologists and sociologists help us?

Both psychologists and sociologists do very important work.

1. They study human behaviour.
2. They find new knowledge.
3. We can use this knowledge.
4. We can make the world a better place.

'Maths and physics cannot change the world. They can only describe the world. Sociologists and psychologists can change the world.'

www.psysoc.com

Student B

Listen to your partner. Complete this map.

Read this description for your partner. Spell names aloud if you need to.

Guatemala has borders in the east with Honduras and in the southeast with El Salvador.
It has a short coastline on the Caribbean Sea to the north and the Pacific Ocean to the south.
The capital is Guatemala City.
There are mountains in the south and centre called the Sierra Madre.
The north of the country has large areas of rainforest. The rainforest is called the Peten.

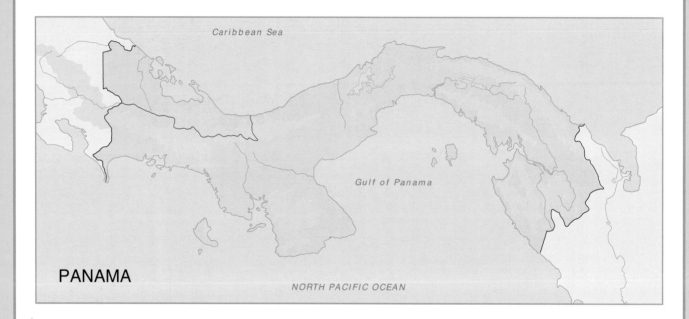

Group B

Do psychologists and sociologists help us?

People often say that psychology and sociology are **not** useful.

1. Psychologists and sociologists do research. But research cannot change human actions.

2. We all have our own personalities. Research cannot change this.

'You can study the mind. You can talk about a person's behaviour. But science can never change people. Only people can change, if they want to.'

The Book of the Mind, M. Lee

Student B

tertiary (*adj*)	
form (*n*)	*Form* is another word for *class* or *year*. In some schools, students are in *forms*, e.g., Form 3A. In other schools, students are in year groups called *forms*, e.g., the fourth form.
set (*v*)	
graduate (*n* and *v*)	A *graduate* is a person with a degree. In other words, he/she has passed a university course.
cram (*v*)	
residential (*adj*)	*Residential* means 'living on the campus'. So in a residential school, you live in the school. You do not go home in the evening.
kindergarten (*n*)	
dormitory (*n*)	A *dormitory* is the place where children sleep at a residential school.

Theme 4: Speaking 4.10

Group C

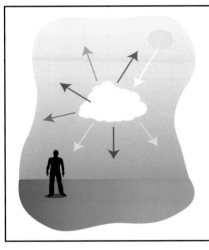

Why are the clouds white?

Light from the sun is white. White light contains all the colours – red, orange, yellow, green and blue. The white light hits water vapour. All the light scatters by the same amount. We see all the colours at the same time. All the colours together make the clouds white.

Theme 1: Speaking 1.10

Group A

What is a good teacher?

Research shows that children have very clear ideas about teachers. Good teachers keep order in the classroom. This means they stop bad behaviour. Good teachers explain things clearly. They show enthusiasm for their subject. In other words, they like their subject and they are excited about teaching it. Good teachers treat the children as individuals. This means they know the names of all their students and they know personal facts about each one. Finally, good teachers have a good sense of humour and make jokes.

Adapted from an article in *The Guardian Unlimited* (October 31, 2000)

Group B
Country   Chile
Continent   S. America (W)
Size   38 / 203

Location

Capital   Santiago
Physical features Andes
                   Atacama Desert
                   forests, volcanoes and lakes
                   + peninsula and many islands

Group B

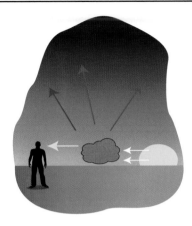

Why is the sky red at sunset?

Light from the sun is white. White light contains all the colours – red, orange, yellow, green and blue. The white light hits dust and smoke in the air. The blue and green light scatters. Some of the red, orange and yellow light comes in a straight line to our eyes.

Group D

Do psychologists and sociologists help us?

We want to live in a safe world. So, three things are very clear.

1. We must study the human mind.

2. We must understand *individual* human behaviour.

3. Then we can understand group behaviour.

In other words, **psychology is the key**. When we understand the human brain, we can have a peaceful world.

www.ideasforum.co.uk

⏱ 1.1

Presenter:	**1.1. Theme 1: Education**
	Lesson 1.1. Vocabulary for listening: Academic life
	Exercise A1. Listen and discuss some statements about education.
Students:	1. At school, English is more useful than Mathematics.
	2. There is no point in studying Art at school.
	3. Writing is the most difficult skill in English.
	4. A teacher should explain everything to the students.
	5. At both university and school, you have lessons and homework.
	6. A university education is not right for everyone.

⏱ 1.2

Presenter:	**1.2. Exercise A2. Listen to some students. Do they agree or disagree with each statement?**
Presenter:	One.
Student A:	At school, English is more useful than Mathematics.
Student B:	I think that's true.
Student C:	Actually, I don't agree. Maths is much more useful than English.
Presenter:	Two.
Student B:	There is no point in studying Art at school.
Student A:	I think Art is important. Everybody needs an Art education.
Student C:	But not modern Art. That's awful.
Presenter:	Three.
Student C:	Writing is the most difficult skill in English.
Student B:	No, it isn't, because you can think about writing. Speaking is more difficult.
Student A:	I agree. Speaking is the most difficult skill.
Presenter:	Four.
Student A:	A teacher should explain everything to the students.
Student B:	No, not everything. We need to work things out for ourselves.
Student C:	Yes, that's right. Teachers should help you, but they shouldn't explain everything.
Presenter:	Five.
Student C:	At both university and school, you have lessons and homework.
Student B:	It's true really.
Student A:	Yes, but they have different names. They are called lectures and assignments.
Presenter:	Six.
Student B:	A university education is not right for everyone.
Student A:	I absolutely agree with that. Some people should not go on to university.
Student C:	Yes. Mechanics and plumbers and electricians don't need a university education, for example.

⏱ 1.3

Presenter:	**1.3. Exercise B2. Listen and check your answers.**
Students:	a. The academic year in my country starts in October. All the university students go back then.
	b. When does the second semester start? Is it in February?
	c. Which faculty are you in? Education? Mathematics? Modern Languages?
	d. Which lecturer gives the Science in Education lectures?
	e. How many staff are in the Faculty of Education? I mean, how many people work there?
	f. Where is the student accommodation at this university? Where do the students live?
	g. This is a large campus. There are ten faculty buildings, the library, the Resource Centre and the Students' Union.
	h. A university student is called a *fresher* in the first year.

⏱ 1.4 DVD 1.A

1.	Student A:	What's the connection between History and Mathematics?
	Student B:	They're both subjects.
2.	Student A:	*Begin* and *end*?
	Student B:	That one's easy. They're opposites!
3.	Student B:	What about *lecturer* and *teacher*?
	Student A:	They both teach.

Student B:	Yes, but a lecturer teaches at a university and a teacher works in a school.
4. Student A:	*In charge of* and *responsible for*?
Student B:	They're the same! They mean 'do a job'.
Student A:	Well, they're not quite the same, are they? *In charge of* goes with a place or group of people, like 'He's in charge of the library' – whereas *responsible for* goes with an action or a thing, doesn't it? 'She's responsible for the schedule.'
5. Student A:	*Head* and *in charge of*?
Student B:	That's easy too. They're the same.
Student A:	Well, not quite. You use them differently, don't you? You say, 'She is the Head of Year 1' or 'She is in charge of Year 1.' Yes, *head* is a noun so we can say *the head*.
6. Student B:	*Accommodation* and *hall of residence*?
Student A:	They are both places to live.
Student B:	*Accommodation* is more general, I think. Yes, *hall of residence* is for students, at a college or university.

🎵 1.5 [DVD] 1.B

Presenter: 1.5. Lesson 1.2. Real-time listening: A speech of welcome

Mr Beech: OK. Let's begin. Welcome to the Faculty of Education. My name is Peter Beech. We all hope that you will have a great time here, and learn a lot, too, of course. OK. First, some important information about people. As I said, I'm Peter Beech. I'm the Dean of Education. That means I'm responsible for this faculty, the Faculty of Education. The bursar is Mrs Pearce. She deals with all the money, so she's a very important person! This is Mrs Pinner. She's the Head of Year 1, and she's responsible for the schedule. After this meeting, Mrs Pinner is going to talk to you about your schedule for the first semester. The Accommodation Manager – that's Mr Heel. He's in charge of the halls of residence on the campus. And finally, Mr Ben Hill looks after the Resource Centre. Ben will help you find the information you need. OK, well that's it from me for the moment. Oh, no. I forgot. One more very important person. Mr Mills. He helps international students if they have any problems. OK, well I will talk to you again later in Freshers' Week. Now I'll hand over to Mrs Pinner…

🎵 1.6 [DVD] 1.C

Mrs Pinner: Thank you, Mr Beech. Right. You need some information about the campus – the university buildings. Firstly, the library is near the main entrance. Next to the library there is the Resource Centre. Resources are things to help you with studying. Ben will help you find the information you need. You can do Internet research in the Resource Centre.

The Administration Block is opposite the library. Go there if you have a problem with fees – that means the money for your course. Behind the Admin block is the Welfare Office. Go there if you have any other problems … You will also find the Medical Centre behind the Admin block.

OK. Next to the Admin block is the JCR and the SCR – that is the Junior Common Room and the Senior Common Room. The common rooms are for the staff, the lecturers. Then on the north of the campus are the halls of residence – in other words, the accommodation for students on campus. We have Hall A, Hall B and Hall C.

Finally, there's the Students' Union – the SU. That's the special place for you. There are lots of facilities for you in the SU. Go and have a look … OK. Now, as Mr Beech said, I'm going to talk to you about your schedule …

🎵 1.7

Presenter: 1.7. Exercise E. Listen and answer the questions.

Voice:
1. What does a dean do at a British university?
2. What does a bursar do?
3. What is a faculty?
4. What's another phrase for *hall of residence*?
5. Where are the social facilities for students?
6. What's the difference between the Welfare Office and the Medical Centre?

🎵 1.8

Presenter: 1.8. Lesson 1.3. Learning new listening skills: Waiting for spoken definitions

Exercise A. Listen to the stressed syllables from some words in this theme. Number the words below.

Voice:
1. ca	4. lec	7. da	10. u
2. bur	5. li	8. spon	11. sour
3. cam	6. sche	9. me	12. fa

🎵 1.9 [DVD] 1.D

Mrs Pinner: OK. As the Dean said, I'm Head of Year 1. That means I'm responsible for the schedule. In Year 1, you have five lectures a week. In two of those lectures, the lecturer will give you an assignment – that is, a piece of work to do on your own. Most assignments have a deadline. That is the time to give it in. The lecturer may say, for example, 'you have one week for this assignment', or 'you must finish this by next Tuesday'.

Don't leave assignments until the last minute. Start work on them immediately. Sometimes assignments involve research – in other words, you must read some articles from journals, um, academic magazines, by scientists and researchers.

There are many journals in the Resource Centre. You can use the Internet to do some research, but be careful – we'll talk more about using Wikipedia and so on for research later on.

You have one tutorial each week. A tutorial is a small discussion with your tutor and some other students.

🔊 1.10

Presenter:	**1.10. Exercise C. Listen to some speakers. They define each word below. Write the definition in each case.**
Students:	1. The SU has a food court – a place with lots of different restaurants.
	2. When the food court is closed, you can use one of the vending machines, which are machines with food and drink.
	3. There's a laundrette in the SU. In other words, you can wash your clothes there.
	4. Did you know? There's a crèche every morning in the SU. It's a place to leave your children for a few hours.
	5. Student A: Is there a gym on the campus?
	Student B: Sorry? What's a gym?
	Student A: It's a place to do exercise.
	Student B: No, I don't think so.

🔊 1.11

Presenter: **1.11. Exercise D. Listen and write the correct consonant in each word.**

Voice:

1.	both	4.	explain	7.	responsible	10.	personal
2.	campus	5.	job	8.	bursar	11.	place
3.	club	6.	pay	9.	people	12.	problem

🔊 1.12

Presenter: **1.12. Exercise E. Listen and tick under the correct vowel sound for each word.**

Voice:

1.	in	3.	teach	5.	begin	7.	meet	9.	it
2.	fee	4.	mean	6.	free	8.	ill	10.	give

🔊 1.13

Presenter: **1.13. Lesson 1.4. Grammar for listening: Defining**

Exercise A2. Listen to some definitions. Which word or phrase is the speaker defining in each case?

Students:
1. It's a place for tennis and squash and football.
2. It's a person in charge of a library.
3. It's a place for lectures.
4. It's a certificate for a university course.
5. It's a restaurant for students. You usually serve yourself.
6. It's a place for plays and sometimes music concerts.
7. It's a place for experiments.
8. It's work outside the university. You visit a place and do research.
9. It's a machine for showing slides, from Powerpoint, for example.
10. It's a person with a degree.

🔊 1.14

Presenter: **1.14. Exercise B. Listen. How does the speaker define each action below?**

Students:
1. revising: It's going over something again, something you have studied before.
2. contributing: It means taking part in something, like a tutorial. It means giving your ideas or your opinion.
3. parting: It means saying goodbye.
4. graduating: It means getting your degree and leaving university.
5. advising: It is telling someone what to do.
6. disagreeing: It is saying you don't agree.

🔊 1.15 DVD 1.E

Presenter: **1.15. Lesson 1.5. Applying new listening skills: Living and studying in Britain**

Mr Mills: Hello. My name is Mills. Tim Mills. I'm sorry I wasn't here earlier in the week. I was feeling really ill. Anyway, I'm fine now so … I want to talk to you for a few minutes about living in the UK. Every culture is different. You are learning a new language. You also need to learn a new culture. International students sometimes have problems because they don't know English very well. But sometimes international students have problems because they don't know British customs. For example, when do you shake hands with someone? Today, I'm going to talk about six things which international students sometimes get wrong.

🔊 1.16 DVD 1.F

Mr Mills: Let's start at the beginning. Greetings – I mean, saying hello to someone. When you meet someone for the first time, you can say 'Pleased to meet you' or 'How do you do?'. Some English people just say 'Hi' or 'Hello'. All of these are fine.

Secondly, be careful when you address people. You can't use titles – I mean Mr, Mrs, Professor – with a first name, like Mr John, or Mrs Mary or Professor Michael. You must use the surname with a title – Mr Williams, Mrs Pearce, Professor Jones. By the way, you call most lecturers at a British university Mr or Mrs or Miss. We only use Doctor if he or she has a PhD. Oh, and Professor. In Britain, a Professor is usually the head of department or faculty. Do not call all lecturers Professor.

Handshakes – shaking hands. We do shake hands a lot in Britain but not with colleagues, that is, people we work with or study with. So don't offer to shake hands with the other students every time you meet them.

What about eye contact? I mean, looking at people. Perhaps, in your country, it is polite to look down when you are talking to an older person, or a person of the opposite sex. But not in Britain. Look people in the eye – your lecturers, the Professor, even the Vice Chancellor. They will not think you are disrespectful.

The next thing is social distance – in other words, how close you should stand to people. In Britain, we stand about 60 centimetres away from colleagues – that's about arm's length.

Next, gender equality. Gender means sex – male or female. So gender equality is the way we think about men and women in Britain. Basically, men and women are equal. You may have male lecturers, or female lecturers or a combination, but they are all equal – same pay, same level in the university.

Finally, participation, which means taking part in something. Lecturers sometimes ask questions during a lecture and they expect you to answer. They sometimes ask for questions at the end of a lecture. It is good to ask questions if you are not sure about something. And of course, lecturers expect active participation in a tutorial.

🎵 1.17

Presenter:	1.17. Lesson 1.6. Vocabulary for speaking: Education systems
	Exercise B1. Listen. Complete each dialogue with a word from the list on the right. Make any necessary changes.
Presenter:	Conversation 1.
Voice A:	When do you sit national examinations?
Voice B:	In Britain, we take them at 16 and at 18.
Presenter:	Conversation 2.
Voice A:	Is education compulsory in your country?
Voice B:	Yes, up to the age of 16.
Presenter:	Conversation 3.
Voice A:	When did you start school?
Voice B:	When I was three. I went to nursery school.
Presenter:	Conversation 4.
Voice A:	Who was your best teacher?
Voice B:	Mr Jarvis. He treated us as adults.

🎵 1.18

Presenter:	1.18. Lesson 1.7. Real-time speaking: Education in the UK
	Exercise A1. Listen to the words on the right. Tick the correct column to show the number of syllables.
Voice:	a. after c. level e. primary g. called i. school
	b. children d. nursery f. secondary h. exam j. sixth

🎵 1.19

| Presenter: | 1.19. Exercise A3. Listen again and repeat the words. |

[REPEAT OF SCRIPT FROM 🎵 1.18]

🎵 1.20

Presenter:	1.20. Exercise B1. Listen to the first part of the talk. Complete Table 1.
Student:	Britain has four kinds of school. They are nursery, primary, secondary and sixth form.
	Many British children go to nursery school at three or four. Children do not take exams at nursery school.
	At five, they move to primary school. Most primary schools are mixed. They stay there for six years and then they move to secondary school. Most children do not take exams at 11, but a few take the 11+ exam.

Secondary school lasts five years. Most secondary schools are mixed. Children take exams called GCSEs at the age of 16. You can leave school after your GCSEs but many children stay at school for two more years.

The last two years are called the sixth form. At the end of the sixth form, teenagers take A levels. You can leave school after A levels, but 50 per cent of British teenagers go on to university.

🕪 1.21

Presenter:	**1.21. Exercise B2. Listen to the second part of the talk.**

Student: I didn't go to nursery school. I started primary school at five. I was good at primary school and I liked the teachers.

I didn't take the 11+ exam. I went to secondary school. I wasn't very good there and I didn't like the teachers. Well, there was one good teacher. I took GCSEs and then A levels.

Then I decided to go to university.

🕪 1.22

Presenter:	**1.22. Exercise C2. Listen and check.**

Student:
a. Britain has four kinds of school. They are nursery, primary, secondary and sixth form.
b. Children don't take exams at nursery school.
c. At four or five, they move to primary school.
d. They stay there for six years and then they move to secondary school.
e. Secondary school lasts five years.
f. Children take exams called GCSEs at the age of 16.
g. You can leave school after GCSEs or A levels. However, about 50 per cent of British teenagers go on to university.
h. I didn't go to nursery school.
i. I was good at primary school and I liked the teachers.
j. I went to secondary school.

🕪 1.23

Presenter:	**1.23. Everyday English: Asking about words and phrases**

Exercise B2. Listen to the conversations. Number the sentences on the right 1 to 6 in the order you hear them.

Presenter:	Conversation 1.

Voice A:	What's a nursery school?
Voice B:	It's a school for young children.
Voice A:	How old are they?
Voice B:	They're between three and five.

Presenter:	Conversation 2.

Voice A:	What does *GCSE* mean?
Voice B:	It's an abbreviation.
Voice A:	I know. But what does it mean?
Voice B:	It means *General Certificate of Secondary Education*.

Presenter:	Conversation 3.
Voice A:	Does *primary* mean 'first'?
Voice B:	Yes, it does.
Voice A:	So does *secondary* mean 'second'?
Voice B:	That's right.

Presenter:	Conversation 4.

Voice A:	What are A levels?
Voice B:	They're exams in Britain.
Voice A:	When do you take them?
Voice B:	You take them at 18.

Presenter:	Conversation 5.

Voice A:	Is sixth form for 17- and 18-year olds?
Voice B:	Yes, it is.
Voice A:	Why is it called *sixth form*?
Voice B:	Because it starts with the sixth year of secondary school.

Presenter:	Conversation 6.

Voice A:	Do you *take* an exam or *make* an exam?
Voice B:	We use the verb *take* with exams.

Voice A:	And what about assignments?
Voice B:	You *do* assignments.

🎧 1.24

Presenter: **1.24. Portfolio: Activities and clubs**

Presenter: Exercise B1. Group 1: the IT club.

Student: IT stands for *information technology* so the IT Club is for anyone interested in computers. Do you like playing games on your computer? Do you use Word or Excel? Do you send e-mails? Would you like to learn how computers work? Then this club is for you.

We meet at 12.30 p.m. on Wednesdays, in the IT Room of course, which is next to Room 16 on the ground floor. The meetings last for one hour so we finish at 1.30 p.m. There is something for everyone. You don't need to bring your laptop. There are 20 computers in the IT room.

What do we do in the meetings? Well, you can learn the latest computer game, get help with computer applications, like Word and Excel, or you can even learn to program in C++.

🎧 1.25

Presenter: **1.25. Exercise B1. Group 2: the Debating Society.**

Student: We are looking for new members for the Debating Society. What is the Debating Society? Well, a debate – that's D-E-B-A-T-E – is like a conversation between two people. But in a debate, one person likes something, and the other person doesn't like it. There are two speeches – one from each person. Then the audience, that's the other members of the Debating Society, the audience chooses between the two people.

So who is the Debating Society for? Well, two kinds of people. Firstly, people who like to speak in public, in front of a group of people. Secondly, for people who like to listen to ideas and opinions.

We meet straight after school in the school hall on Thursdays for an hour – so that's from 4.00 p.m. to 5.00 p.m. Each week, there is a debate. You can lead a debate or just sit in the audience and choose the best speaker at the end.

🎧 2.1

Presenter: **2.1. Theme 2: Psychology and sociology**
Lesson 2.1. Vocabulary for listening: What groups do you belong to?

Exercise B2. Listen. Complete the text below with words from the list on the right. Make any necessary changes.

Lecturer: A person is an individual. Psychology is about individuals. Psychologists ask questions like: *What is the mind? How does it control human behaviour?*

People have relationships with other people. Sociology is about human behaviour in groups. Sociologists ask questions like: *Why do people form groups? Why do groups sometimes behave badly?*

In the diagram, the circle for **my family** is separate from the other three circles. Why? Because my family is different from my friends, my neighbours and my colleagues. Why are these three circles linked? Because some of my friends live in my neighbourhood and some of my friends are also my colleagues.

Sociologists call the four inner circles the primary groups. The people in your primary groups are very important to you.

🎧 2.2

Presenter: **2.2. Exercise C2. Listen to a student explaining one word in each pair. Tick the word.**

Student: 1. Oh that's the person. You know, the person who studies human behaviour.
2. Well, it's a science. It's the study of the mind, I think.
3. That's where children go. From about 5 to 11 years, isn't it?
4. It's a physical part of your body. The organ in your head.
5. It's everyone in the world. We are thinking of them as one group.
6. Well, I think it means 'one person'.

🎧 2.3 DVD 2.A

Presenter: **2.3. Lesson 2.2. Real-time listening: An introduction to sociology**

Part 1
Lecturer: In this lecture, I'm going to talk about sociology. Now, firstly, I'm going to mention the aims of the science. Secondly, I will give a little bit of history – some key names and quotes from each person. Finally, I'm going to talk about sociology today.

Part 2
Lecturer: So, first. Sociology has three main aims. Firstly, sociologists *study* human behaviour in groups. They ask the question: *How do people behave in groups?* Secondly, they try to understand human behaviour in groups. They ask the question: *Why*

do they behave in those ways? Finally, they try to predict human behaviour in groups. They ask the question: *How will people behave in groups in certain situations*?

Part 3
Lecturer: In 1838, a Frenchman called Auguste Comte used the word *sociology* for the first time. Today, Comte is often called 'The Father of Sociology'. He said 'Human behaviour has rules and patterns.' So the name *sociology* is quite new, but interest in human behaviour is very, very old. For example, in the 4ᵗʰ century BCE, Plato had ideas about people and groups. He said 'People live in groups for friendship. They also live in groups for safety. Groups must have rules of behaviour.'

Nearly two thousand years later, in the 14ᵗʰ century, in Tunisia, a man called Ibn Khaldun wrote about people in groups. He said 'Groups are like animals. They are born, they grow and then they die. This happens to all groups.'

Part 4
Lecturer: In the nineteenth century, Auguste Comte used the term *sociology*. Perhaps you did not know the name of Comte. But I'm sure you know the name of the next man. In 1848, Karl Marx, a German, wrote a famous book. At that time, there was a lot of unrest in many countries. Poor people were unhappy. They started to fight for their rights. Marx wrote about this situation. He said, 'People from different groups must fight each other.' In 1904, another German, Max Weber, said: 'There are three important things for groups. They are religion, work and money.'

Part 5
Lecturer: In the past, we called people like Plato and Ibn Khaldun philosophers. These days, we call them sociologists. In the 1960s, sociology became an important subject. Today, pupils even study sociology at secondary school. They look at the ideas of modern sociologists like Anthony Giddens. He wrote a famous book in 1984. He says: 'People make groups ... but then the groups make people.' The relationship between the individual and the group works in both directions.

🕲 2.4

Presenter: **2.4. Lesson 2.3. Learning new listening skills: Recognizing time signposts**

Exercise A2. Listen. Tick the word you hear in each case.

Voice:
a. Nowadays we call the study of groups *sociology*.
b. We are all part of the human race.
c. Sociologists study human behaviour.
d. People lived together for friendship.
e. They also wanted to feel safe.
f. Would you like to study sociology?
g. What are the main aims of the course?
h. What did the people say?
i. There was a lot of unrest about rights.
j. According to Plato, groups must have rules of behaviour.

🕲 2.5

Presenter: **2.5. Exercise C. Listen to sentences from other lectures. Is each sentence about the past or the present?**

Voice:
1. In 1789, there were a lot of changes in France.
2. In the 1970s, there was a lot of research into sociology.
3. At one time, people thought the mind was in the heart.
4. Later, scientists found that the brain controlled the body.
5. Nowadays, a lot of sociologists talk about the philosopher Confucius.
6. Today, university students study philosophers from Ancient Greece.
7. In the nineteenth century, the term *gender studies* didn't exist.
8. In 1904, Weber wrote a famous book.

🕲 2.6

Presenter: **2.6. Exercise D3. Listen and check your answers.**

Voice:
a. Do you all have a book?
b. Let me start with …
c. It's an important part of the topic.
d. He's called 'The Father of Sociology'.
e. He began writing in 1957.
f. It's important to understand this.

🕲 2.7

Presenter: **2.7. Lesson 2.4. Grammar for listening: Recognizing past-time sentences**

Exercise A1. Listen to some verbs. Say *present* or *past* in each case.

Voice:
| 1. are | 3. became | 5. go | 7. grew | 9. had |
| 2. were | 4. become | 6. went | 8. grow | 10. have |

🎵 2.8

<table>
<tr><td>Presenter:</td><td>2.8. Exercise A2. Listen to some sentences. Say present or past in each case.</td></tr>
<tr><td>Voice:</td><td>
1. He's a sociologist.
2. He was a psychologist.
3. They knew the answer.
4. We know the reason.
5. I made a mistake.
6. They thought about important questions.
7. People say sociology is not a real science.
8. Most of the students take two main subjects.
9. The assignment was difficult.
10. He did experiments to check his ideas.
</td></tr>
</table>

🎵 2.9

<table>
<tr><td>Presenter:</td><td>2.9. Exercise B1. Listen to some verbs. Say present or past in each case.</td></tr>
</table>

Voice:

1. predict	4. graduated	7. contributed	10. edited	13. edit
2. predicted	5. collected	8. record	11. collect	14. recorded
3. contribute	6. deleted	9. delete	12. graduate	

🎵 2.10

<table>
<tr><td>Presenter:</td><td>2.10. Exercise B2. Listen to the same verbs in sentences. Say present or past in each case.</td></tr>
<tr><td>Voice:</td><td>
1. We predicted the results.
2. I contribute to tutorials.
3. They graduate in the summer.
4. We collected a lot of data.
5. The scientists record their results in a table.
6. I edited my work.
</td></tr>
</table>

🎵 2.11

<table>
<tr><td>Presenter:</td><td>2.11. Exercise C1. Listen to some sentences. Say present or past or I don't know in each case.</td></tr>
<tr><td>Voice:</td><td>
1. They called these people philosophers.
2. The problems happened lots of times.
3. Scientists analyze data.
4. Some students drop Geography.
5. They managed three shops.
6. Many students plagiarize the articles on Wikipedia.
</td></tr>
</table>

🎵 2.12

<table>
<tr><td>Presenter:</td><td>2.12. Exercise C2. Listen to the same sentences with time expressions. Say present or past or I don't know in each case.</td></tr>
<tr><td>Voice:</td><td>
1. At one time, they called these people philosophers.
2. In the past, the problems happened lots of times.
3. Nowadays, scientists analyze data.
4. Every year, some students drop Geography.
5. In the 1990s, they managed three shops.
6. Today, many students plagiarize the articles on Wikipedia.
</td></tr>
</table>

🎵 2.13

<table>
<tr><td>Presenter:</td><td>2.13. Lesson 2.5. Applying new listening skills: An introduction to psychology

Exercise A. Listen and complete the phrases.</td></tr>
</table>

Voice:

1. human behaviour	5. main aims
2. modern sociologists	6. famous book
3. important people	7. people in groups
4. twentieth century	8. in the past

🎵 2.14 DVD 2.B

<table>
<tr><td>Lecturer:</td><td>In today's talk, I'm going to answer some very basic questions about psychology: First, what is it? Secondly, how does psychology help us in our day-to-day lives? Finally, who are the important names in the history of psychology?

OK, let's answer the first question. What is psychology? Psychology is the study of the mind. It is not the study of the brain. The brain is physical. You can see a brain, you can touch it, you can even cut it open. The mind is in the brain but</td></tr>
</table>

you can't see it or touch it. We now believe that the mind controls our behaviour. So psychologists study the human mind. Then they try to understand human behaviour.

We must understand the mind. Then we can understand the way we think. We can understand the things we say. We can understand the things we do.

2.15 DVD 2.C

Lecturer: A long time ago, in the 4th century BCE, the Greek philosopher Aristotle wrote the first book about the mind. It was called *Para Psyche*. *Psyche* means 'mind' in ancient Greek. *Para* means 'about'. In the 17th century, Locke in England and Descartes in France asked the same question: *How do the mind and the body work together?* At that time, we called these people philosophers not psychologists. They thought about important questions but they did not do scientific experiments.

In 1879, a German scientist, Wilhelm Wundt, opened the first psychology school. The science of Psychology was born. At the end of the 19th century, Ivan Pavlov in Russia asked the question: *How do people learn?* He did experiments to check his ideas. In the early 1900s, Sigmund Freud in Germany asked: *What do dreams mean?* At the same time, Watson, an American, said: 'We can only study behaviour. We cannot study the mind.' But in1967, Ulric Neisser said: 'We must study the mind.' It was the start of cognitive psychology. *Cognitive* means 'knowing'.

2.16 DVD 2.D

Lecturer: Finally, I want to mention three modern psychologists.

Elizabeth Loftus was born in 1944. In 1970, she obtained a PhD in Psychology. At that time, she was interested in learning. But in 1974, she started to study memory. Today, she works with the police in criminal cases.

Stephen Pinker was born in 1954. In 1979, he obtained his doctorate in Psychology. In 1994, Pinker wrote a famous book called *The Language Instinct*. At that time, he was a Psychology teacher. Today he does a lot of research into language and the mind.

Elizabeth Spelke was born in 1949. In the 1980s, she carried out experiments on babies and young children. In 2000, Elizabeth Spelke described new ideas about the minds of babies. Today, she teaches Psychology in the USA.

2.17

Presenter: **2.17. Lesson 2.6. Vocabulary for speaking: Personality**

Exercise B1. Listen and complete the conversations with words from the list on the right.

Presenter: Conversation 1.

Voice A: Do you like being on your own?
Voice B: It depends. Sometimes I like being with other people.

Presenter: Conversation 2.

Voice A: Is personality the same as behaviour?
Voice B: Well, I think it influences behaviour.

Presenter: Conversation 3.

Voice A: What is personality?
Voice B: I think it's similar to behaviour.

Presenter: Conversation 4.

Voice A: Can people change their behaviour?
Voice B: Yes, but they can't change completely.

2.18

Presenter: **2.18. Lesson 2.7. Real-time speaking: Personality *vs* behaviour**

Exercise A1. Listen and mark the stress on these words.

Voice: a. behaviour   c. completely   e. difference   g. important   i. personality
          b. changes   d. depend   f. friendly   h. influences   j. situation

2.19

Presenter: **2.19. Exercise A2. Listen again and repeat the words.**

[REPEAT OF SCRIPT FROM 2.18]

🔊 2.20 [DVD] 2.E

Student 1: I think behaviour and personality are the same thing. You can say 'He is a very happy person' or you can say 'He smiles a lot', and it's the same thing. There is no difference between personality and behaviour … I think …

Student 2: Well, I read that behaviour and personality are two completely different things. Behaviour changes depending on your situation. But your personality is always the same. You like some things but you don't like other things.

Student 3: But I found an article. It says … um … I've got a quote here. 'Personality influences behaviour. An aggressive person acts in one way in a situation. In the same situation, a friendly person acts in a different way.' So your personality is more important. What do you think?

Student 4: OK, but, no, I think your behaviour is much more important, because you learn good behaviour when you're a child. But your personality changes all the time. Your personality depends on your friends, the places you go, and so on.

🔊 2.21

Presenter: **2.21. Everyday English: Asking for information**

Exercise B2. Listen to the conversations. Number the sentences on the right in the correct order.

Presenter: Conversation 1.

Voice A: Is this the way to the bookshop?
Voice B: Yes. I'm going that way too.
Voice A: Do you mind if I go with you?
Voice B: No, not at all.

Presenter: Conversation 2.

Voice A: Excuse me. Where's the library?
Voice B: It's in the other building.
Voice A: Thanks. Which floor is it on?
Voice B: The second.

Presenter: Conversation 3.

Voice A: Do you give a student discount?
Voice B: Yes, with a student ID card. It's 10 per cent.
Voice A: Oh, great. Can I pay for these books then?
Voice B: Certainly.

Presenter: Conversation 4.

Voice A: When does the library tour start?
Voice B: Ten o'clock, I think.
Voice A: How long does it last?
Voice B: An hour.

Presenter: Conversation 5.

Voice A: How do you reserve a book?
Voice B: You have to fill in a form.
Voice A: OK. Sorry. Where are the forms.
Voice B: They're next to the index.

Presenter: Conversation 6.

Voice A: How much does this book cost?
Voice B: It's on the back.
Voice A: Oh, yes. Thank you.
Voice B: No problem.

🔊 2.22

Presenter: **2.22. Lesson 2.8. Learning new speaking skills: Taking turns**

Exercise C2. Listen. Complete the sentences.

Voice: a. I found a good article in the library.
b. I think we should discuss sociology first.
c. Well, what is the difference between them?
d. I read that a lot of psychologists are women.
e. OK, and what about old people?
f. I found a quote about that on the Internet.
g. Yes, but that's not a new idea.
h. I heard that it's an interesting website.

Presenter:	**2.23. Exercise D2. Listen. Are these examples of good or bad turn-taking?**
Presenter:	Example 1.
Student A:	Well I've seen a –
Student B:	I've got a good quote here from the article.
Presenter:	Example 2.
Student C:	… and that's all really. That's all I wanted to say. Yes, that's all.
Student D:	Hmm. OK. I think it's an interesting idea.
Presenter:	Example 3.
Student E:	I read that psychologists and sociologists don't help in our everyday life.
Student F:	Well I read something different. I have it here.
Presenter:	Example 4.
Student G:	There is one more thing that I found. It was on the Internet.
Student H:	I looked on the Internet too. I saw an article there.
Presenter:	Example 5.
Student I:	So maybe we should work in pairs to find the information. What do you think?
Student J:	I think that's a good idea.

3.1

Presenter:	**3.1. Theme 3: Work and business** **Lesson 3.1. Vocabulary for listening: Responsibilities at work** **Exercise A2. Listen to descriptions of the jobs above. Number the pictures in order.**
Presenter:	One.
Voice 1:	I'm a medical assistant. I work in a hospital.
Presenter:	Two.
Voice 2:	I'm an engineer. I work on big public projects.
Presenter:	Three.
Voice 3:	I am a businessperson. I work in a small company.
Presenter:	Four.
Voice 4:	In my office we make plans for towns and cities. I'm an office worker.
Presenter:	Five.
Voice 5:	I work as a waiter. A waiter, and sometimes a cook. I also have to wash up sometimes.
Presenter:	Six.
Voice 6:	I'm a park ranger. I look after the animals and the plants.

3.2

Presenter:	**3.2. Exercise B1. Listen. The people in the pictures above are talking about their jobs. You will hear two of the words or phrases below in each description. Number the words.**
Presenter:	One.
Voice 1:	I'm responsible for the equipment in the hospital. My job is to clean it and keep it in order.
Presenter:	Two.
Voice 2:	We make roads and water systems and other things for everybody to use. So our customers are people like you and me – the public.

Presenter:	Three.
Voice 3:	We work fast. It's important for us to finish tasks on time. If we can't, another company gets the job, and we lose the money.
Presenter:	Four.
Voice 4:	We go to a lot of meetings for work to discuss projects. We need to travel sometimes and we're very busy, so we organize our time carefully. We also have to wear good clothes, and be punctual.
Presenter:	Five.
Voice 5:	I work with food, so it's very important that my workspace is always clean and tidy. It's important too that our customers are always satisfied. That way they come back.
Presenter:	Six.
Voice 6:	I think of myself as a kind of teacher. My colleagues and I teach people, usually children, to enjoy and respect nature.

🔊 3.3 [DVD] 3.A

Presenter:	**3.3. Lesson 3.2: Real-time listening: behaviour at work**
Businessman:	How do you get a good job when you leave university? Well, here's an idea. Start thinking about it NOW! Change the way that you think about university. Think of university as a kind of job – your first real job.

So university should be a job. But what is a job? What do employers want? I'm going to tell you eight important things. I'm talking about *work*, but all of these things are important at *university* too.

Number one: You must go to work every day. Of course, if you are sick, you can't go. Phone and tell your manager, and stay at home. But you must phone.

Secondly, you must be punctual – that means, you must always be on time. You must be on time for work, for meetings, and when you come back to your desk after lunch. If you are not punctual, people are waiting for you, and they get angry. Why? Because you waste their time. In addition, the company loses money.

Number three: You must respect your manager – the person who gives you your tasks, your pieces of work. You must also respect your colleagues – that is, the people who you work with. Finally, you must also respect the customers, in other words, the people who buy things from the company.

Fourthly, you must do all the tasks on time, but fifthly, you must not rush work in order to finish on time. You are responsible for the quality of your work – whether it is good or bad.

Sixthly. Now, this one is a big problem nowadays. You must only use the company's equipment – that is, the phones and computers – for work, and not for personal things. Many companies have software to check your computer usage. If you misuse your computer, your manager will probably find out.

Seven. You must keep your workspace tidy – that means your desk, and any shelves or cupboards that you use.

And, finally, you must also organize your work files sensibly – in alphabetical order, or chronologically – that means by date.

We have heard about a lot of *rules* at work. In the next part of my talk, I will give *reasons* for these rules.

🔊 3.4

Presenter:	**3.4. Lesson 3.3. Learning new listening skills: Recognizing sentence stress**
	Exercise A. Listen to the sentences. What is the next word?
Voice:	1. Always arrive on time. It's important to be [PAUSE] punctual.
	2. You must keep your shelves, your desk and your cupboards [PAUSE] tidy.
	3. Your files must be in date order or in alphabetical [PAUSE] order.
	4. At university, your tutor gives you instructions. He or she is your [PAUSE] manager.
	5. If your work is bad, it is your fault. You are [PAUSE] responsible.
	6. Do your work on time. Complete all your [PAUSE] tasks.

🔊 3.5

Presenter:	**3.5. Exercise B3. Listen. Underline the stressed words.**
Voice:	a. Companies want college or university graduates.
	b. All employers want critical thinking.
	c. 'But how can I *get* work skills?' you might ask.
	d. You can learn management skills in university clubs.
	e. You must show that you want to learn.
	f. You must take responsibility for your mistakes.

🔊 3.6

Presenter:	**3.6. Exercise C2. Listen and note the key words in each sentence.**

Voice:	a. How do you keep a good job?
	b. How old do you need to be?
	c. You learn new skills from your colleagues.
	d. Your employer will give you orders.
	e. Practise your skills to make them better.

🔊 3.7

Presenter:	**3.7. Exercise D3. Listen and check your answers.**

Voice:	change, begin, get, job, university, young, wage

🔊 3.8

Presenter:	**3.8. Lesson 3.4. Grammar for listening: Negative sentences; reasons**

	Exercise A1. Listen to some verbs. Say *positive* or *negative* in each case.

Voice:	1. goes	3. 'll do	5. doesn't like	7. won't make	9. 'd like
	2. don't tell	4. see	6. has	8. didn't take	10. wouldn't go

🔊 3.9

Presenter:	**3.9. Exercise A2. Listen to some sentences. Say *positive* or *negative* in each case.**

Voice:	1. He works in a bank.
	2. Managers don't like workers to come late.
	3. I'll finish the work tomorrow.
	4. The company has a big office.
	5. The woman doesn't know the way.
	6. The secretary has a lot of experience.
	7. They won't buy any new machines.
	8. I didn't make a mistake in the letter.
	9. They'd like me to work at the weekend.
	10. I wouldn't do that. It's dangerous.

🔊 3.10

Presenter:	**3.10. Exercise B1. Listen to some verbs. Say *positive* or *negative* in each case.**

Voice:	1. are	4. must go	7. isn't	10. mustn't come
	2. aren't	5. shouldn't leave	8. were	11. should have
	3. can't wear	6. is	9. can be	12. weren't

🔊 3.11

Presenter:	**3.11. Exercise B2. Listen to some sentences. Say *positive* or *negative* in each case.**

Voice:	1. You can't be rude to customers.
	2. They're important people.
	3. She's the manager.
	4. They weren't late yesterday.
	5. You aren't responsible for the files.
	6. The papers were on your desk.
	7. You must arrive before nine.
	8. Everyone should be in the office now.
	9. I mustn't leave before six.
	10. You shouldn't wear those clothes.
	11. This isn't a difficult problem.
	12. You can be in charge this afternoon.

🔊 3.12

Presenter:	**3.12. Exercise C1. Listen to some sentences. Does the speaker give a reason? Say *Yes* or *No*.**

Voice:	1. You must finish on time. Why? Because other people need that information.
	2. We must arrive before eight o'clock; we have lunch at twelve; we finish at five.
	3. You must be responsible for your work … other people can't do it for you.
	4. Customers must complete a form with their name, address and telephone number.
	5. Office employees must be polite. Rudeness makes people angry.
	6. I must go because I have a meeting at three o'clock.

Presenter: 3.13. Exercise C2. Listen. Is the second sentence a reason or a new point?

Voice:
1. A new employee must work hard. He or she usually has a lot to learn in his or her new job.
2. So you must always come on time. Now let's think about wages.
3. Big companies want diplomas and degrees. They need knowledge.
4. Employees mustn't waste time. Time is money!
5. You mustn't take things from the office. Another point is critical thinking.

3.14

Presenter: 3.14. Exercise C3. Listen. The speaker gives a silly reason! Correct the reason in each case.

Voice:
1. You mustn't play games on the computers at work because the level is too difficult for you.
2. You must be polite to colleagues – they will buy lunch for you every day.
3. You must respect your manager. Why? Because he is taller than you.
4. You must go to work because it's boring at home.
5. You mustn't wear shorts to work – you might be cold.
6. You must be nice to customers. Why? Because they are poor.

3.15

Presenter: 3.15. Lesson 3.5. Applying new listening skills: Reasons for good behaviour at work

Exercise A2. Listen and tick the phrase you hear.

Businessman:
a. If you are ill and can't work, stay in bed, but phone.
b. The company doesn't want to waste money.
c. It's important to respect your colleagues and customers.
d. You're responsible for your office equipment.
e. Organize your files in chronological order.
f. Make sure your workspace is organized.

3.16 [DVD] 3.B

Presenter: 3.16. Lesson 3.6. Vocabulary for speaking: Employment

Businessman: OK. How to be a good employee. I have told you some of the things which you must do. But why must you do these things? Sometimes, people don't see the reason for some of the things. They say 'Oh no, it's just more rules. It's just the same as school.' But there is a reason for each thing. Lets look at each thing and suggest a reason.

Firstly, you must go to work every day because people rely on you – they need you to do your work so they can do their work. A company needs reliable employees.

My second point – that you must be punctual – is connected to this. You must be punctual because people expect to start at a certain time. If you are late, you waste their time. People get angry and, sometimes, the company loses money.

Next, you must respect people. You must respect your manager and your colleagues because you must work together every day. It's very difficult to work with a person if he or she behaves badly or is rude to you.

You must respect the customers. Why? Because, in the end, they pay your wages. Think about it. It is not the manager. It is not the company. It is the customers. They buy things from the company and the company uses the money to pay you.

You must complete all the tasks your manager gives you. Why? Because other people need the information. And you must do all the tasks well because it is very bad if a customer is not satisfied with a product or service.

A few final points. You must not use the company's phones and/or the email to talk to your friends – this is a waste of
time. It is also a waste of the company's money.

You must keep your workspace tidy because untidiness is rude to the other people in your workplace. Also, perhaps colleagues need to use the same space. They need to find things. For the same reason, you must organize your work files sensibly. You might be ill one day. Then a manager or colleague will have to find urgent papers in your work files.

3.17

Presenter: 3.17. Exercise B1. Listen and check.

Presenter: Conversation 1.

Voice A: You look smart.
Voice B: Thanks. I'm on my way to a recruitment agency.
Voice A: Oh, what for?
Voice B: I've got an interview for a summer job.
Voice A: Well, good luck!

Presenter:	Conversation 2.
Voice A:	Could you put an advert in the paper for a summer job?
Voice B:	Yes, of course. What's the exact job title?
Voice A:	Um. Sales assistant, I think.
Voice B:	Full-time or part-time?
Voice A:	Part-time.

Presenter:	Conversation 3.
Voice A:	Did you have a good summer?
Voice B:	Not really. I was working for a building company.
Voice A:	In the office?
Voice B:	No, I wasn't doing clerical work. I was outside.
Voice A:	So manual work, then.
Voice B:	That's right. It was hard work, but the pay was good.

🎧 3.18

Presenter:	**3.18. Exercise C4. Listen to some sentences and check your ideas.**
Voice:	1. There are lots of job advertisements in today's paper.
	2. I am advertising my bike on the university website.
	3. The careers advisor's office is next to the library.
	4. There is lots of interview advice on the Internet.
	5. It's important to make a good impression at an interview.
	6. My boss is very hard to impress.
	7. The organization of the office is not very good.
	8. I need to organize my desk before I start work.
	9. I did lots of preparation before my interview.
	10. Good managers prepare for meetings.
	11. Banks have reduced recruitment recently.
	12. We need to recruit more staff for the tourist season.

🎧 3.19

Presenter:	**3.19. Lesson 3.7. Real-time speaking: Talking about summer jobs**
	Exercise C. Listen. Julia is talking to her friend, Carla. Fill in the form below for Carla.
Carla:	Hi, Julia. What are you doing?
Julia:	I'm using this webpage to help me find a summer job. It says a good summer job for me is … nursery school assistant or shop assistant. I think that's a stupid suggestion. I don't like working with children and I don't like selling things!
Carla:	Are you going to get a job in the university holidays?
Julia:	I'd like to. What about you?
Carla:	Yes, I think so.
Julia:	What would you like to do?
Carla:	I'm not sure.
Julia:	Would you like to work abroad?
Carla:	Yes, I would. I'd love to work in another country.
Julia:	Do you like working alone or with other people?
Carla:	With other people definitely. I don't enjoy working alone. But I would prefer to do something with adults because I have no experience with children.
Julia:	Do you like working inside or outside?
Carla:	Mm. Let me think. Inside. No, I'll change that. Outside.
Julia:	OK. So I just click *Find* and …
Carla:	Why are you laughing?
Julia:	It says … a good job for you is… camp counsellor.
Carla:	Well, I agree. I think that's a good suggestion.
Julia:	Oh, look at the time. I must go. I'm late for a lecture.

🎧 3.20

Presenter:	**3.20. Exercise D. Listen. Write one or two words in each space.**
Carla:	Are you going to get a job in the university holidays?
Julia:	I'd like to. What about you?
Carla:	Yes, I think so.
Julia:	What would you like to do?
Carla:	I'm not sure.
Julia:	Would you like to work abroad?
Carla:	Yes, I would. I'd love to work in another country.
Julia:	Do you like working alone or with other people?
Carla:	With other people definitely. I don't enjoy working alone. But I would prefer to do something with adults because I have no experience with children.
Julia:	Do you like working inside or outside?
Carla:	Mm. Let me think. Inside. No, I'll change that. Outside.

3.21

Presenter:	**3.21. Everyday English: Talking about days and times**
	Exercise A2. Listen and match a conversation with each picture.

Presenter:	Conversation 1.
Voice A:	Excuse me. Have you got the time?
Voice B:	Yes, it's just after three forty.
Voice A:	Thank you.
Voice B:	That's OK.

Presenter:	Conversation 2.
Voice A:	Excuse me. What day is our test?
Voice B:	Next Monday.
Voice A:	What time does it start?
Voice B:	At nine thirty.

Presenter:	Conversation 3.
Voice A:	What's the date today?
Voice B:	Let me check. The ninth.
Voice A:	So what's the date next Wednesday?
Voice B:	The fifteenth.

Presenter:	Conversation 4.
Voice A:	Hurry up! We're late!
Voice B:	What time is it?
Voice A:	It's nearly eight fifteen. The bus is at half past.
Voice B:	OK. I'll be as quick as I can.

3.22 [DVD] 3.C

Presenter:	**3.22. Lesson 3.8. Learning new speaking skills: How to be a good interviewee**
Careers advisor:	What sort of summer job would you like?
Female student:	I'm not sure.
Careers advisor:	Well, for example, do you like working with people?
Female student:	Mm, yes.
Careers advisor:	And how about children?
Female student:	Maybe.
Careers advisor:	OK. I know there is a job at Macdonald's. You could apply for that.
Female student:	Oh no, I wouldn't like to work inside.
Careers advisor:	I see. Well, let me have a look what I can find for you out of doors …

3.23 [DVD] 3.D

Careers advisor:	What sort of summer job would you like?
Male student:	Well, I'm doing an education course so perhaps something with children. Also I have two younger brothers and I like looking after them.
Careers advisor:	That's a good idea. Would you like to work in this country or abroad?
Male student:	I would like to work abroad, if possible. I like travelling.
Careers advisor:	Well, there are lots of jobs in holiday camps for children in the USA.
Male student:	Ah, that sounds interesting. Can you tell me more about them?
Careers advisor:	Yes, of course. And I have some leaflets you can take away with you …

3.24

Presenter:	**3.24. Exercise A. Listen and give true answers with *Yes, …* or *No, …* .**
Voice:	1. Do you go to university?
	2. Have you got a job?
	3. Can you drive a car?
	4. Would you like to work in a bank?
	5. Did you go out last night?
	6. Are you a student?
	7. Were you late for class today?
	8. Have you been to another country?
	9. Can you ride a horse?
	10. Do you live in a flat?

🎵 3.25

Presenter: **3.25. Exercise B. Listen and give true answers. Select the first choice or the second choice.**

Voice:
1. Would you like to visit Russia or America?
2. Would you like to have a manual job or a clerical job?
3. Would you prefer to live in a city or in a village?
4. Would you prefer to eat Chinese food or Indian food?
5. Would you like to travel in your job or stay in one place?
6. Would you prefer to work with children or adults?
7. Would you like to live in a flat or a house?
8. Would you prefer to work in the daytime or at night?
9. Would you like to be a manager or a worker?
10. Would you like to have your own desk or share a desk?

🎵 3.26

Presenter: **3.26. Portfolio: Jobs**

Presenter: Exercise B1. Group A.

Teacher: I'm going to tell you a little bit about my job. I'm a primary school teacher. At primary schools in the UK, we have children between the ages of 5 and 11. After 11, they go on to secondary school. So I teach children between 5 and 11. I teach all the subjects, like History and Geography. At primary schools, we don't have special teachers for Maths or Science.

I think you have to be a special kind of person to be a primary teacher. I don't mean very intelligent. I mean patient. You have to say the same things again and again, and you must not get angry with the children. In fact, you must like children very much.

Primary schools are open from 8.45 a.m. to about 3.45 p.m., but a teacher's day is longer. I work from about 8.00 a.m. to about 5.00 p.m. Schools are open five days a week, Mondays to Fridays. But of course, my work does not finish when I go home. I have to prepare lessons, mark homework, write reports for the school or the government. I also manage an after-school club.

Some people think teachers have an easy life because schools are only open for about 40 weeks each year. But I have to go into the school when the children are on holiday and there is a lot of preparation for the next term.

You must have a teaching certificate – that takes three years. You must then work as a practice teacher for one year.

The best work experience for this job is having younger brothers and sisters. You learn to be patient. If you don't have brothers or sisters, get a job in a school in the summer holidays. Teachers need a lot of help in the classroom.

A newly qualified teacher can earn about £18,000 per year at first.

🎵 3.27

Presenter: **3.27. Exercise B1. Group B.**

Solicitor: I'm going to tell you a little about my job. I'm a solicitor. A solicitor is a person who helps if you have a legal problem, or if you want to write a legal document. For example, you need a solicitor when you buy or sell your house.

Solicitors must be patient and they must be good at listening. They must listen to their customers' problems and give them advice. They must also be very careful because their advice must be correct, in the law.

Solicitors work a 37-hour week usually, Monday to Fridays. However, you are often on call at night or at the weekend. On call means that people can call you on your mobile and you have to talk to them or even go and see them at any time.

New solicitors usually start with small companies but they can go on to work with very large companies. Many solicitors start their own companies after some years.

You must have a degree in law or a diploma. A degree takes three years and a diploma takes at least two years.

The best work experience for this job is working with a local solicitor, in his or her office. You get a good idea of the different jobs. Some are very interesting, some are quite boring!

A newly qualified solicitor can earn about £14,000 per year at first.

🎵 3.28

Presenter: **3.28. Exercise E. Listen to a talk about the job of retail manager.**

Voice: The job is retail manager. *Retail* is another word for 'selling' so a retail manager is in charge of a shop or a store. At first, a retail manager usually manages a department – that is, one small part of the store. He or she manages different departments in the first two or three years and then, finally, manages a complete store.

A retail manager must organize the work of the staff – the people in the department. He or she must also check the stock – the things for sale – and make sure there are enough things for customers to buy. A manager must be confident. A manager must be able to deal with people – staff and customers. The normal working hours are nine to five, six days a week, but there is lots of overtime. This is not paid for in many cases. A manager usually gets discounts on purchases from the store. In other words, a manager can buy things from the store for 10 or 20 per cent less than other customers.

You need a degree for most stores. A degree in business or retail management is obviously the best. Stores are looking for people with sales experience. You can get this in the summer holidays or in the evenings and at weekends. The starting salary is quite low – about £12,000 in a small company, perhaps £17,000 in a large company.

🎧 4.1

Presenter:	4.1. Theme 4: Science and nature Lesson 4.1. Vocabulary for listening: Tables, graphs, experiments Exercise A1. Listen. Add the information to the table and the graph.
Teacher:	Add the word *London* to the first column of the table. Write the data for London in the table. You can get it from the graph. Write one number in each block. Add the missing months to the graph. Write them on the horizontal axis. Now write the missing temperatures on the vertical axis. Add the data for Abu Dhabi to the graph and draw the line.

🎧 4.2

Presenter:	4.2. Exercise A2. Listen and answer the questions.
Teacher:	a. What do the table and the graph compare? b. Which one displays the information more clearly? Why? c. What does the dotted line in the graph represent? d. What is another way you can display results in a graph? e. Why is it useful to organize information in this way? f. Which websites are useful for research about average temperatures?

🎧 4.3

Presenter:	4.3. Exercise B. Listen. Tick the correct column to show the stressed syllable.
Voice:	1. average 3. circle 5. compare 7. display 9. result 2. axis 4. column 6. data 8. research 10. table

🎧 4.4

Presenter:	4.4. Exercise C. Listen. Complete the text with words from the list on the right.
Lecturer:	Science is the study of how things work in the world. A scientist usually works in a laboratory. He or she works with many different kinds of materials, for example plastic or metal, and liquids. A scientist tests things to prove a hypothesis. A hypothesis is an idea that something is true. Scientists must collect all the facts first. Then he or she often puts the facts in a table with columns of information, or in a graph, with blocks or lines that represent the information.

🎧 4.5

Presenter:	4.5. Lesson 4.2. Real-time listening: Scientists and the scientific method Exercise A2. Listen to the introduction and answer the first two questions.
Arthur Burns:	This week on *So you want to be* ... we are looking at the job of a scientist. What is science? What do scientists do? And, possibly, the most important question of all: Is science the right career for you? First, what is science? Science is the study of how things work in the world. The word *science* comes from Greek and Latin words meaning 'to know'. What do scientists do? Well, scientists are not satisfied just to think something is true. They must prove it. Proving means showing that something is always true. In this way, scientists are different from other people. Let me show you the difference. I know that plants need sunlight and water to live. At least, I think that's true. But thinking is not enough for a scientist. If a scientist thinks something is true, he or she wants to prove it.

🎧 4.6

Presenter:	4.6. Exercise B. Listen and complete the notes below about the scientific method.
Arthur Burns:	How exactly can scientists prove that something is true? They must follow the scientific method. A method is a way of doing something. But what is the scientific method? It works like this: Firstly a scientist makes a hypothesis, which means an idea of the truth. Then he or she tests the hypothesis. Scientists can test a hypothesis in two main ways. They can do an experiment, which means a test in a laboratory. Scientists study

what happens during the experiment. Or they can do research, which means looking up information. They usually do research in a library or, nowadays, on the Internet. With research, scientists look at what happened in the past.

In both cases – experiments and research – they collect data. Data is information before it is organized. Then they display the results in a table or graph. They draw conclusions. Conclusions are what you learn from an experiment. The hypothesis is proved – or disproved.

Does this sound interesting to you? Is science the right career for you?

🎧 4.7

Presenter:	**4.7. Lesson 4.3. Learning new listening skills: Predicting the next word** **Exercise B2. Listen to some of Arthur's sentences from the radio programme. Number a word in the table in Exercise A each time Arthur pauses.**
Arthur Burns:	1. Science is the study of how things work in the … 2. The word *science* comes from Greek and Latin words meaning to … 3. Scientists must prove that something is … 4. They must follow the scientific … 5. Scientists must collect … 6. They display the results in a table or …

🎧 4.8

Presenter:	**4.8. Exercise C1. Listen and predict the next word.**
Arthur Burns:	I made a … Plants need things to help them … I think they need sunlight and … I bought three … I tested the … I put one plant in a cupboard so it did not get any … The plant went … The second plant did not get any … The plant … I put the third plant in … I gave it … It grew … It did not go … I proved my …

🎧 4.9

Presenter:	**4.9. Exercise C2. Listen to the complete talk. Check your ideas.**
Arthur Burns:	I made a hypothesis. Plants need things to help them grow. I think they need sunlight and water. I bought three plants. I tested the hypothesis. I put one plant in a cupboard so it did not get any sunlight. The plant went yellow. The second plant did not get any water. The plant died. I put the third plant in sunlight. I gave it water. It grew well. It did not go yellow. I proved my hypothesis.

🎧 4.10

Presenter:	**4.10. Exercise D. Listen and copy each word from Arthur's talk into the correct column.**
Arthur Burns:	that, the, they, both, then, there, with, hypothesis, thing, truth

🎧 4.11

Presenter:	**4.11. Exercise E1. Listen. Which is the odd one out?**
Voice:	test, when, then, pen, she, bed, many, any, head, again

🎵 4.12

Presenter: **4.12. Lesson 4.3. Grammar for listening: Articles; introduction phrases**

Exercise B. Listen and check your answers.

Radio presenter: Firstly, a scientist makes a hypothesis, which means an idea of the truth. Then he or she tests the hypothesis. Scientists can test a hypothesis in two main ways. They can do an experiment, which means a test in a laboratory. Scientists study what happens during an experiment. Or they can do research, which means looking up information. They usually do research in a library or, nowadays, on the Internet.

🎵 4.13

Presenter: **4.13. Exercise C. Listen and check your ideas.**

Voice:
1. I know that plants need water.
2. I think that sugar damages teeth.
3. I don't believe that the research is finished.
4. It means that we don't have enough data.
5. It proves that the hypothesis is correct.
6. The graph shows us that the average temperature in summer is 17°C.
7. Scientists have proved that seawater temperatures are getting warmer.

🎵 4.14

Presenter: **4.14. Lesson 4.5. Applying new listening skills: Proving a hypothesis: Drinks can damage your teeth**

Exercise B. Listen. Put these groups of words in the correct order.

Student: Remember: my hypothesis is that cola and other sugary drinks damage your teeth.

The experiment: I bought four types of drink: cola, fruit drink, fresh fruit juice and water. I also brought in some clean eggshells. Why eggshells? Because they are made of similar material to human teeth.

🎵 4.15

Presenter: **4.15. Exercise C1. Listen to the student describing the experiment. When she stops speaking, tick the correct word from each pair of words below.**

Student: Remember: my hypothesis is that cola and other sugary drinks damage your [PAUSE] teeth.
The experiment: I bought four types of drink: cola, fruit drink, fresh fruit juice and [PAUSE] water. I also brought in some clean [PAUSE] eggshells. Why eggshells? Because they are made of similar material to human teeth.
I put each drink into a different [PAUSE] glass.
I made a small hole in each shell with a [PAUSE] pin.
I tied each piece of eggshell onto a piece of [PAUSE] thread.
Then I hung each piece of thread so that the eggshell was in the [PAUSE] liquid.
I left the four glasses of liquid for one week.
After one week I compared the pieces of egg [PAUSE] shell.
The eggshells from the glasses of cola and fruit drink were very soft.
The eggshells from the glasses of fruit juice and water were not [PAUSE] damaged.
My conclusion is: cola and fruit drinks damage your teeth.

🎵 4.16

Presenter: **4.16. Lesson 4.6. Vocabulary for speaking: Diagrams and explanations**

Exercise B. Listen and number the words below in the order that you hear them.

Lecturer: Isaac Newton explained about sunlight over 300 years ago. He said that sunlight contains seven colours. Light from the Sun hits the Earth. It passes through the atmosphere. When white light from the Sun hits water, it splits into seven colours. This produces a rainbow in the sky. The opposite is also true. If you mix the seven colours of natural light together, you get white light.

🎵 4.17

Presenter: **4.17. Exercise C1. Listen and check.**

Presenter: Conversation 1.

Voice A: What is the water cycle?
Voice B: I'm not sure. Is it something to do with rain?

Presenter: Conversation 2.

Voice A: What's that noise?
Voice B: I think it's thunder.

Presenter:	Conversation 3.
Voice A:	What are clouds made of?
Voice B:	Water vapour, I think.
Presenter:	Conversation 4.
Voice A:	Why do we have tides at the coast?
Voice B:	I don't know. Perhaps the wind causes them.

🔊 4.18 [DVD] 4.A

Presenter: **4.18. Lesson 4.7. Real-time speaking: The water cycle**

Ruth:	Can I help?
Martha:	Yes, please. We've got to study the pictures and the information, and on Tuesday we have to explain it to the other students in our group and draw a picture to show them.
Ruth:	Can you use notes?
Martha:	No.
Ruth:	What's it about?
Martha:	We're doing weather. My topic is rain: 'Why does it rain?' What do you think?
Ruth:	Why does it rain? ... That's easy. It's because ... um ... I don't know.
Martha:	OK. Shall I try out my talk on you?
Ruth:	Yes, go ahead.
Martha:	OK. I'll draw a picture for you, too. Right. (*She draws*) This is the sky. This is the land. These are rivers and lakes. Now, rain is part of the water cycle.
Ruth:	The what?
Martha:	The water cycle. Look. The Sun is here (*She draws*), and it heats up the surface of the water, here. The water is a liquid, of course, but it heats up and it turns into a gas. The gas is called water vapour. The water vapour rises into the air, like this (*She draws*).
Ruth:	What's that?
Martha:	That's the water vapour rising. It rises because it's hot.
Ruth:	OK.
Martha:	But the atmosphere here (*She points to the sky on her drawing*), above the Earth, is cold. The vapour makes clouds because it cools. Here are the clouds (*She draws clouds*). The clouds move with the wind. They collect more and more water, and get bigger and bigger, like this (*She draws more and bigger clouds*). Finally, they are full of water, and burst. The water falls from the clouds. In other words, it rains.
Ruth:	Ahhh ...
Martha:	This is the rain falling (*She draws*). Some rain falls directly into the rivers, lakes and seas. The rest falls onto the land, and from there it travels back to the seas, rivers and lakes. And the cycle continues, round and round, like this (*She draws*).
Ruth:	That's great.

🔊 4.19

Presenter: **4.19. Everyday English: Offering and requesting, accepting and refusing**

Exercise C. Listen to the conversations. Then practise them in pairs.

Presenter:	Conversation 1.
Voice A:	Are you OK there?
Voice B:	I don't understand this assignment.
Voice A:	Let me have a look.
Voice B:	Thank you.
Presenter:	Conversation 2.
Voice A:	Would you like some help with that?
Voice B:	No, thanks. I can manage.
Voice A:	Are you sure?
Voice B:	Yes, I'm fine. Thanks anyway.
Presenter:	Conversation 3.
Voice A:	Can I help you?
Voice B:	Yes, please. Black coffee please.
Voice A:	Medium or large?
Voice B:	Mm. Large.
Presenter:	Conversation 4.
Voice A:	Could you help me with this?
Voice B:	I'm afraid I can't. I haven't finished myself.
Voice A:	OK. Don't worry.
Voice B:	Give me a few minutes.

Presenter:	Conversation 5.

Voice A:	Could you help me with this?
Voice B:	Of course.
Voice A:	Sorry to trouble you.
Voice B:	It's no trouble.

Presenter:	Conversation 6.

Voice A:	Have you got a moment?
Voice B:	No, sorry. I'm in a hurry.
Voice A:	OK. That's fine.
Voice B:	Sorry.

4.20 DVD 4.B

Presenter:	**4.20. Lesson 4.8. Learning new speaking skills: Scientific explanations**

Student 1:	The title of my talk is 'Why is the sky blue?'. This is white light travelling from the Sun. And the light contains all the colours. Here's orange, here's yellow, here's red, this is green, and this is blue. The white light hits dust and the smoke in the atmosphere, like this. And the blue light scatters more than any other colour. And that's why the sky is blue.

Student 2:	My explanation is about why the sky is red at sunset. This is white light travelling from the Sun. White light contains all the colours. These are the colours; this is red, this is orange, here's yellow … and green, and this is blue. The white light hits dust and smoke in the atmosphere, like this. The blue and green light scatters, like this. This is the red, orange and yellow light. Some of it comes in a straight line to our eyes, like this.

Student 3:	Why are clouds white? My explanation will answer that question. This is white light travelling from the Sun. White light contains all the colours. These are the colours; this is red, this is orange, this is yellow … this is green, and blue. The white light hits water vapour, like this. All the light scatters by the same amount. We see all the light at the same time, like this. All the colours together make the clouds white, like this.

4.21

Presenter:	**4.21. Portfolio: Natural events**

Presenter:	Exercise B1. Group 1.

Lecturer:	I'm going to talk to you today about tides. Tides, spelt T-I-D-E-S, are regular changes in the height of the sea. There are low tides and high tides at certain times in the day everywhere in the world. High tide is when the sea covers a lot of the beach. Low tide is when the sea is far out. But why do we have tides?
	Tides are caused by gravity. Gravity usually means the attraction or pull towards the centre of the Earth. The gravity of the Earth causes things to fall to the ground. However, the *Earth's* gravity does not cause tides. The gravity of the *moon* causes tides. As the Earth turns, one side and then the other is close to the moon. When the sea is closer to the moon, the moon's gravity pulls the sea towards it so the sea gets deeper on that side, and shallower at the North Pole and the South Pole.

4.22

Presenter:	**4.22. Exercise B1. Group 2.**

Lecturer:	I'm going to talk to you today about the wind. Wind is air moving from one place to the other. Sometimes it moves fast and sometimes it moves slowly. Sometimes it hardly moves at all. Why?
	The wind always blows from an area of high pressure to an area of low pressure. *Pressure* – spelt P-R-E-S-S-U-R-E comes from the verb *press*. The air presses on the Earth all the time. But in some places the pressure is high and in some places it is low. Why is that?
	Cold air is heavier than hot air. When air gets hot, it rises. This causes low pressure. When it gets cold, it falls. This causes high pressure. So, all the time, there are areas of high pressure and areas of low pressure all around the world. The wind blows from an area of high pressure to an area of low pressure.

5.1

Presenter:	**5.1. Theme 5: The physical world**
	Lesson 5.1. Vocabulary for listening: Location in the world, physical features
	Exercise B1. Listen to descriptions of six countries and look at the map. Number each country in the correct order on the map.

Voice:	1. It is in North America. It is north of the USA.
	2. It is in Asia. It is southeast of Pakistan.
	3. It is in Africa. It is west of Egypt.
	4. It is in Europe. It is west of Spain.

5. It is in Oceania. It is a large island. It is on the Tropic of Capricorn. It is near New Zealand.
6. It is in South America. It is between the Equator and the Tropic of Capricorn. It is north of Argentina.

🎧 5.2

Presenter: **5.2. Exercise B2. Listen. Is each sentence true or false?**

Voice:
1. The Equator runs through Central Africa.
2. New Zealand consists of four islands.
3. The whole of India is between the Tropics.
4. This map gives geographical information.
5. The map shows ten continents.
6. The area north of the Equator contains most of the world's countries.

🎧 5.3

Presenter: **5.3. Exercise C1. Listen to the pronunciation of ten words for physical features. Find and number them in the list on the right.**

Voice:
1. border	3. freshwater lake	5. island	7. rainforest	9. volcano
2. coastline	4. gulf	6. peninsula	8. mountain range	10. ocean

🎧 5.4

Presenter: **5.4. Exercise C2. Listen to a sentence about each physical feature. Find an example of each feature on the map.**

Voice:
a. A peninsula is a piece of land with water on three sides.
b. An island is a piece of land surrounded by water.
c. A gulf is an area of water with land on three sides.
d. A lake is an area of water surrounded by land.
e. An ocean is a very large area of water.
f. The coastline of a country is where the land meets the sea or the ocean.
g. A border is one where country meets another country.

🎧 5.5 [DVD] 5.A

Presenter: **5.5. Lesson 5.2. Real-time listening: The countries of Central America**

Lecturer: Let's focus on Nicaragua. This is a map of central America, as you can see. Nicaragua is located at 13 degrees north, between the Equator and Tropic of Cancer. It's 85 degrees west. It is the largest country in Central America, with an area of 129,500 square kilometres.

The capital city, Managua, which is spelt M-A-N-A-G-U-A, is in the west of the country, on a lake. There are two large lakes in the country. I'll tell you about the other one in a moment. Nicaragua is bordered to the northwest by Honduras, here, and to the south by Costa Rica. You can see that Central America is long and thin. Like most of the countries in Central America, Nicaragua has two coastlines – one to the east, on the Caribbean Sea, and one to the west, on the Pacific Ocean. The word *nicaragua* apparently means 'surrounded by water' in a native language.

Student: Excuse me. How do you spell *Caribbean*?

Lecturer: *Caribbean* has one R and two Bs: C-A-R-I-B-B-E-A-N. Now, the country consists of three main areas: rainforest in the eastern region, then mountains in the north, here, including a lot of volcanos. These mountains are the Central Highlands – in Spanish, the *Altiplano*. Then we have the warm Pacific Coast area in the west, where we find the largest freshwater lake in Central America, Lake Nicaragua. There are two volcanoes on the island in the middle of this lake. It's a very beautiful place. There are a lot of volcanoes in the country – perhaps you know the San Cristobal volcano. Nicaragua also has the largest river in Central America, the river Coco.

Student: Sorry. Where is the river?

Lecturer: The river Coco forms the border with Honduras to the north here. It's just spelt C-O-C-O.

🎧 5.6

Presenter: **5.6. Exercise D2. Listen to the words and tick the pronunciation that you hear.**

Voice: river, south, west, bordered, Cancer, kilometre, north, freshwater

🎧 5.7

Presenter: **5.7. Lesson 5.3. Learning new listening skills: Transferring information to a map**

Exercise A1. Listen and tick the form of the word that you hear in each case.

Voice:
a. tropical	c. locates	e. bordering
b. centre	d. rainforest	f. coastline

Lecture extract 1:

The capital city of Honduras is Tegucigalpa. It's located in the south-central area of the country – just here. I'll spell it for you: T-E-G, U-C-I, G-A-L, P-A.

Lecture extract 2:

So mark on your map the Sierra Madre mountains. It's a large mountain range that covers the south and the west. Be careful to copy the correct spelling: S-I-E, double-R-A, and Madre: M-A-D-R-E.

Lecture extract 3:

The highest peak in Honduras is Celaque at 2,827 m. It's situated in the west of the country, in the mountains of the Celaque National Park.

Lecture extract 4:

Central America's second longest river is in Honduras, the river Patuca. It begins here in the south-central area of the country, to the east of the capital. It flows northeast, like this, to the Atlantic Ocean.

Lecture extract 5:

The country's largest lake, Lake Yojoa, is located in the western part of the country, to the east of Celaque.

Lecture extract 6:

Honduras is bordered by Nicaragua to the south, of course, and by Guatemala to the northwest, and El Salvador to the southwest.

Lecture extract 7:

There is a group of islands off the north coast called the Bay Islands. These islands belong to Honduras.

♫ 5.9

Presenter:	**5.9. Exercise C2. Listen. Circle the word in each row with a different vowel sound.**
Voice:	a. what, four, not, on
	b. sorry, wash, come, from
	c. more, coast, fall, for
	d. long, not, was, north
	e. locate, border, draw, for
	f. before, small, home, warm

♫ 5.10

Presenter:	**5.10. Exercise C3. Listen and write the words you hear.**
Voice:	sort, common, corner, top, watch, saw, forest, orange, autumn, hot, morning, always, dawn, honest, block

♫ 5.11

Presenter:	**5.11. Lesson 5.4. Grammar for listening: *There* as replacement subject**
	Exercise A2. Listen and check.
Voice:	1. There's a lake in the south.
	2. There are many natural features in the country.
	3. There are several islands in the gulf.
	4. There is a long thin peninsula in the south of the capital.
	5. There isn't a mountain range in the east.

♫ 5.12

Presenter:	**5.12. Exercise B. Listen. Mark the features on the map on the right.**
Voice:	There are a lot of mountains in the north and east of the country. There's a large volcano in the mountains in the north, but there aren't any volcanoes in the other mountains. There's a large lake in the centre of the country. There's a river from the mountains in the north to the lake. There's another river from the lake to the coast to the east of the peninsula. There's a city on the west side of the lake. There's another city on the west side of the peninsula. It's very dry in the east but there aren't any deserts there.

Presenter: 5.13. Exercise D. Listen. Which piece of information will come next?

Voice:
1. There are some containers in the lab.
2. There's a plant in a pot.
3. There are some students in the cafeteria.
4. There aren't any people in the room.
5. There's an exam in the hall today.
6. There isn't any coffee in the pot.

5.14 DVD 5.C

Presenter: 5.14. Lesson 5.5. Applying new listening skills: Mexico: location and physical features

Student: Mexico, officially the United Mexican States, is located on the Tropic of Cancer at 23 degrees north and 102 degrees west.

It has a long border in the north with the USA – over 3,000 kilometres – while to the southeast it has borders with Guatemala and with its smallest neighbour, Belize. It has a coastline to the west on the Pacific Ocean, again a very long coastline, and also to the east on the Gulf of Mexico. Where it meets Belize in the east, Mexico has a coastline on a third body of water, the Caribbean Sea. You can see why this country is popular with people who want a holiday at the beach.

The country's capital, Mexico City, is in the south-central area of the country, about the same distance from the west and east coasts.

Many people do not think of Mexico as a large country, but it actually has a total area of 1,972,550 square kilometres – about a fifth of the area of the USA. Much of the country consists of a mountain range called the Sierra Madre. These mountains run in two parts down the west and east sides of the country. These mountains continue from the USA in the north. Between the west and east parts of the Sierra Madre is the high Central Plateau. Some of the largest cities, including Mexico City, are on the Central Plateau. Careful with the spelling of *plateau*: P-L-A-T-E-A-U.

A chain of volcanoes runs east to west across the country in the south. Many of them are active. In the far southeast of Mexico, there is a lowland peninsula called the Yucatán Peninsula. That's spelt Y-U-C-A-T-A-N. It is a low, flat area. The southern part has dense rainforest. Yucatán is home to the Mayan people. If you do history, maybe you also know that central Mexico contains the area of the ancient Aztec culture – ruled by the Mexican people.

Thank you.

5.15

Presenter: 5.15. Lesson 5.6. Vocabulary for speaking: Continents

Exercise C1. Listen and check.

Presenter: Conversation 1.

Voice A: We have a big mountain range in my country.
Voice B: What is a *range*?

Presenter: Conversation 2.

Voice A: Is your country landlocked?
Voice B: No, it has a coastline on the Mediterranean.

Presenter: Conversation 3.

Voice A: What's a *plain*?
Voice B: It's a big flat area of land.

5.16

Presenter: 5.16. Lesson 5.7. Real-time speaking: Croatia

Exercise A1. Listen to the words. Tick the correct column to show the number of syllables.

Voice: Europe, capital, coastline, feature, low, mountainous, north, plain, range, rocky

5.17

Presenter: 5.17. Exercise A2. Listen again and repeat the words.

[REPEAT OF SCRIPT FROM 5.16]

5.18. Exercise C1. Listen. Make notes beside each heading in the table at the bottom of the page.

Student: I am going to talk about my country, which is Croatia, in southern Europe. First of all, I will describe the size and the location. Then I'll tell you about the capital city. Finally, I'll mention some of the physical features of the country.

OK. The country is quite small. We are 127th out of 203 countries in the world. The country has a strange shape. It looks like a dog's back leg!

Croatia is north of Bosnia-Herzegovina and south of Hungary and Slovenia. We have a border with Serbia to the northeast. There is also a tiny border with Montenegro in the far southeast. In the south and west there is a coastline on the Adriatic Sea.

The capital city is Zagreb, Z-A-G-R-E-B, Zagreb, which is in the north of the country. In fact, I don't live in the capital. My hometown is a small place in the north called Ludbreg, which is north of Zagreb.

Croatia is a very beautiful country. There are low mountains in many parts of the country, including the north and the northeast. There is a flat plain along the border with Hungary. There are many rivers which cross this plain. The Danube river, which is the second longest in Europe, forms part of the border with Serbia. There are also many lakes, including the Plitvice – that's P-L-I-T-V-I-C-E, lakes which are part of a national park with forests and waterfalls. In fact, this is a UNESCO World Heritage site. Finally, there is a beautiful rocky coastline. Off the coast there are over 1,000 islands.

5.19

Presenter: **5.19. Everyday English: Going places**

Exercise B. Listen and check your ideas.

Presenter: Conversation 1.

Voice A: Excuse me.
Voice B: Yes, sir. Can I help you?
Voice A: Yes, please. Where's the nearest tube station?
Voice B: Go straight down this road. It's on the next corner.

Presenter: Conversation 2.

Voice A: Where are we on this map?
Voice B: Let's see. We're here.
Voice A: And where's the hotel?
Voice B: Mm. About a ten-minute walk, I think.

Presenter: Conversation 3.

Voice A: Which room are we in?
Voice B: J32. But I'm not sure where it is.
Voice A: Here we are. It's on the fourth floor.
Voice B: OK. We'd better take the lift.

Presenter: Conversation 4.

Voice A: Are you going to the meeting about fees?
Voice B: Yes, I am. I think it's in the main hall.
Voice A: Where's that?
Voice B: Not far. I'll show you.

Presenter: Conversation 5.

Voice A: How far are we from the bus station?
Voice B: I think it's in the next road on the left.
Voice A: No it isn't! It's the second on the right.
Voice B: Oh, yes. I've got the map the wrong way round!

Presenter: Conversation 6.

Voice A: Hi you two! Where are you going?
Voice B: We're on our way to the café.
Voice A: Can I join you?
Voice B: Yeah, sure. But hurry up, we're starving.

⏺ 5.20

Presenter:	5.20. Lesson 5.8. Learning new speaking skills: Introducing a talk

Exercise A1. Listen to these sentences. What is the sound of the letter *s* in each case?

Voice:	a. Where's that?
	b. Yes, that's right.
	c. How do you spell that?
	d. Sorry. What did you say?
	e. It goes through the capital.

⏺ 5.21

Presenter:	5.21. Lesson 5.9. Grammar for speaking: Location: *which*

Exercise A2. Listen. Which place are they talking about in each case?

Voice 1:	It's on a river near the coast.
Voice 2:	It's in the centre of the country.
Voice 3:	It's in the mountains near the border.
Voice 4:	It's on a lake in the east.
Voice 5:	It's between the centre and the northern border.
Voice 6:	It's on the northeast border.

⏺ 5.22

Presenter:	**5.22. Portfolio: Comparing countries**
Presenter:	Exercise B1. Group A: Kuwait.

Voice: I'm going to talk to you today about one of the countries of the Middle East. The name of the country is Kuwait – in English that spelt K-U-W-A-I-T. Kuwait is located between latitudes 29 and 30 north and longitudes 47 and 48 east.

The capital is Kuwait City. It is located on the edge of the country, by the coast. However, Kuwait is not the largest city. That is Al Salimiyah, which is very close to Kuwait City.

The country is very small. It covers an area of only 17,820 square kilometres.

Kuwait is only bordered by Iraq and Saudi Arabia, but it is very near Iran.
Kuwait's land is mostly flat, desert. Its highest point is an unnamed location which is 306 metres high. Kuwait does not have much natural fresh water or any rivers.

⏺ 5.23

Presenter:	**5.23. Exercise B1. Group B: Yemen.**

Voice: I'm going to talk to you today about one of the countries of the Middle East. The name of the country is Yemen. Yemen is located between latitudes 14 and 17 north and longitudes 43 and 53 east.

The capital is Sana'a. It is in the Jebel an Nabi Shu'ayb mountains, which contain the highest point of the country at 3,760 metres.

Aden, spelt A-D-E-N in English, is the second biggest city. It is on the south coast. The city of Mocha on the coast of Yemen is famous for its chocolatey coffee.

The country covers an area of 527,970 square kilometres.

Yemen is on the Gulf of Aden to the south. It is bordered by Oman in the east and Saudi Arabia in the north.

Yemen's land comprises a narrow coastal plain in front of flat-topped hills and rugged mountains.

A		
ability (*n*) [= skill]	1.6, 3.11	
abroad (*adj*)	3.6	
academic (*adj*)	1.1	
access (*n* and *v*)	1.1, 5.16	
accommodation (*n*)	1.1	
accurate (*adj*)	1.11	
act (*v*)	2.1	
act on impulse	2.16	
active (*adj*) [of a volcano]	5.16	
ad (*n*)	3.6	
address (*n*)	1.16	
advantage (*n*)	5.16	
advert (*n*)	3.6	
advertisement (*n*)	3.6	
advisor (*n*)	3.6	
affect (*v*)	4.11	
Africa (*n*)	5.6	
aggressive (*adj*)	2.6, 2.16	
agricultural (*adj*)	5.16	
agriculture (*n*)	5.11	
aim (*n* and *v*)	2.1	
almost (*adv*)	5.11	
alone (*adj*)	2.1	
along (*prep*)	5.11	
alphabetical order	3.1	
always (*adv*)	2.11	
America (*n*)	5.6	
amount (*n*)	4.6	
analyze (*v*)	1.11	
ancient (*adj*)	2.1	
and so on	2.6	
annual (*adj*)	5.16	
appearance (*n*)	3.16	
applicable (*adj*)	1.16	
applicant (*n*)	1.16	
application (*n*)	1.16	
apply (*v*)	1.16	
appoint (*v*)	3.16	
appointment (*n*)	3.16	
appropriate (*adj*)	1.16, 3.11	
architect (*n*)	3.11	
architecture (*n*)	3.11	
area (*n*)	4.6, 5.1	
area (*n*) [= location]	5.16	
around (*prep*) [= approximately]	6.16	
arrow (*n*)	3.16	
article (*n*)	1.1	
Asia (*n*)	5.6	

assignment (*n*)	1.1
assistant (*n*)	3.6
atmosphere (*n*)	4.6
attachment (*n*) [= document]	1.11
attitude (*n*)	2.16, 3.16
average (*adj*)	4.1, 4.11
axis (*n*)	4.1

B		
background (*n*)	5.16	
background (*n*) [= upbringing]	2.11	
bank (*n*) [of a river]	5.16	
base (*n*)	4.11, 4.16	
basic (*adj*)	2.16	
bay (*n*)	5.16	
behave (*v*)	2.1	
behaviour (*n*)	1.6, 2.1, 2.6	
behind (*prep*)	5.6	
benefit (*n* and *v*)	3.11	
best (*adj*)	1.6	
between (*prep*)	5.6, 5.11	
block (*n*)	4.1	
block capital	1.16	
body (*n*)	2.11	
body language (*n*)	3.6	
border (*n* and *v*)	5.1, 5.6	
brain (*n*)	2.1	
bully (*n* and *v*)	2.11	
bursar (*n*)	1.1	
burst (*v*)	4.6	
businessperson (*n*)	3.1	

C		
calm (*adj*)	2.16	
campus (*n*)	1.1	
candidate (*n*)	3.16	
career (*n*)	3.6	
career-entry (*adj*)	3.11	
careers advisor	3.6	
central (*adj*)	5.1	
centre (*n*)	4.11	
centre of attention	2.16	
century (*n*)	2.1	
certificate (*n*)	1.6	
chain (*n*)	5.11	
change (*v*)	2.6	
charge (*n*) [electrical]	4.6	
chronologically (*adv*)	3.1	
clear (*adj*)	2.6	
clerical (*adj*)	3.6	
cloud (*n*)	4.6	

everybody (*n*)	2.11	
everyone (*n*)	2.11	
exactly (*adv*)	5.6, 5.11	
examination (*n*)	1.6	
excitement (*n*)	2.16	
excuse me	2.6	
executive (*n*)	3.16	
expand (*v*)	4.6	
expect (*v*)	3.1	
experience (*n* and *v*)	3.11	
experience (*n*)	1.16, 3.16	
experiment (*n* and *v*)	4.1	
experiment (*n*)	1.11	
explain (*v*)	4.6	
explanation (*n*)	4.6	
extinct (*adj*)	5.11	
extracurricular (*adj*)	1.11	
extreme (*adj* and *n*)	2.16	
extremely (*adv*)	4.11	
extrovert (*n*)	2.16	
eye contact (*n*)	3.6	

F

face (*n*)	2.11
fact (*n*)	4.1
factor (*n*)	4.11
faculty (*n*)	1.1
fairly (*adv*)	5.11
fall (*v*)	4.6
farmland (*n*)	5.11
feature (*n*)	5.1, 5.6, 5.11
fee (*n*)	1.1
fertile (*adj*)	5.16
field trip	1.1
fifth (*n*)	5.1
figure (*n*)	4.16
file (*n* and *v*)	3.1
fill (*v*)	4.16
fit (*v*)	2.16
flat (*adj*)	5.1, 5.6, 5.16
flood (*n* and *v*)	5.16
flow (*v*)	4.16
flow chart	3.16
force (*n*)	4.16
foreground (*n*)	5.16
form (*n*)	1.6, 1.16
form (*v*)	2.1
freelance (*adj* and *n*)	3.11
fresher (*n*)	1.1
freshwater (*adj*)	5.1

friendly (*adj*)	2.6, 2.16
friendship (*n*)	2.1
full (*adj*)	4.6
full (*adj*) [name]	1.16
full-time (*adj*)	3.6
furthest (*adj*)	4.11

G

gas (*n*)	4.6
geographical (*adj*)	5.1, 5.6
graduate (*n* and *v*)	1.1, 1.6
graph (*n*)	4.1
gravity (*n*)	4.6
ground (*n*)	4.11
group (*n*)	2.1
gulf (*n*)	5.1

H

hall of residence	1.1
head (*n*) [of]	1.1
heading (*n*)	1.11
heat (*n* and *v*)	4.6
height (*n*)	2.11, 4.16, 5.11
hemisphere (*n*)	4.11
hide [one's] feelings	2.16
high (*adj*)	4.16
hit (*v*)	4.6
hobby (*n*)	1.16
hole (*n*)	4.16
hometown (*n*)	5.1
honest (*adj*)	3.6
horizon (*n*)	4.11
horizontal (*adj*)	4.1
human (*adj* and *n*)	2.6
human (*n*)	2.1
human race	2.1
hypothesis (*n*)	4.1

I

identity (*n*)	2.1, 2.6
ill (*adj*)	3.1
impact (*n*)	5.16
implication (*n*)	4.16
impolite (*adj*)	3.6
impression (*n*)	3.6, 3.11
in charge [of]	1.1
in order (*adv* and *n*)	3.1
in the centre of (*prep*)	5.6
indicate (*v*)	4.16
individual (*n*)	2.1
industry (*n*)	5.16
influence (*n* and *v*)	2.6, 4.11
inland (*adj* and *adv*)	4.11

inland (*adv*)	5.11	
insect (*n*)	5.16	
intelligence (*n*)	3.16	
interact (*v*)	2.16	
interest (*n*)	1.16	
(the) Internet (*n*)	1.11	
interpersonal (*adj*)	3.16	
interview (*n and v*)	3.16	
interview (*n*)	3.6	
interviewee (*n*)	3.6	
interviewer (*n*)	3.6	
introduction (*n*)	4.16	
introvert (*n*)	2.16	
investigate (*v*)	4.16	
involve (*v*)	3.1	
island (*n*)	5.1	

J job title (*n*) — 3.6
journalist (*n*) — 3.11

K keep (*v*) [order] — 1.6
key (*adj*) — 2.1
kind (*adj and n*) — 2.11
kindergarten (*n*) — 1.6
kindness (*n*) — 3.11

L laboratory (*n*) — 4.1
lake (*n*) — 4.6
landlocked (*adj*) — 5.6
landscape (*n*) — 5.11
last (*v*) — 1.6
latitude (*n*) — 4.11
lazy (*adj*) — 3.6
lecture (*n*) — 1.1
lecturer (*n*) — 1.1
left (*n*) — 5.6
level (*n*) — 1.16
librarian (*n*) — 1.1
lie (*v*) — 5.11
lift (*v*) — 4.16
light (*n*) — 4.6
lightning (*n*) — 4.6
line (*n*) — 4.1
link (*n and v*) — 5.16
link (*n*) — 1.11
link (*v*) — 2.1
liquid (*n*) — 4.1
locate (*v*) — 4.11, 5.1
location (*n*) — 5.1
longitude (*n*) — 4.11

look (*v*) [= appear] — 3.6
look up (*v*) — 1.1, 4.1
lose [one's] temper — 2.16
low (*adj*) — 5.1
lower case — 1.16
lowland (*n*) — 5.11

M main (*adj*) — 5.1
major (*adj*) — 5.11
majority (*n*) — 5.11
make fun of — 2.11
manage (*v*) — 1.11
manager (*n*) — 3.1
manual (*adj*) — 3.6
mark (*n and v*) — 1.11
mark (*v*) — 4.16
marsh (*n*) — 5.16
(the) mass media (*n*) — 3.11
material (*n*) — 4.1
measure (*v*) — 4.16
measurement (*n*) — 4.11
medicine (*n*) — 2.1
meet a deadline — 3.11
meeting (*n*) — 3.1
member (*n*) — 3.16
membership (*n*) — 1.16
memory (*n*) — 2.1
mentally (*adv*) — 2.11
meridian (*n*) — 4.11
mess (*n*) — 3.1
method (*n*) — 4.1
middle (*n*) — 5.16
(the) Middle East (*n*) — 5.6
mind (*n*) — 2.1
mind (*v*) — 2.6
minus (*prep*) — 4.11
miserable (*adj*) — 2.11
mix (*v*) — 4.6
mixed (*adj*) — 1.6
mixture (*n*) — 2.16
money (*n*) — 3.1
mostly (*adv*) — 5.11
motivate (*v*) — 3.11
motivation (*n*) — 3.16
mountainous (*adj*) — 5.1, 5.6

N natural (*adj*) — 4.6
negative (*adj*) — 4.6
neighbour (*n*) — 2.1, 5.11
never (*adv*) — 2.11

next to (*prep*)	5.6	
no one (*n*)	2.11	
nobody (*n*)	2.11	
normal (*adj*)	2.11	
northern (*adj*)	4.11	
notes (*n pl*)	5.11	
nursery (*adj*) [school]	1.6	

O

occupy (*v*)	5.11
ocean (*n*)	5.1
Oceania (*n*)	5.6
officially (*adv*)	5.11
often (*adv*)	2.11
on time (*adv*)	3.1
opinion (*n*)	1.11
opposite (*prep*)	5.6
optimistic (*adj*)	2.16
organization (*n*)	3.6
organize (*v*)	1.16, 3.1, 4.1
original (*adj*)	3.16
other (*adj*)	2.6
out (*adj*) [= not in a library]	1.11
outgoing (*adj*)	3.6
outside (*adj*)	3.6
overtime (*n*)	3.11
own (*pron*)	2.6

P

paragraph (*n*)	1.16
part of speech	3.11
participate (*v*)	1.16
participation (*n*)	1.1
part-time (*adj*)	3.6
pass through (*v*)	4.6
password (*n*)	1.11
paste (*v*)	1.11
pattern (*n*)	2.1
pay (*n and v*)	3.6
peak (*n*)	4.11, 5.1
peninsula (*n*)	5.1, 5.11
perk (*n*) [= work benefit]	3.11
permanent (*adj*)	5.11
permission (*n*)	1.11
personal (*adj*)	3.1
personal qualities	3.11
personality (*n*)	2.1, 2.6
pessimistic (*adj*)	2.16
petroleum engineer	3.16
philosopher (*n*)	2.1
physical (*adj*)	5.1, 5.6
physically (*adv*)	2.11

plagiarism (*n*)	1.11
plagiarize (*v*)	1.11
plain (*n*)	5.6, 5.16
plateau (*n*)	5.1
plot (*v*) [on a graph]	4.16
point (*n*)	4.16
pole (*n*)	4.11
polite (*adj*)	2.16
port (*n*)	5.11
portal (*n*)	1.11
positive (*adj*)	4.6
predict (*v*)	2.6
prefer (*v*)	2.16
pressure (*n*)	4.16
prevailing (*adj*)	5.16
primary (*adj*) [= main]	2.1
primary (*adj*) [research]	1.11
primary (*adj*) [school]	1.6
print (*v*)	1.16
process (*n*)	3.16
professor (*n*)	1.1
program (*n*)	1.11
projector (*n*)	1.1
prove (*v*)	4.1
provide (*v*)	5.16
psychiatrist (*n*)	2.16
psychologist (*n*)	2.1, 2.6
psychology (*n*)	2.1, 2.6
punctual (*adj*)	3.1
punctuation (*n*)	1.16
punishment (*n*)	1.6
pupil (*n*)	1.6
put (*v*)	4.16
put in (*v*)	3.16

Q

qualification (*n*)	1.16
qualifications (*n*)	3.11
quality (*n*)	3.1
quote (*n*)	2.6

R

race (*n*) [= ethnic]	2.11
rainbow (*n*)	4.6
rainfall (*n*)	4.11, 5.16
rainforest (*n*)	5.1
range (*n*)	5.1, 5.6
rarely (*adv*)	2.11
reach (*v*)	5.11
reason (*n*)	3.1
record (*n and v*)	1.11
record (*v*)	5.11

recruitment (n)	3.6, 3.11	self-motivated (adj)	3.6
referee (n)	1.16, 3.16	semester (n)	1.1, 1.6
reference (n)	3.16	sensibly (adj)	1.11
region (n)	5.11	sensibly (adv)	3.1
relationship (n)	2.1	separate (adj)	2.1
relax (v)	1.11	set (v) [an exam]	1.6
reliability (n)	3.11	shape (n)	4.16
religion (n)	2.1	shelf / shelves (n)	3.1
rely on (v)	3.1	shelter (n)	5.16
remind (v)	1.11	shift (n) [= work period]	3.11
represent (v)	4.1	short list (n)	3.16
require (v)	1.16	show (v)	4.16
requirement (n)	3.11	show [one's] feelings	2.16
research (n)	1.1, 4.1	shy (adj)	2.16, 3.6
research (v)	3.11	sick (adj)	3.1
residential (adj)	1.6	similar (adj)	2.16
resource centre	1.1	similar (adj) [to]	2.6
respect (n and v)	3.1	single (adj)	4.11
respect (v)	1.11	single-sex (adj)	1.6
responsibility (n)	3.1, 3.11	sit (v) [an exam]	1.6
responsible [for]	1.1	situated (adj)	5.11
result (n)	4.1, 4.16	situation (n)	2.6
retail (adj)	3.6	sixth form	1.1
reward (n)	1.6	sixth form college	1.1
rewrite (v)	1.16	slightly (adv)	4.11
right (n)	5.6	slope (n and v)	5.11
rights (n)	2.1	smart (adj)	3.6
rise (n and v)	3.11	smile (n and v)	2.6
rise (v)	4.6	smoke (n)	4.6
river (n)	5.6	sociable (adj)	2.16
rocky (adj)	5.6	social (adj)	2.1
row (n)	4.11	socialize (v)	1.1
rude (adj)	2.11, 3.6	society (n)	2.6
rule (n)	2.1	sociologist (n)	2.1, 2.6, 2.16
run (v) [= go]	4.11	sociology (n)	2.1, 2.6
		soft (adj)	4.1
S salary (n)	3.6	sometimes (adv)	2.11
satisfied (adj)	3.1	sound (n and v)	3.6
scale (n)	4.16	sound (n)	4.6
schedule (n)	1.1	source (n)	1.11, 4.11, 5.16
science (n)	4.1	space (n)	1.16
scientific (adj)	4.1	spend (v)	3.1
scientist (n)	4.1	split (v)	4.6
sea level (n)	5.11	square (adj)	5.1
search engine	1.11	staff (n)	1.1, 3.16
secondary (adj) [research]	1.11	stage (n)	3.16
secondary (adj) [school]	1.6	stand out (v)	2.16
select (v)	1.16	statement (n)	1.16
selection (n)	3.16		

status (n)	1.16	
stay on (v)	1.6	
storm (n)	5.16	
stranger (n)	2.16	
strong (adj)	2.16	
Students' Union	1.1	
stupid (adj)	2.11	
subheading (n)	1.11	
subject (n)	1.1, 1.16	
successful (adj)	3.16	
sunlight (n)	4.1	
surface (n)	4.6, 4.16	
surname (n)	1.16	
surround (v)	5.16	
system (n)	3.1	

T

table (n)	5.11
table (n) [data]	4.1
take (v)	4.16
take (v) [an exam]	1.6
take up (v)	3.16
task (n)	3.1
technology (n)	3.11
teenager (n)	2.11
temperature (n)	4.11
term (n) [= name]	2.1
tertiary (adj)	1.6
test (n and v)	4.1
the same as	2.1
through (adv)	5.6
thunder (n)	4.6
thunderstorm (n)	4.11
tide (n)	4.6
tidy (adj)	3.1
tilt (v)	4.11
together (adv)	2.6, 4.6
topic (n)	1.11
trainee (n)	3.11
transport (n)	5.16
treat (v) [= behave towards]	1.6
(the) Tropic of Cancer (n)	5.1
(the) Tropic of Capricorn (n)	5.1
true (adj)	4.1
trust (n and v)	2.16
truth (n)	4.1
turn (v)	4.16
tutorial (n)	1.1, 1.6

U

undergraduate (n)	1.1
unemployment (n)	3.11

unfriendly (adj)	2.16
uninhabited (adj)	5.11
unit (n)	4.11
unkind (adj)	2.11
unpaid (adj)	3.11
unsociable (adj)	2.16
unsuccessful (adj)	3.16
unsuitable (adj)	3.16
useful (adj)	2.6
usually (adv)	2.11

V

vacancy (n)	3.16
vacation (n)	3.6
valley (n)	5.6, 5.11
vapour (n)	4.6
vertical (adj)	4.1
vice chancellor (n)	1.1
virus (n)	1.11
volcano (n)	5.1
volume (n)	4.16

W

wages (n pl)	3.1
warm (adj)	2.16
waste (v)	3.1
waterfall (n)	5.6
weak (adj)	2.16
webpage (n)	1.11
website (n)	1.11
weigh (v)	4.16
weight (n)	2.11, 4.16
western (adj)	5.6
whole (adj)	5.1
wireless (adj)	1.11
worker (n)	3.11
working hours (n)	3.11
workplace (n)	3.11
workspace (n)	3.1
world (n)	5.11
worry (v)	2.11
worst (adj)	1.6